PUBLICATIONS OF THE NEW CHAUCER SOCIETY

THE NEW CHAUCER SOCIETY

Officers and Board of Trustees

CHARLES MUSCATINE
President 1980–82
University of California, Berkeley

DEREK S. BREWER Cambridge University	E. TALBOT DONALDSON University of Indiana
JOHN H. FISHER University of Tennessee	ROBERT W. FRANK Pennsylvania State University
DONALD K. FRY State University of New York, Stony Brook	DONALD R. HOWARD Stanford University
ALICE S. MISKIMIN Yale University	DONALD M. ROSE *Deputy Executive Director* University of Oklahoma

PAUL G. RUGGIERS
Executive Director
University of Oklahoma

JOHN H. FISHER *Compiler of Bibliography* University of Tennessee	CHRISTINE G. PEARCY *Assistant to the Editor* University of Oklahoma

Studies in the Age of Chaucer, the yearbook of The New Chaucer Society, is published annually in May. Each issue contains a limited number of substantial articles, reviews of books on Chaucer and related topics, and an annotated Chaucer bibliography. Articles explore such concerns as the efficacy of various critical approaches to the art of Chaucer and his contemporaries, their literary relationships and reputations, and the artistic, economic, intellectual, religious, scientific, and social and historical backgrounds to their work.

Manuscripts, in duplicate, accompanied by return postage, should follow the *MLA Handbook for Writers* (1977). Unsolicited reviews are not accepted. Authors receive free twenty offprints of articles and ten of reviews. All correspondence concerning manuscript submissions should be addressed to Roy J. Pearcy, Editor, Department of English, The University of Oklahoma, 760 Van Vleet Oval, Norman, Oklahoma 73019.

All correspondence regarding subscriptions to The New Chaucer Society and information about the Society's activities should be directed to Donald M. Rose at the above address.

Studies in the Age of Chaucer

Studies in the Age of Chaucer

Volume 3
1981

EDITED BY ROY J. PEARCY • PUBLISHED

ANNUALLY BY THE NEW CHAUCER SOCIETY

THE UNIVERSITY OF OKLAHOMA, NORMAN

The frontispiece design, showing the Pilgrims at the Tabard Inn, is adapted from the woodcut in Caxton's second edition of *The Canterbury Tales*.

Copyright 1981 by The New Chaucer Society, The University of Oklahoma, Norman. Manufactured by Pilgrim Books, Norman. First edition.

ISBN 0–933784–02–3

ISSN 0190–2407

CONTENTS

The Presidential Address, 1980:
What Amounteth Al This Wit?—Chaucer and Scholarship
    Charles Muscatine   3

ARTICLES

Fate and Freedom in The Knight's Tale
    Edward C. Schweitzer   13

Politics and the Paralysis of Poetic Imagination
in The Physician's Tale
    Sheila Delany   47

The Poet as Petitioner
    J. A. Burrow   61

The Order of The Canterbury Tales
    Larry D. Benson   77

REVIEWS

David Aers, *Chaucer, Langland, and the Creative*
    Imagination (Elton D. Higgs)   121

C. David Benson, *The History of Troy in Middle English*
    Literature: Guido delle Colonne's Historia
    destructionis Troiae *in Medieval England* (McKay
    Sundwall)   124

Juliette de Caluwé–Dor, trans., *Les Contes de Cantorbéry* (Roy J. Pearcy)   128

Norman Davis, Douglas Gray, Patricia Ingham, and Anne Wallace–Hadrill, comps., *A Chaucer Glossary* (W. Bruce Finnie)   134

D. H. Green, *Irony in the Medieval Romance* (Paul G. Ruggiers)   138

Douglas Kelly, *Medieval Imagination: Rhetoric and the Poetry of Courtly Love* (James I. Wimsatt)   142

Gregory Kratzmann, *Anglo–Scottish Literary Relations 1430–1550* (Barrie Ruth Straus)   148

John P. McCall, *Chaucer among the Gods: The Poetics of Classical Myth* (George D. Economou)   152

Thomas E. Maresca, *Three English Epics: Studies in Chaucer, Spenser, and Milton* (Gwenn Davis)   156

Priscilla Martin, Piers Plowman: *The Field and the Tower* (Mary Carruthers)   161

John Norton–Smith, introd., *Bodleian Library MS. Fairfax 16* (Donald C. Baker)   165

Maureen Quilligan, *The Language of Allegory: Defining the Genre* (Paul Strohm)   169

Mary Salu, ed., *Essays on* Troilus and Criseyde (C. David Benson)   171

Tsutomu Satow, *Sentence and Solaas: Thematic Development and Narrative Technique in* The Canterbury Tales (Thomas W. Ross)   176

Nathaniel B. Smith and Joseph T. Snow, eds., *The Expansion
and Transformation of Courtly Literature* (H. A. Kelly)   179

Siegfried Wenzel, *Verses in Sermons:* Fasciculus Morum *and
its Middle English Poems* (James J. Wilhelm)   183

Charles R. Young, *The Royal Forests of Medieval England*
(Sumner Ferris)   185

BIBLIOGRAPHY

John H. Fisher, *An Annotated Chaucer Bibliography 1979*   189

    Classifications   191

    Journal Abbreviations   193

    Citations   195

    Author Index   257

VARIA

    Notes on Contributors   260

    Abbreviations for Chaucer's Works   261

    General Index   263

Studies in the Age of Chaucer

"What Amounteth Al This Wit?"— Chaucer and Scholarship

Charles Muscatine
University of California, Berkeley

"WHAT AMOUNTETH AL THIS WIT?" The question, taken out of context and applied to Chaucerian scholarship and criticism, is not often asked among Chaucerian scholars and critics; it seems like one of those questions which, if you have to ask it, you probably would not understand the answer. We are, as a group, rightly assured of certain certainties—of the values of literature and history, and of the unchallengeable importance of Chaucer. In a particular sense, as medievalists, we know perhaps better than anyone else what the preservation of learning means. Our memory of the survival of scholarship and of its value for our culture goes back to barbarian times of a thousand years ago and more. In us, the preservation of learning is an unquestioned piety.

I bring this question—this rude question—into this company only because we seem currently to have entered times more barbarous than they were before, and because in the last decade we seem to be more and more surrounded by outsiders who in various ways are asking this question of us.

"What amounteth al this wit?" The question asked contemptuously by the hardened American anti-intellectual perhaps still does not merit a reply. But I must confess that I am moved to make an answer when the question is posed by persons who are young, and if not anti-intellectual then *un*intellectual, by persons who are not irremediably hostile, but who ask the question indirectly by refusing or ignoring what we have to teach. An answer is needed, too, for legislators and donors who have to weigh the claims of education and scholarship against those of other benefits to society.

The question takes on some added point when it is made in terms of

3

social and cultural distinctions. Is it not true, we are being asked, that insofar as most of you work and teach in colleges and universities—is it not true that your whole discipline and approach to teaching was formed for the education of upper-class (mostly male) students? Until recently your audiences have always come to you already conditioned with socially based assumptions about the value of literature and history. They have come with a knowledge of the Bible and of classical mythology, and perhaps some French learned in school or abroad. They have had the leisure, based on economic security, that afforded them the time to spend on your literature and your arcane philology. But now the last vestiges of nineteenth-century elitist education are being swept away (with the last vestiges of nineteenth-century culture). The demographic base in colleges has vastly widened to include persons (both washed and unwashed) of every sort of social and cultural origin. Many of them are completely oblivious of the Western tradition, if not hostile to it, and most of them are economically insecure. Why shouldn't the number of *your* students be dwindling, even though college enrollments in the last decades have doubled several times over? What have you medievalists got to offer to people from the ghettos and barrios and immigrant ships and endless plastic suburbs—people getting ready to face life (if that is what it will be called) in the next millennium? What amounteth al this wit?

We are not hearing the question for the first time at this meeting, and our very presence here in fact constitutes an astonishingly emphatic and optimistic reply: "Chaucer scholarship is alive and well, you people, no matter what you may think of it." But we have been giving less optimistic replies, too, along with the majority of the humanities establishment, with the virtual dissolution of the liberal arts curriculum in many places in the 1960's, and with our slowness, so far, to re-think and re-locate the role of our studies in the life experience that faces our students. Some of us have already gone into psychological seclusion, as if the continued dwindling of our audience would leave us finally in a noble new monasticism.

As for me, I want that audience back; I want us to reach the new (and newly indifferent) student. Confidence in the value of what we have to offer calls for sympathetic advance, not retreat. But advance, I think, will be made more convincingly, our answer will be more credible, to the extent that it does not merely depend on the ancient a priori pieties about scholarship and learning. It must also relate our work as directly as possible to the central concerns of our culture.

Taking thus a position in favor of the re-validation of scholarship and criticism in these times, I am comforted by the idea that Chaucer would be in complete agreement. Of course, one does not get a sense from Chaucer that scholarship was in serious difficulties vis-à-vis the central concerns of his own culture; and we know that from his day on the fortunes of scholarship—with minor ups and downs—were to be on the rise for a long time. But Chaucer does give us a sense that scholarship must tend to its filiations with the culture. Chaucer is, a bit ingenuously for modern taste, an unabashed commender of relevance:

> For seint Paul seith that al that writen is,
> To oure doctrine it is ywrite, ywis;
> Taketh the fruyt, and lat the chaf be stille.
> (*NPT*, 3441–43)

The matter is a complicated one, and I am not prepared here to speculate on how much Chaucer's notions of scholarship and learning derive primarily from the study of the Bible and thus perhaps make "relevance" an idea too vast to be useful. But we can see from Chaucer's lifelong activity—if not as a professional scholar then as a part-time gifted amateur and as an intermediary between professional scholars and a less than intellectual but interested public—we can see in Chaucer's notorious love of books coupled with his unfailing sense of an audience a sympathetic model for our own activity:

> For out of olde feldes, as men seyth,
> Cometh al this newe corn from yer to yere,
> And out of olde bokes, in good feyth,
> Cometh al this newe science that men lere.
> (*PF*, 22–25)

The *bokes* in Chaucer are always old, but the knowledge provided by their reading is made new. Elsewhere he says:

> . . . if that olde bokes weren aweye,
> Yloren were of remembrance the keye.
> Wel oughte us thanne on olde bokes leve,
> There as there is non other assay by preve.
> (*PLGW*, G25–28)

"There as there is non other assay by preve." The reservation is utterly Chaucerian and, as with so much else in Chaucer, makes his attitudes all the more acceptable by showing that he does not come by them uncritically. The world of books and authority is balanced off against the world of experience in Chaucer's mind and life in just the way we would wish for ourselves.

No small sense of Chaucer's feeling for the nonscholarly audience for learning comes from his mostly comic recognition of anti-intellectualism or the cult of practical wisdom:

> Now is a nat that of God a ful fair grace
> That swich a lewed mannes wit shal pace
> The wisdom of an heep of lerned men?
> (*GP*, 573–75)

> "Straw for thy Senek, and for thy proverbes!
> I counte nat a panyer ful of herbes
> Of scole-termes."
> (*MerT*, 1567–69)

> "So ferde another clerk with astromye;
> He walked in the feeldes, for to prye
> Upon the sterres, what ther sholde bifalle,
> Til he was in a marle-pit yfalle;
> He saugh nat that."
> (*MilT*, 3457–61)

> "Myn hous is streit, but ye han lerned art;
> Ye konne by argumentes make a place

> A myle brood of twenty foot of space.
> Lat se now if this place may suffise,
> Or make it rowm with speche, as is youre gise."
> (*RvT*, 4122–26)

At points one is uncertain where Chaucer's amusement with redneck hostility to learning shades off into a shared satire of the excesses and limitations of scholarship itself. Chaucer is sensitive to the layman's response to the complexity of scholarly argument, sensitive and sympathetic too. Dorigen, contemplating the black rocks that threaten her husband's life, makes a moving appeal that has no use for argument:

> I woot wel clerkes wol seyn as hem leste,
> By argumentz, that al is for the beste,
> Though I ne kan the causes nat yknowe.
> But thilke God that made wynd to blowe
> As kepe my lord! this *my* conclusion.
> To clerkes lete I al disputison.
> (*FranT*, 885–90)

The *clerkes* do not necessarily come out on top in sympathy here. Elsewhere Chaucer can have fun with clerkly complexity, and make fun of it too. For this his favorite topic is free will and predestination:

> Witnesse on hym that any parfit clerk is,
> That in scole is greet altercacioun
> In this mateere, and greet disputisoun,
> And hath been of an hundred thousand men.
> But I ne kan nat bulte it to the bren
> As kan the hooly doctour Augustyn,
> Or Boece, or the Bisshop Bradwardyn . . ."
> (*NPT*, 3236–42)

and the Nun's Priest concludes, after a brief but skillful summary of the issues:

> I wol nat han to do of swich mateere;
> My tale is of a cok, as ye may heere . . .
> (NPT, 3251–52)

Perhaps the high point of this fun comes with the seventeen stanzas of speculation that Chaucer gives to Troilus, punctuated with the despairing cry:

> "O, welaway! so sleighe arn clerkes olde,
> That I not whos opynyoun I may holde."
> (TC IV, 972–73)

Chaucer's good sense and balance concerning scholarship are validated, finally, by the evidence that he, too, has often enough become intoxicated with the thing itself. The amassing of notes, the piling up of instances, the gaudy display of erudition—Chaucer knew those sweet seductions. According to the *Prologue* to *The Legend of Good Women*, he has a collection of "sixty bokes olde and newe" about women. We can imagine a comparable collection (or at least a good set of notes) about dreams and about alchemy, and we know how much pedantic sport he had—sanctioned by the rhetoric of amplification—with these and other subjects. In his later years, though by no means cured of amplification, he came to see the potential pompousness in it; Chauntecleer shows us that—as Alice of Bath shows us the helpless desperation of an audience whom the next in a seemingly endless list of exempla might drive to violence; and Nicholas shows us the arrogance of intellectual pride itself.

As a user and transmitter of learning, then, Chaucer is on both sides of the transaction. In balance, he respects learning; but he does not accept it uncritically. He responds *most* sympathetically to learning when it promises a connection with practical virtue. His poor Parson, we remember, is "also a lerned man, a clerk," whose teaching is validated by practice: "first he wroghte, and afterward he taughte." It is similarly a practical or instrumental aspect of learning that is exemplified in his own best efforts at pedagogy. In the *Astrolabe* and the second Book of *The House of Fame*, in the clarity of the exposition, and in the tender regard for the wits of his audience, we get perhaps our best glimpse of the kind of scholar or teacher Chaucer would have been had he chosen that profession at all:

> "lo, so I can
> Lewedly to a lewed man
> Speke, and shewe hym swyche skiles
> That he may shake hem be the biles,
> So palpable they shulden be."
> (HF, 865–69)

Chaucer, lover of books but also practical man of affairs, vis-à-vis learning was a popularizer, and would have been proud to have been recognized as such. Indeed, some such idea may well have been on the mind of Eustache Deschamps when he called Chaucer a *grant translateur*.

After offering this brief reminder of some of Chaucer's opinions and practice, I am, however, not going to invoke him as a guide to what any one of us ought to be doing in Chaucer scholarship or criticism. Our subject is rich and difficult, and one could not define the degree of even the most arcane learning or of the most complex abstraction that might not still afford us profit, or at least scholarly pleasure. While it does look as if it would be highly un-Chaucerian to be too solemn or too pious about Chaucer scholarship, none of us is under the obligation, after all, to be Chaucerian. Chaucer would have been the first to insist, rather, on our being ourselves, and doing well what our talents and temperaments fit us for:

> "What amounteth al this wit?
> What shul we speke alday of hooly writ?
> The devel made a reve for to preche,
> Or of a soutere a shipman or a leche."
> (Prologue of *Rvt*, 3901–04)

Chaucer admires his Clerk perhaps as much for his being himself, pursuing his own bent, as for his clerkship. For another man "upon a book in cloystre alwey to poure" would drive him crazy. Chaucer has substantial sympathy for both; nor am I about to recommend the conversion of the reeves among us into preachers, much less the preachers into reeves.

Yet, the health of the profession in these and coming times will, I think, be better served by some moves in scholarship than in others. In this sense, if we cannot or should not try to remake ourselves or each other, we can at least be aware of what new talents the profession most needs, what recruits it might most welcome, what directions might be for us corporately most rewarding.

In this sense the Chaucerian advice might well be to look sympathetically toward our new audience—massively *lewed* as it may be—and to try to re-locate and re-define the connections between our activity and the culture in which we find ourselves.

The pedagogical aspect of moving in this direction is quite simply to make a generous outreach to students and to try to formulate—even at the expense of re-thinking them for ourselves—understandable answers to their questions about the value of humanistic scholarship.

On the professional side, the logic of the same argument would suggest that as researchers and critics, we would be best served if for a time we looked outward rather than inward—that we gave less emphasis to source studies and textual studies and narrow explication, and more emphasis to cultural history and the reading of medieval culture itself. We will, of course, always need and always profit from new textual discoveries, and explication will never go out of style. But we are in any case manifestly at the end of a phase in textual studies—conspicuously to be marked by the *Chaucer Library* and the *Variorum*; and we need some relief from the flood of explication that in its increasing inwardness and high focus seems to be telling us more and more about the lenses of the critics and less and less about Chaucer and his time.

By the time you hear this, our Program's first topic, *Contemporary Literary Theory and Chaucer*, will have been presented, and the matter may be already settled. I hope that we have already decided that for Chaucer studies it will be better that our messages be lucid and communicable rather than opaque and private; that the literary text be kept more important than the critic; that the text have a unique importance, but that part of its importance be its importance as cultural history. Looking outward—from Chaucer to his culture and to its place in cultural history—will take some of the emphasis away from ourselves and bring us into fresh contact with other fields, especially with sociology, historiography, and ethnography, themselves becoming more and more implicated in the procedures of literary discourse and analysis. The direction is an important and promising one suggested by modern critical theory itself. Viewing literature not so much as a separable part of culture but as one of its central traits; viewing literature not merely as illustrating history or as being illustrated by it, but as constituting the deepest history itself—this would be an exciting and productive direction to go. A new study of the place of Chaucer in cultural history might even turn up a new appreciation of the place of Chaucer studies in cultural history as well.

Fate and Freedom
in *The Knight's Tale*

Edward C. Schweitzer
Louisiana State University

L ARGE in theme, rich in concrete detail and philosophical allusion, complex in style and structure, enigmatic in its final effect, *The Knight's Tale* is the most often and the most variously interpreted of *The Canterbury Tales*, and no aspect of *The Knight's Tale* is so difficult to interpret as the circumstances of Arcite's death. It is, in fact, Arcite's death and the manner of its presentation that above all make the meaning of the whole elusive. But I will argue here that Arcite's death is not only just but poetically inevitable and that Chaucer's presentation of it points to the perspective from which the diverse elements of the tale form a coherent pattern in which apparent contradiction becomes significant paradox.[1]

I

If there were some difference between Palamon and Arcite sufficient to explain why the one should win Emelye and the other should lose her, Arcite's death might appear to serve a higher order. The tale's repeated references to a higher order imply that there is such a difference, but despite ingenious and contradictory efforts to discover it, the two lovers are essentially interchangeable. Apart from the gods they serve, they are even more alike than Boccaccio's Palemone and Arcita. Though they are

[1] Research for this essay was supported in part by a grant from LSU's Council on Research. Abbreviated versions of an early draft were read at meetings of the International Courtly Literature Society, in Athens, Georgia, April 1977, and the South Central Modern Language Association, in Hot Springs, Arkansas, October 1977.

continually at odds not only in their rivalry for Emelye but in all their opinions and arguments, they are at one in the folly each can see in the other but not in himself.[2] And that the lover defeated in the tournament should win the lady denied the victor only emphasizes the arbitrariness of the outcome. If Palamon deserved to live, it is hard to see why Arcite deserved to die and harder still to see why he deserved to die so horribly as he does, for Chaucer emphasizes the wretchedness of Arcite's end, describing it with such particularity that it is difficult to see in it, at the climax of the tale, that general significance which the overall abstractness of the narrative impels us to expect. As Charles Muscatine puts it, Chaucer "involves the reader not in moral conclusions, but in complicated *physical* data with associations so cold and scientific that no moral conclusion can possibly be drawn."[3] And if Arcite's fall is as arbitrary and his death as meaningless as they seem, then it is difficult to find support in the tale for the cosmic order and justice Theseus proclaims at the end. If the gods have overthrown Arcite ruthlessly and capriciously and rewarded Palamon with equal injustice, then Palamon's and Arcite's speeches lamenting the malice and cruelty of the gods—which seemed at first to demonstrate confusion, measured against the norm of their source, Boethius' *Consolation of Philosophy*—become far more complexly and disturbingly ironic, for in the end it seems Palamon and Arcite were

---

[2] Where Arcite tells Palamon, in argument, that neither of them is likely to enjoy Emelye's favor since they are condemned to perpetual imprisonment (1172–76), in the *Teseida*—ed. Alberto Limentani, *Tutte le opere di Giovanni Boccaccio*, II (Verona: Mondadori, 1964)—Palemone, 9.24, recognizes the folly of his own hopeless love. When Arcita is released from prison he *almost* says he prefers prison to exile (3.69), "Ma la ragion . . . subita prevenne / alla volonta folle di costui" (3.70. 1–2) with three arguments, two of which Chaucer omits, giving the third (3.71) to Palamon to use against Arcite (1283–90). Similarly, Palemone is *almost* jealous of Arcita's release (3.60), and when he weeps, it is first of all because of the loss of Arcita's companionship (3.77); when Arcita tells Palemone that he would prefer prison to exile (3.73), he does so to comfort his cousin, just as when Palemone reminds Arcita, as Arcita has already reminded himself, that he can do much free that Palemone cannot do in prison (3.78), that reminder is itself consolation rather than rebuke. All subsequent references to the *Teseida* are to the Mondadori edition. There is a convenient translation by Bernadette Marie McCoy, *The Book of Theseus* (New York: Medieval Text Association, 1974). On the relationship between the *Teseida* and *The Knight's Tale* in general, see Robert A. Pratt, "Chaucer's Use of the *Teseida*," *PMLA*, 62 (1947), 613–21. All references to Chaucer are to F. N. Robinson, *The Works of Geoffrey Chaucer*, 2nd ed. (Boston: Houghton Mifflin, 1957).

[3] *Chaucer and the French Tradition: A Study in Style and Meaning* (Berkeley: U. of California P, 1957), p. 186.

right all along, vindicated by the final events of the tale; the Boethian vision of cosmic order is the delusion; and Arcite's dying question is unanswerable—despite Lady Philosophy's answer. And so, while *The Knight's Tale* celebrates for some the order of the noble life as a bulwark against chaos, for others it is a cynical demonstration that, whatever they pretend to themselves, men are mere pawns of superhuman forces beyond their control and beyond their understanding.[4]

All these problems of interpretation grow out of the fact of Arcite's death, which Chaucer took over from Boccaccio. But they are all problems Chaucer has created, and they constitute an essential part of the new and larger significance with which Chaucer charged Boccaccio's highly personal tale of misfortune in love. For while he abbreviated and condensed Boccaccio's *Teseida*, focusing on the story of Palemone's and Arcita's love for Emilia but stripping Boccaccio's characters of their individual humanity, making Palamon and Arcite virtually interchangeable and Emelye a cipher, Chaucer turned Boccaccio's love story into the vehicle for a philosophical poem. He generally heightened the abstract pattern of symmetry and correspondence in the tale which impels its readers to look through the particular details of its action for some underlying meaning. He added the detailed and medically exact diagnosis of Arcite's love sickness in Thebes and of his fatal injury in Athens, added the series of speeches echoing the *Consolation* and raising those profound and awkward questions about man's place in the universe, and added the god who embodies disorder, Saturn, making him, not Venus, responsible for Arcite's death. And although Chaucer took the fury infernal that frightens Arcite's horse from the *Teseida*, it is only the most obvious of several points, all the others added by Chaucer, at which superhuman forces appear to control the fates of the tale's human actors.

---

[4] The most influential argument for the dominant order of *The Knight's Tale*, and the single most influential interpretation of the entire tale, from which the figure of the bulwark comes, is Muscatine's, pp. 175–90. The case for the dominance of disorder is put most effectively by Elizabeth Salter, *Chaucer: The Knight's Tale and the Clerk's Tale* (London: Edward Arnold, 1962), pp. 9–36, Joseph Westlund, "The *Knight's Tale* as an Impetus for Pilgrimage," *PQ*, 43 (1964), 526–37, and Kathleen A. Blake, "Order and the Noble Life in Chaucer's *Knight's Tale*," *MLQ*, 34 (1973), 3–19. The depth of the division may be suggested by the fact that Alfred David, *The Strumpet Muse: Art and Morals in Chaucer's Poetry* (Bloomington: Indiana UP, 1976), p. 87, calls Elizabeth Salter's "the closest and most perceptive reading of the tale," while Robert Burlin, *Chaucerian Fiction* (Princeton: Princeton UP, 1977), p. 264, n. 20, calls it "perverse."

In the *Teseida* Mars and Venus signify the irascible and concupiscible appetites,⁵ moral forces acting from within; Chaucer, however, presents them primarily, and Saturn (his own addition to the tale) exclusively, as planets,⁶ cosmic forces acting from without. The pattern of planetary influence is so pervasive—informing the portraits of the champions Lygurge and Emetreus, and extending to the hours of the day at which the protagonists pray to their patron deities, the day of the tournament, the hour of Arcite's accident, and the day and manner of his death—that Curry at least concluded that the motivating force of *The Knight's Tale* was the "impelling influence of the stars" and indeed "that the real conflict behind the surface action of the story is a conflict between the planets, Saturn and Mars."⁷ And since Curry wrote, Brooks and Fowler on the one hand and North on the other have further strengthened his case, arguing independently that both the location of the temples around the circumference of the stadium and the relative position of Palamon's and Arcite's forces as they take the field on a Tuesday morning in early May correspond to the position of the zodiac and symbolize astrological relationships: Palamon enters from the east, they explain, under the temple of Venus, as Taurus, a domicile of Venus, rises in the eastern sky; Arcite enters from the west, under the temple of Mars, as Scorpio, a domicile of Mars, sets in the west; Capricorn, a domicile of Saturn, is at

---

⁵ Boccaccio's notes on the houses of Mars and Venus (7.30 and 50) make the point explicitly and at length, but even if Chaucer did not have access to those notes—as is argued by Robert A. Pratt, "Conjectures Regarding Chaucer's Manuscript of the *Teseida*," *SP*, 42 (1945), 745–63—their significance is implicit in the text, especially in the conventional detail of the description of their houses, and represents one of the main traditions of medieval mythography; see Jean Seznec, *The Survival of the Pagan Gods: The Mythological Tradition and Its Place in Renaissance Humanism and Art*, trans. Barbara Sessions (New York: Pantheon, 1953), pp. 84–121.

⁶ On this physical tradition of mythography, see Seznec, pp. 37–88. Failure to take Saturn seriously as a planet but only as "a metaphorical elaboration of the unfortunate aspects of Venus and Mars" vitiates the otherwise suggestive essay by Alan T. Gaylord, "The Role of Saturn in the *Knight's Tale*," *ChauR*, 8 (1973), 171–90 (quotation from p. 174).

⁷ See Walter Clyde Curry, *Chaucer and the Medieval Sciences*, 2nd ed. (New York: Barnes & Noble, 1960), pp. 119–54 (quotations are from pp. 119–20). Similarly Dorothy Bethurum Loomis, "Saturn in Chaucer's *Knight's Tale*," in *Chaucer und seine Zeit: Symposion für Walter F. Schirmer*, ed. Arno Esch, Buchreihe der *Anglia*, 14 (Tübingen: Niemeyer, 1968), pp. 149–61: Hamilton M. Smyser, "A View of Chaucer's Astronomy," *Speculum*, 45 (1970), 359–73, quoted below at n. 18.

the zenith; and Cancer, a domicile of the moon, is at the *imum medium coelum*, conventionally north, like the temple of Diana.⁸

Their suggestion that the stadium is an image of the zodiac is persuasive and is supported by the changes Chaucer has here made in the *Teseida*.⁹ But their further suggestion that the disposition of forces at the beginning of the tournament also reflects the zodiac and so symbolizes the underlying disposition of cosmic forces must be rejected for the simple reason that the tournament does not begin at sunrise, as both Brooks and Fowler and North assert. Chaucer specifies that "it nas nat of the day yet fully pryme" when Theseus took his seat in the stadium and Arcite's and Palamon's forces came onto the field (2575-86). But although *prime* is ambiguous in Middle English, referring, as Skeat explained, "sometimes to the *beginning*, sometimes to the *end* of the period from 6 to 9, or again sometimes to the *whole* of the period," the phrase *high prime* or, as here, "fully Pryme" means unequivocally 9:00.¹⁰ The tale itself makes clear that the knights arm themselves "whan that day gan sprynge" (2491-93), and only after a long series of events (2494-567) do they ride to the stadium. The correspondence between the stadium and the zodiac, then, cannot extend to the tournament itself, but it is nevertheless astrologically significant that the tournament begins at 9:00.

North argues incisively that Saturn's remark that he does "vengeance and pleyn correccioun" when he dwells "in the signe of the leoun" (2461-62) implies that Saturn is then in Leo—and here his argument does not depend on the hour at which the tournament begins—and he concludes that the date Chaucer imagined for the tournament in *The Knight's Tale* must have been Tuesday, May 5, 1388, when Saturn was in the seventh degree of Leo, since that date accords perfectly with the chronology of the tale and of Chaucer's career and is the only one in

---

⁸ Douglas Brooks and Alastair Fowler, "The Meaning of Chaucer's *Knight's Tale*," *MÆ*, 39 (1970), 128-30; J. D. North, "Kalenderes Enlumyned Ben They: Some Astronomical Themes in Chaucer," *RES*, 20 (1969), 154.

⁹ In the *Teseida* (5.97) the stadium has been built long before the tournament; the temples are not part of the stadium but are located in the city itself (7.22-23, 42); before the tournament, Arcita enters from the east and Palemone from the west (7.114, 118), directions Chaucer has reversed.

¹⁰ W. W. Skeat, note to *Piers Plowman*, C 9.119, *The Vision of William Concerning Piers the Plowman in Three Parallel Texts* . . . (Oxford: Oxford UP, 1886; repr. 1965), II, 110. See *OED, prime*, sb.¹ 2, and *NPT*, VII, 3196-99.

Chaucer's literary lifetime which does so.[11] On that date Saturn is in favorable sextile aspect with Venus, in 15° Gemini, and in near opposition to Mars, in 17° Aquarius, a domicile of Saturn, so that the relationship between Chaucer's Saturn, Venus and Mars—and the outcome of the tournament, which follows from it—reflects the configuration of the planets within the zodiac on the day of the tournament. North's argument is all the more convincing because Chaucer changed the date of the tournament from the end of May in Boccaccio to the beginning.[12] And it appears to provide compelling evidence that Arcite and Palamon are helpless victims of cosmic forces beyond their control:

> "Som wikke aspect or disposicioun
> Of Saturne, by som constellacioun,
> Hath yeven us this, although we hadde it sworn;
> So stood the hevene whan that we were born.
> We moste endure it; this is the short and playn."
> (1087–91)

Though we cannot know the configuration of the heavens at the time of their birth, it seems we can know it at the time of the tournament that decides their destiny. And indeed in London on Tuesday, May 5, 1388, the sign of Leo, with Saturn in its seventh degree, began to rise above the eastern horizon a little before 9:00 a.m., so the tournament itself begins

---

[11] North, pp. 150–54. Palamon and Arcite, however, cannot meet on a Friday, as North claims, since they would then duel on Saturday, May 4, and assemble for Theseus' tournament either the corresponding Saturday (May 2, 1388) or the corresponding day of the month (a Monday in 1388), whereas the champions assemble on Sunday (2188). There is no good reason, however, not to understand that Palamon escaped in the early hours of May 4, confronted Arcite on Saturday, fought on Sunday, and returned to Athens the corresponding Sunday one year later, May 3, 1388. Chaucer's comparison of Palamon's behavior to the proverbially eccentric weather of Fridays (1528–39) provides no evidence that the day is Friday: because they are dominated by Venus, lovers' behavior is *always* variable, just as the weather on Friday, her day, is proverbially different from the rest of the week. It is at least as appropriate to have the meeting on a Saturday—Saturn's day—as May 4, 1387, was. And since we know the assembly was a Sunday and the interval between it and the duel is calculated in weeks, the duel was probably on a Sunday too.

[12] "Verso l'uscita di maggio," note to 7.104.5–6; the text of the poem itself, 7.94, indicates that the sun is in Gemini.

with Saturn in the ascendent,[13] in the sign of Leo, where by his own account he does "vengeance and pleyn correccioun," and in the first ten degrees of that sign, in his own face, signifying according to Albohazen Haly cruelty, evil deeds, violence, suffering to be endured, audacity, and lust.[14] Furthermore, according to the tradition which discovers a correspondence between every part of the body and a sign of the zodiac, a tradition to which Chaucer refers in his *Treatise on the Astrolabe* (1.21.70–77, p. 549), Leo governs the heart.[15] And it is about the heart that Arcite is injured by his fall: he is carried "with herte soor" (2695) to Theseus' palace, where, despite the best efforts of his physicians, the breast swells and "the soore / Encreeseth at this herte moore and moore" (2743–44). Even the lungs, which swell with the corrupting blood Arcite cannot expel, are effectively an extension of the heart, for they have in medieval physiology the twofold function of tempering the heart's natural heat and expelling its excess fumosity.[16] And Curry taught us long ago that

---

[13] I have calculated the ascendent using astrolabes constructed from plates in Andrew Edmund Brae, *The Treatise on the Astrolabe of Geoffrey Chaucer* (London: Russell Smith, 1870), and W. W. Skeat, *Chaucer's Treatise on the Astrolabe*, EETS, ES, 16 (London: Oxford UP, 1872), and, with the assistance of Martha Moseley, using modern tables of ascendents, *Concise Planetary Ephemeris for 1950–2000 A.D. at Noon* (Medford, Mass.: Hieratic Publishing, 1978) and *Simplified Scientific Tables of Houses, Latitudes 1 to 66 Degrees, North and South* (Oceanside, Calif.: Rosicrucian Fellowship, 1949), which show 2° Leo ascendent in London at 9:00 a.m., May 15 (= Chaucer's May 5), 1952 (a leap year like 1388). Chaucer explains in the *Astrolabe*, 2.4, that any planet within 5° above and 25° below the horizon is considered in the ascendent. Given that range and accepting North's argument that Saturn's reference to Leo suggests he is then in that sign, it is scarcely necessary to know the exact day, much less the year, for this calculation, since Leo begins to rise above the eastern horizon around 9:00 throughout the first week of May.

[14] Albohazen Haly filius Abenragel, *Liber de iudiciis astrorum* (Basel, 1551), 1.3, p. 4ª: "Prima facies Leonis est Saturni, completa forma, et est crudelitatis, maleficiorum, et violentiarum, sustinendi labores, audaciae, ac libidinis."

[15] So Albumasar, probably the most important of the Arabic astrologers for the Latin Middle Ages, *Introductorium in astronomiam Albumasaris abalachi octo continens libros partiales* (Augsburg, 1489), 6.11, fol 49ʳ: "[Signum leonis] os stomachi superius quod meri dicunt, cor, epar, nervi, lacerti, ossa, dorsum, eorumque accidentia"; Bartholomeus Anglicus, *De rerum proprietatibus* (Frankfurt, 1601; rpt. Frankfurt a. M.: Minerva, 1964), 8.14, p. 391: "In homine signum leonis cooperatur stomacho, lacertis, cordi, et dorso"; in the Brussels MS. Royal 4862–69 of Chaucer's *Treatise on the Astrolabe*, fol. 67ʳ, reproduced as an appendix to P. Pintelon, *Chaucer's Treatise on the Astrolabe* (Antwerp: De Sikkel, 1940), there is an astronomical man with the annotation, "Leo . . . habet potestatem de corpore hominis cor, stomachum, latus, et dorsum."

[16] See Vincent of Beauvais, *Speculum naturale* (Douai, 1624; rpt. Graz: Akademische Druck-u. Verlagsanstalt, 1964), 28.58, col. 2031.

the retentive virtue, which in Arcite's case prevents the expulsion of corrupting blood, is govered by Saturn.[17]

The stars then seem to determine not only the general outcome of the tournament and the brute fact of Arcite's downfall but the hour of his accident, the area of his injury, and the manner and day of his death. Because, with all its weight and complexity, the astrological machinery which overwhelms Arcite is more universal and less conventional than the arbitrary intervention of anthropomorphic gods, it implies even more than the intervention of the gods that he is a passive victim, not a free agent, and so is not responsible for his own actions but is instead crushed by ineluctable forces set in motion even before his birth. "Shapen was my deeth erst than my sherte" (1566); so Arcite laments before Palamon confronts him in the grove, and so the astrological machinery Chaucer added to the tale seems to suggest. And if the stars determine Arcite's death and Palamon's triumph, both undeserved, then cosmic order itself appears cruel and malicious, just as Palamon and Arcite said it was from the beginning, and even more than the arbitrary intervention of the gods, that appearance of universal malice exposes to withering irony the tale's network of allusions to the *Consolation*, with their promise of universal order.

II

But if *The Knight's Tale* is, as the circumstances of Arcite's death suggest, "a story of rivalry in human love in which not the merits nor the valor of the lovers determines the outcome, but the powers of planetary gods,"[18] then it is a most remarkable paradox[19] that Chaucer should have set this elaborate astrological machinery in motion to "determine"

---

[17] See p. 147. More pertinent references than Curry's are Roger Bacon, *The Opus Majus*, ed. John H. Bridges, I (Oxford: Oxford UP, 1897), 386, and Albertus Magnus, *The Book of Secrets*, ed. and trans. Michael R. Best and Frank H. Brightman (London: Oxford UP, 1973), p. 66. The connection follows from the fact that both Saturn and the retentive virtue are by nature cold and dry. So Bartholomeus, *De rerum prop.*, 5.3, p. 124, explains that the third ventricle of the brain is cold and dry "ut in ea melius fieret retentio."

[18] Smyser, p. 368.

[19] Noted by Richard Neuse, "The Knight: The First Mover in Chaucer's Human Comedy," *UTQ*, 31 (1962), 307.

precisely what the protagonists freely choose for themselves: Arcite wins the victory and Palamon wins Emelye, just as each of them prayed he would before the tournament, and it does no violence to the text to conclude that Emelye is married to the knight who desired her most, just as she prayed she would be. There is, I suggest, an exactly comparable paradox in the fury infernal that frightens Arcite's horse and in the injury it causes. Sent by Pluto at Saturn's request, the fury strikingly epitomizes the arbitrary and amoral determinism about which Palamon and Arcite both complain and which Chaucer seems to have incorporated into the very structure of his tale. Yet the cosmic forces acting from without through that fury can be seen, paradoxically, as the dramatic projection of moral forces acting from within, for Arcite's downfall enacts the progress of the lover's malady of *hereos* from which Arcite suffered in the first half of the tale, as that malady was explained by the medical authorities of Chaucer's time.

The symptoms of Arcite's love-sickness, like his fatal accident and the fury which caused it, Chaucer found in the *Teseida*, but as John Livingston Lowes demonstrated in a magisterial and now classic article Chaucer rearranged and recast them to support the explicit diagnosis provided in the text: Arcite suffers from a disease of the brain widely discussed by medieval physicians, "the loveris maladye / Of Hereos," verging on mania (to which *hereos* could lead) in Arcite's agitation and wild shifts of mood.[20]

> His slep, his mete, his drynke, is hym biraft,
> That lene he wex and drye as is a shaft;
> His eyen holwe, and grisly to biholde,
> His hewe falow and pale as asshen colde,
> And solitarie he was and evere allone,
> And waillynge al the nyght, makynge his mone;

[20] "The Loveres Maladye of Hereos," *MP*, 11 (1914), 491–546; on Chaucer and Boccaccio, p. 525, n. 1. See also Bruno Nardi, "L'amore e i medici medievali," in *Studi in onore di Angelo Monteverdi* (Modena: Società Tipografica Editrice Modenese, 1959), II, 517–42, and Stephan Kohl, *Wissenschaft und Dichtung bei Chaucer, dargestellt hauptsächlich am Beispiel der Medizin* (Frankfurt: Akademische Verlagsgesellschaft, 1973), pp. 218–308. D. W. Robertson, *A Preface to Chaucer* (Princeton: Princeton UP, 1963), pp. 457–60, provides translations and summaries of parts of treatises by Arnald of Villanova and Bernard of Gordon.

And if he herde song or instrument,
Thanne wolde he wepe, he myghte nat be stent.
So feble eek were his spiritz, and so lowe,
And chaunged so, that no man koude knowe
His speche nor his voys, though men it herde.
And in his geere for al the world he ferde,
Not oonly lik the loveris maladye
Of Hereos, but rather lyk manye,
Engendred of humour malencolik,
Biforen, in his celle fantastik.
And shortly, turned was al up so doun
Bothe habit and eek disposicioun
Of hym, this woful lovere daun Arcite.
(1361–79)

Anticipating the even more medically detailed account of Arcite's injury, the passage as a whole "might almost be a paraphrase of a chapter on *hereos* from one of the medical treatises themselves,"[21] or part of one. What Chaucer says about *amor hereos* is "correct" down to the smallest detail, but however detailed Chaucer's list of symptoms, however exact his diagnosis, however precise his summary of its effect, Chaucer does not define this lover's malady of *hereos* or explain its cause, as the medical treatises regularly do. And while the diagnosis and summary conclusion in themselves provide a link to the circumstances of Arcite's death and

[21] Lowes, p. 525, with a catalogue of detailed parallels, pp. 525–26. The shifts of mood, the one symptom Chaucer adds to those described by Boccaccio (4.26–29), are typical of lovers—as Chaucer reminds us later, 1528–39, playing on the same word, *geere* (on which see *OED, gere*)—and they appear among the symptoms of *amor hereos* listed by, among others, Avicenna (in Lowes, p. 513), and Bernard of Gordon (in Lowes, p. 500). Frenzied physical activity is, however, a specific symptom of mania, which Avicenna—*Canon* (Venice, 1582), lib. 3, fen 1, tract. 4, c. 15, fol. 203^v—uses to distinguish mania from melancholia, of which *hereos* is a special type: "Et melancholia quidem est cum malitia existimationis et cogitatione corrupta, et timore, et quiete, et non est in ipsa agitatio vehemens. Mania vero tota est agitatio, et saltus, et inquisitio cum manibus, seu motio manuum ad aliquid inquirendum"; and c. 18, fol. 204^r: "Cumque melancholia componitur cum rixa et saltu, contentione, seu pugna permutatur, et nominatur mania." The same chapters explain that mania and melancholia are both caused by melancholic humor, though of different types, and that strictly speaking mania is an infection of the anterior ventricle of the brain, as Chaucer notes, and melancholia is an infection of the middle ventricle. See also the *Glosulae quatuor magistrorum super chirurgiam Rogerii et Rolandi*, quoted in Lowes, p. 527.

point toward its significance, to see clearly how they do so we must understand not only what Chaucer says but what he assumes and leaves unsaid.

According to medieval physicians, *amor hereos* is a kind of melancholy, and like the disease of melancholy in general and the mania to which *hereos* can lead, it is engendered from melancholic humor, infecting the middle ventricle of the brain in melancholia and the anterior ventricle in mania. It is caused by thinking continually about the beloved and concentrating on her image, or phantasm, fixed so firmly in the *vis imaginativa* (which retains and combines the images of sense experience)—located in the foremost of the three ventricles of the brain, the "celle fantastik"—that the lover can think of nothing else, at least for long. And since the *vis estimativa* (which apprehends insensible intentions, distinguishes good from evil, and discerns what is to be pursued and what avoided) in the middle ventricle depends upon the images transmitted to it by the *vis imaginativa*, the rational power in its turn becomes corrupted, failing to discern correctly and judging that the beloved is the greatest possible good, offering the greatest possible happiness. The rational power, which ought to rule, is thus subjected to the delusions of the senses, the natural operations of the body are upset—as Chaucer says, "turned was al up so doun / Bothe habit and eek disposicioun"—and the lover, obsessed with the thought of his beloved, cannot eat or drink or sleep. And if the malady is allowed to run its course, according to the physicians, the melancholia of *amor hereos* will degenerate into mania, "engendred of humour melancolik / Biforen, in [the] celle fantastik," as Chaucer suggests Arcite's love-sickness has, in perfect agreement with the traditional accounts. The prognosis then is death.

Once we know so much, the correspondence between the conventional course of *amor hereos* and the circumstances of Arcite's death is, I think, inescapable and striking. The fury appears while Arcite is looking at Emelye and she at him (2678–83), though there is no such connection between Arcita and Emilia in the *Teseida*, just as Arcite's malady ultimately began with the figurative wound or hurt (1114–16) caused by his first sight of Emelye. The fury is summoned by Saturn just as *hereos* is a variety of Saturnian melancholia and is engendered, like the mania to which it leads, from that Saturnian humor; and in *The Knight's Tale* the fury rises up "out of the ground"—and the earth is cold and dry like

Saturn and melancholy—whereas in the *Teseida* it comes down into the stadium from above ("giù nel campo." 9.7.3). This psychological significance of the fury is obscured in the *Teseida*, if it is present at all, since Boccaccio calls his fury by name, Erinys (9.4.6), and devotes a full stanza (9.5) to the description of her long serpent-like hair, her green hydras belching sulphurous flames, and the whip of snakes in her hands; nevertheless, lust, avarice, and wrath are traditional significances of the Furies, because, according to Isidore of Seville, they all create great perturbation in men's souls.[22] Horse and rider, furthermore, are an almost commonplace figure for the control of sensuality by reason,[23] and that significance gives point to the fact that in Chaucer, unlike Boccaccio, Arcite's horse does not simply rear up at the sight of the fury and fall over backwards onto him, crushing his chest with its saddle;[24] instead, "er that Arcite may taken keep" (2688), it first throws him off onto "the pomel of his heed" (2689)—emblematically upside down—just as the image of Emelye in Arcite's imagination overthrew his reason and "turned . . . al up so doun / Bothe habit and eek disposicioun" (1377–78). In fact, *hereos* is called *amor furiosus* and a *furia* by Arnald of Villanova, Chaucer's "Arnold of the Newe Toun" (VIII, 1428).[25] Closer still to Chaucer's "furie infernal," in a tradition which goes back to Isidore's *Etymologies*, Arnald explains *mania*, to which Chaucer likened Arcite's malady in Thebes (1374), by deriving it from *Manes*: "mania quasi manium, id est, deorum infernalium insania."[26] And Chaucer's younger contemporary, the physician Valescus of Tarenta, says flatly, "Mania etiam dicitur quaedam furia infernalis."[27] As in Thebes Arcite

---

[22] *Etymologiae*, ed. W. M. Lindsay (Oxford: Clarendon Press, 1911), 8.11.95; see also Pierre Bersuire, *De formis figurisque deorum* (Utrecht: Instituut voor Laat Latijn der Rijksuniversiteit, 1966), p. 44.

[23] For references to this tradition, which goes back to the *Phaedrus*, see Beryl Rowland, "The Horse and Rider Figure in Chaucer's Works," *UTQ*, 35 (1966), 246–59; John B. Friedman, "A Reading of Chaucer's *Reeve's Tale*," *ChauR*, 2 (1967), 8–19.

[24] Arcita is never thrown from his horse and must be lifted down from its back after the accident (9.9.2–3), doubtless a far more realistic outcome than Chaucer's; and Boccaccio emphasizes that he is injured more by his saddle than by his horse (9.8.1–4, 9.9.1–2, 9.13.6–8).

[25] *Amor Furiosus* in *De amore heroyco*, c. 1, *Opera* (Lyons, 1504), fol. 255^v; *furia, ibid.* and three times in c. 24, fol. 256^r; Avicenna, *Canon*, lib. 3, fen 1, tract. 4, c. 24, fol. 207^r, calls it "species quaedam daemonis."

[26] *De parte operativa*, *Opera* (Lyons, 1504), fol. 128rb, in Lowes, p. 496; Isidore, *Etym.*, 4.5.8.

[27] *Philonium* (Lyons, 1535), 1.12, fol. 24^v.

could not expel Emelye's image from his imagination, with the result that the normal operation of his body was upset and he could not eat or drink or sleep, so in Athens he cannot expel the corrupted blood from his chest, with the result that "Nature wol nat wirche" (2759) and he dies. And as in Thebes the fire of love made Arcite "pale as asshen colde" (1364), so in Athens he is literally "brent to asshen colde" (2957), in the very grove where he suffered the "hoote fires" of love (2862), a correspondence doubly striking because it is here noted by Theseus himself (2860–64) and because Chaucer's apparent eagerness to mark the corrrespondence creates an inconsistency in the text; for Theseus has already destroyed the grove to make way for the stadium and so, it seems, to realize another metaphor by constructing actual lists on the site where he found Palamon and Arcite fighting "as it were in a lystes roially" (1713).

Among so many correspondences between Arcite's accident and the progress of *amor hereos*, there is probably one more in the striking detail, unparalleled in the *Teseida* and not further developed in *The Knight's Tale*, that after Arcite was thrown from his horse onto his head,

> As blak he lay as any cole or crowe,
> So was the blood yronnen in his face;
> (2692–93)

and this further correspondence gives precise point to the fact that the fury appears while Arcite and Emelye exchange glances. Arnald of Villanova, whose discussion of the lover's malady in *De amore heroyco* is unusually full, explains what is elsewhere only hinted at or passed over altogether: the mechanism by which the estimative power comes to err in thinking the beloved much better than she is and by which, accordingly, reason is subjected to the delusions of the senses. The estimative power— which is part, though the highest, of the sensible soul—wavers (or "stumbles"—"claudicat"—as Arcite's horse "foundred" [2687] while leaping sideways, frightened by the fury) and errs in its operation because it is overwhelmed and confused by the sudden rush to it of vital spirits from the heart. For when the soul perceives something delightful (and in details original with Chaucer Arcite is looking at Emelye, "and she agayn hym caste a freendlich ye" [2679–80] just as the fury starts from the ground), the vital spirits contained in the heart, those subtle and airy substances which connect body and soul,[28] are abruptly multiplied and enflamed; because of their heat, they rush most abundantly to the head (as Arcite's blood rushes to his), passing through the anterior ventricle, or *celle fantastik*, to the middle ventricle, where they confuse the judgment of the estimative power with their turbulent motion in the brain, and those so afflicted "judge with fallacy and error like drunken men." Because the flow of heat and moisture from the anterior to the middle ventricle leaves the *celle fantastik* colder and drier and so more retentive than normal, the imaginative power then holds tenaciously to the image of the beloved, creating still greater agitation.[29] Agitation, in turn, increases the production of melancholic humor[30] (suggested in Chaucer's narrative by the blackness of Arcite's face), which engenders both *hereos* and mania and which, as Avicenna explains, corrupts the estimative power because melancholy is cold and dry and so contrary to the naturally

---

[28] See, e. g., Bartholomeus Anglicus, *De rerum prop.*, 3.22, pp. 74–76: Lynn Thorndike, *History of Magic and Experimental Science*, I (New York: Macmillan, 1929), 658–60.

[29] C. 2, fols. 255vb–256ra with some additonal punctuation: "Causa vero propter quam estimativa virtus in opere vel iudicio suo claudicat sic et errat necessario sumenda videtur ex parte instrumentorum quibus dicta virtus suas perficit actiones, medie scilicet concavitatis cerebri et spirituum receptorum in ea. . . . Et ad hoc non tantum organicitas operatur sed ipsorum spirituum calefactio aliunde contracta sicut et bene consideranti apparere videbitur. Cum enim anime gratum seu delectabile presentatur, ex gaudio delectabili apprehensi spiritus in corde multiplicati subito, prout in 'De motibus animalium' inquisitum est in ea parte qua de motu cordis agitur, delegantur ad membra corporis universa. Cum sint igitur calidi vel quasi ferventes, ad organum estimative virtutis copiose, ad [*read* et] organum quia siccum et inde exacuens aut etiam calidum nequit illorum caliditatem reprimere; tunc quasi motu mixtionis turbate volvuntur, quapropter confundunt virtuale iudicium et velut ebrii iudicant cum fallacia vel errore. . . . Cum itaque firma retentio formarum in multis quibuslibet nequaquam effici valeat sine sicco, necessario sequitur cerebellarem partem imaginative virtutis aliqualiter exiccari. Hoc vero ex pretactis sic ostenditur: videtur tamen etiam fortis et frequens sit transitus caloris spirituum ad cellam extimative fluentium ad iudicium celebrandum; pars anterior in qua virtus imaginativa residet propter humiditatis consumptionem a calore spirituum relicta remanet necessario siccior seu minus humida quam fuerit, . . . maxime si aliqua frigiditas coniungatur, quod forma imaginationis in organo firmius retinetur necnon multa sollicitudo validius excitatur."

[30] E. g., Bernard of Gordon, *Lilium medicinae* (Lyons, 1574), 2.19, p. 209: "Causa igitur immediata [maniae et melancholiae] est humor melancholicus corruptus, inficiens cerebrum. Causae autem antecedentes, sunt omnia illa qua multiplicant melancholiam, sive per se, sive per accidens, sive per viam adustionis et corruptionis. Ista autem sunt multa, scilicet timor, et tristitia, et solicitudo, et similia."

warm and moist qualities of the middle ventricle of the brain.[31] If, in accord with Arnald's explanation of how the lover's judgment is overwhelmed when he sees his beloved, we understand that the friendly glance Emelye cast upon Arcite just before the appearance of the fury *causes* the overthrow of Arcite's reason by spirits which rush to his brain as the blood rushed to his head, then the accident realizes with technical precision Arcite's earlier and fundamentally figurative (or at least conventional) complaint, "Ye sleen me with youre eyen, Emelye!" (1567), providing one last star in the constellation of such correspondences between Arcite's love-sickness in the first half of the tale and his fatal injury in the second.

The medically detailed account of Arcite's injury which Chaucer added in Part IV thus corresponds in substance as well as style to the medically detailed account of Arcite's malady which he added in Part II, and the correspondence gives the very physical account of Arcite's injury a moral significance despite its cold and scientific detail. Indeed, the cold and scientific detail which describes the debilitating consequences of the injury extends the correspondence and hence re-emphasizes the significance, for Arcite dies when "nature hath no dominacioun," when:

> The vertu expulsif, or animal,
> Fro thilke vertu cleped natural
> Ne may the venym voyden ne expelle.
>   (2749–51)[32]

He dies despite the artificial aid of emetics, laxatives, and bloodletting, all aimed at removing the corrupted blood from the region around the heart, just as the cure for *hereos* consists in distracting the lover from his obsession, removing that delusive image from his consciousness.[33]

---

[31] *Canon*, lib. 3, fen 1, tract. 4, c. 18, fol. 204^r.

[32] Chaucer refers here to two of the three powers by which the soul acts upon the body. See the pseudo-Augustinian *De spiritu et anima*, 20–22, *PL* 40. 794–95, quoted in Vincent of Beauvais, *Spec. nat.*, 24.3, col. 1711, and Curry, pp. 140–42.

[33] Valescus, *Philonium*, 1.11, 23^v: "tota cura stat in distractione imaginationis. . . . Si ergo hec opinio seu imaginatio removetur, similiter et tota egritudo"; Bernard of Gordon, *Lilium medicinae*, 2.20, p. 217 (in Lowes, p. 501): "Patiens . . . removeatur ab illa falsa imaginatione"; Arnald of Villanova, *De parte operativa*, fol. 141va: "specialis cura heroys divertere cogitationem a re desiderata."

W. C. Curry and Pauline Aiken have both demonstrated in detail the technical accuracy of Chaucer's description of Arcite's injury, the complications which result from it, and the treatment it receives—all quite different from Boccaccio's account[34]—though they disagree on whether Chaucer's observation that the expulsive or the animal virtue could not expel the venom from the natural virtue means that Arcite could not cough or that he could not breathe. In fact, breathing and coughing—like urination and defecation—are both "composite motions," in which the *virtus expulsiva* and the *virtus animalis* act together,[35] since both are partly voluntary and partly involuntary. Choosing either of those possibilities, however, substantially alters Chaucer's text and obscures its significance, which lies precisely in its generality, since that generality carries us beyond the external fact of Arcite's injury to the breakdown in the normal interaction of inner forces which follows from it—the loss of rational control and nature's "dominacioun"—a breakdown which corresponds exactly to the breakdown in the interaction of reason and imagination characterizing *amor hereos*. Inability to cough, or to breathe, is just one more symptom, from which the underlying cause must be inferred, but it is the underlying cause that provides the link between Arcite's injury and his love-sickness, and it is the underlying cause that Chaucer specifies.

In his commentary on Guido Cavalcanti's poem *"Donna me prega,"* the Italian physician Dino del Garbo provides, in an account of *amor hereos*, a remarkable parallel to Chaucer's account of Arcite's injury and strikingly

---

[34] Curry, pp. 138–45; Pauline Aiken, "Arcite's Illness and Vincent of Beauvais," *PMLA*, 51 (1936), 361–69; See *Teseida* 9.8.2–4; 9.23; 10.13.8.

[35] E. g., Galeazzo de Santa Sofia, *Opus medicinae practicae saluberrimum . . . in nonum tractatum libri Rhasis ad regem Almansorem* (Hagenau, 1533), c. 55, fol. 41^r: "Tussis est motus compositus, id est, ex naturali et animali motibus factus, propter expellere nocumentum in pectore et partibus propinquis"; Bernard of Gordon, *Lilium medicinae*, 4.4, pp. 358, 361: "motus virtutis expulsivae aliquando est virtutis naturalis, sicut in corde, pulmone, hepate et fere in toto corpore: aliquando est compositus ex animali et naturali, ut in egestione, urina, tussi et sternutatione"; "iste autem motus in tussi, sternutatione et singultu, est motus compositus ex animali et naturali"; Avicenna, *Canon*, lib. 3, fen 3, tract. 4, c.1, fol. 268^r: "sputum est operatio quae completur duabus virtutibus, quarum una est naturali maturativa, et expulsiva etiam, et altera est voluntaria expulsiva"; Vincent of Beauvais, *Speculum doctrinale* (Douai, 1624; rpt. Graz: Akademische Druck-u. Verlagsanstalt, 1964), 14.83, col. 1335: "tussis est motus, animatae et naturali virtuti iunctus." I find no evidence of the "violent controversy" on this point referred to by Curry, p. 141.

corroborates the correspondence between illness and injury just suggested. Describing love's effects on the body as a whole, Dino explains that love kills by impeding with its vehemence the operation of the vegetative or vital powers of the soul: "amor tunc interficit quando est adeo uehemens, quod propter ipsum impediuntur opera uirtutis uegetatiuae uel uirtutis uitalis, que conseruat uitam et operationes eius in corpore humano."[36] Though the term *virtus vegetabilis* is Aristotelian, it is exactly equivalent here to Chaucer's "vertu cleped natural,"[37] and it is precisely when the operation of Arcite's animal virtues is impeded as a result of his injury that he dies. Dino's explanation is unusual only for its generality, since it is the impeded operations of the natural and vital virtues which produce the conventional outward symptoms of *hereos* that Chaucer catalogues in Part II of *The Knight's Tale*; but because he emphasizes the disorder underlying the particular symptoms of the disease, just as Chaucer emphasizes the underlying disorder of the injury, Dino puts into relief the correspondence between them despite the outward difference in symptoms. In the same way, Chaucer's generalization that in suffering from *hereos* Arcite's "habit and eek disposicioun" were turned upside down anticipates Arcite's fatal accident more clearly and directly than do the particular symptoms of *hereos* Chaucer describes, conventional though they are.

If it is the symbolic re-enactment of what has gone before, then the conclusion which seemed arbitrary and unpredictable becomes almost inevitable, and if Arcite is responsible for his infatuation with Emelye—and there seems no reason to suppose he is not, though the medical terms in which that infatuation is described make it difficult for the reader to identify or sympathize with him[38]—then by the logic of poetry he is responsible, too, for the fury sent by Saturn, and the death he suffers becomes an emblem of the end of those who persist in loving unreasonably. And the fury, while epitomizing the intervention of cosmic forces

---

[36] "La glossa latina di Dino del Garbo a 'Donna me prega' del Cavalcanti," ed. G. Favati, *Annali della Scuole Normale Superiore di Pisa*, NS 21 (1952), 96.

[37] Cf. Bartholomeus Anglicus, *De rerum prop.*, 3.8, p. 52: "Huic autem virtuti vegetabili quatuor deserviunt, scilicet virtus appetitiva . . . , digestiva . . . , retentiva . . . , expulsiva," corresponding exactly to the description of the *virtus naturalis* cited in n. 32; see also Vincent of Beauvais, *Spec. nat.*, 24.63, col. 1757, quoting Aristotle, *De anima*, 2.4.415^a.

[38] See Robertson, p. 49.

to determine the course of events, epitomizes also the paradox that those cosmic forces determine only what the human protagonists have freely chosen.

III

But what is the point of the paradox? If Saturn and the fury dramatize the consequences of human choice, then what is the significance of the elaborate pattern of astrological influence which Chaucer went to such lengths to construct and of which the fury is only the most obvious example? The answer can be found, I suggest, in the very network of allusions to Boethius which that astrological machinery and especially the circumstances of Arcite's death made appear so problematic.

The *Consolation of Philosophy*, indeed, provides a virtual commentary on Arcite's death and all the action of the tale, partly because it aims to reconcile just such apparent misfortune or injustice with the existence of divine providence, the problem pointedly raised by Arcite's dying question,

> "What is this world? what asketh men to have?
> Now with his love, now in his colde grave,
> Allone, withouten any compaignye,"
>
> (2777–79)

but also and more crucially because it demonstrates that the appearance of misfortune and injustice in the world is an illusion that follows from mistaking the nature of the true good, the source of true happiness. And *amor hereos* is, in essence, just such a mistake, since the lover, deluded by his senses, expects to find both true good and true happiness in his beloved. So Bernard of Gordon:

> The cause of this passion is the corruption of the estimative power on account of a firmly fixed form and figure. Consequently when some man is overcome with love for some woman, he so intently imagines her form and figure and manner that he believes and thinks she is better, more

beautiful, more worthy, more fair, and more richly endowed in appearance and character than any other woman, and therefore he desires her ardently, excessively and extravagantly, thinking that if he could attain his end it would be his felicity and beatitude.[39]

It is precisely this delusion that Chaucer reveals in Arcite through the pointedly ironic echoes of the *Consolation* in Arcite's lamenting and still mistaken speech at the end of Part I, just before Chaucer describes and diagnoses Arcite's love malady. Complaining with comical exaggeration of the "aventure" (1235) that leaves Palamon dwelling "Ful blisfully in prison . . . / In prison? certes nay, but in paradys!" and himself condemned to a purely figurative "prisoun worse than bifor . . . / Noght in purgatorie, but in helle" (1224–37), Arcite feels no inconsistency in asking (with regard to his earlier complaints about imprisonment [1081–91], not his present complaints about freedom):

> "Allas, why pleynen folk so in commune
> On purveiaunce of God, or of Fortune,
> That yeveth hem ful ofte in many a gyse
> Wel bettre than they kan hemself devyse?
> Som man desireth for to han richesse,
> That cause is of his mordre or greet siknesse;
> And som man wolde out of his prisoun fayn,
> That in his hous is of his meynee slayn.
> Infinite harmes been in this mateere.
> We witen nat what thing we preyen heere:
> We faren as he that dronke is as a mous.
> A dronke man woot wel he hath an hous,
> But he noot which the righte wey is thider,
> And to a dronke man the wey is slider.
> And certes, in this world so faren we;
> We seken faste after felicitee,

---

[39] *Lilium med.*, 2.20, p. 216, in Lowes, p. 499; similarly Arnald of Villanova, *De amore heroyco*, c. 1, fol. 255[va]; Dino del Garbo, *Glossa latina*, p. 95; and texts by Arnald of Villanova and John of Tornamira in Lowes, pp. 496, 504. Avicenna, *Canon*, lib. 3, fen 1, tract. 4, c. 7, fol. 202[r], explains that whenever a patient "putat esse bonum quod non debet putari bonum, et sperat quod non est sperandum, et inquirit quod inquirendum non est," the physician can infer that the middle ventricle of the brain has been affected.

> But we goon wrong ful often, trewely.
> Thus may we seyen alle, and namely I,
> That wende and hadde a greet opinioun
> That if I myghte escapen from prisoun,
> Thanne hadde I been in joye and perfit heele,
> Ther now I am exiled fro my wele.
> Syn that I may nat seen you, Emelye,
> I nam but deed; ther nys no remedye."
>   (1251–74)

If the inconsistency were not enough, Arcite's equation of "purveiaunce of God, or of Fortune," would at once signal his philosophical confusion, and the speech as a whole drives the point home, for every sentence contains some dramatic irony. Even as he complains of his "misfortune," it must be clear to the reader, as it is to Palamon (1281–98), that freedom is a greater gift than Arcite could ever have devised. Arcite wants no riches—he has them already—but his desire for Emelye will cause his death, not through murder, though he is prepared to risk violent death at the hands of his cousin and blood brother, but through "great siknesse." Arcite himself is proof, though not in the sense he understands, that we all seek felicity but often fail to find it because we look in the wrong place: the figure of the drunken man who knows he has a house but cannot find it comes from Book 3, Prose 2, of the *Consolation*, the same passage that exposes both riches and "voluptuous delyt" as delusory partial goods, and it signifies there exactly what it signifies here—the natural search for happiness, true felicity, in which men so often go astray. The Boethian context, however, reminds us what the true good and source of true felicity is, and so emphasizes the extent of Arcite's confusion, for, Boethius would argue, Arcite can no more find "joye and perfit heele" in Emelye than he has found it in physical release from prison, since man can find true felicity only in God, the one true good, not in any creature of flesh and blood. His unreasoning pursuit of happiness in Emelye, not his inability to see her, brings Arcite to death: "in hire presence I recche nat to sterve" (1398). The irony is especially sharp if, as already suggested, Emelye's "freendlich ye" somehow "causes" the fury that frightens Arcite's horse so that it throws him off onto his head, fatally injuring him. There *is* a remedy, the remedy Lady Philosophy offers Boethius: reason and understanding. And thus, just as mistaking the nature of the good causes a spiritual *maladye* in the *Consolation*[40] so, to use Bernard of Gordon's words, seeking *felicitas* and *beatitudo* in possession of a woman causes a physical disease, "the loveris maladye of Hereos," and in his passion for Emelye Arcite is doubly ill, as Chaucer makes clear through philosophical allusion and medical diagnosis.

Arcite's earlier speech to Palamon reveals, though more obliquely, the same confusion and suggests its consequences. One of the several contradictory arguments Arcite uses to defend himself against Palamon's charge of treason appeals to the authority of the "olde clerkes sawe,/ . . . 'who shal yeve a lovere any lawe?'" (1163–64), which Arcite takes to prove that "A man moot nedes love, maugre his heed./ He may nat fleen it, thogh he sholde be deed" (1169–70). But the reference is to the story of Orpheus and Eurydice in the twelfth and final meter of the *Consolation's* third book, and if we follow the allusion to its source, we find Arcite as self-serving and as wrong here as in the conclusion he draws from the exemplum of the two hounds that fought over a bone and so lost it to a kite.[41] For Boethius' story of Orpheus and Eurydice does *not* show that a man must love "maugree his heed" (and the ironic force of the idiom here is put in relief by the parallel and equally ironic exclamation "by my pan" four lines before); on the contrary, it shows that the consequences of loving unreasonably, putting creatures before their creator, is the very death Arcite mentions so triumphantly—"He may nat fleen it, thogh he sholde be deed."[42] Orpheus sought Eurydice in hell and charmed the infernal powers into releasing her, though on the condition that he should not look back until out of hell—a condition he could not keep, for "what is he that may yeven a lawe to loveris?"—and at the very edge of hell "Orpheus lokede abakward on Erudyce his wif, and lost hire, and was deed." The meter itself then interprets the story to make clear its general application:

This fable apertenith to yow alle, whosoevere desireth or seketh to lede his

---

[40] E. g., 1, pr. 6, 67, 81; 2, pr. 3, 20. These and all other references to the *Consolation* are to Chaucer's translation in Robinson's edition of his works.

[41] Robertson, pp. 107–08; on the irony in 1165, p. 106.

[42] Flight is, ironically, a conventional remedy for mad love: Jean de Meun, *Roman de la rose,* ed. Félix Lecoy (Paris: Champion, 1965), 4321–28; 4780–84 in the Chaucerian translation.

thought into the sovereyn day (*that is to seyn, into cleernesse of sovereyn good*). For whoso that evere be so overcomen that he ficche his eien into the put of helle (*that is to seyn, whoso sette his thoughtes in erthly thinges*), al that evere he hath drawen of the noble good celestial he lesith it, whanne he looketh the helles (*that is to seyn, into lowe thinges of the erthe*).[43]

Arcite's allusion to the story of Orpheus and Eurydice, then, reveals both Arcite's folly and its fatal consequence, thereby emphasizing the dramatic irony of his own reference to death. And it suggests, further, that the earth from which Chaucer, unlike Boccaccio, later makes his infernal fury spring on its way up from hell should be associated not only with Saturn and melancholy but with all the "lowe thinges of the erthe" in which men mistakenly attempt to find happiness.

The spiritual progress that Boethius epitomizes in the story of Orpheus and Eurydice, to which Arcite alludes with unconscious irony, is itself a figurative "maladye." And in both the confusion with which it began and the death to which it leads, it corresponds to the course of Arcite's lover's malady of *hereos* and to the parallel course of Arcite's injury. Arcite's dying question,

> "What is this world? what asketh men to have?
> Now with his love, now in his colde grave
> Allone, withouten any compaignye,"
>
> (2777–79)

emphasizes the correspondence by recalling at the end of the tale, while Arcite's body suffers the fatal disorder that reflects the disorder of *hereos* in his brain, the Boethian context established at the beginning, thus marking the comparable depth of Arcite's philosophical confusion. Though it is a pathetic question, it becomes problematic only if we choose to share Arcite's blindness, ignoring the fact that it is precisely his pursuit of Emelye—a creature, however alluring (and Chaucer has made

---

[43] See 3, m. 12, 52–70; on this meter and traditional commentaries on it, see John Block Friedman, *Orpheus in the Middle Ages* (Cambridge, Mass.: Harvard UP, 1970), pp. 86–145.

Emelye far less alluring than Boccaccio's Emilia)—who has, in Boethian terms, exiled him from the true good and brought him to the isolation of the grave. In his speech to Emelye (2782), as in his speech to Palamon in the first part of the poem (1084), "love of God" is an empty exclamation. And the creatureliness of the woman in whom he *has* sought felicity is implicit in the absurd but pertinent lament of the women of Athens: "'Why woldestow be deed,' thise wommen crye, / 'And haddest gold ynough, and Emelye?'" (2835–36). For Arcite has chosen death by seeking felicity in Emelye just as some other seeks it in "richesse, / That cause is of his mordre or greet siknesse" (1255–56)—by pursuing "blynde lust, the which that may nat laste," rather than the one true good; "the wrastling for this world axeth a fal."[44]

From this Boethian perspective, the stadium appears not only an image of the zodiac but an image of the cosmos, binding together the warring elements of fire, air, water, and earth, and an image of that supreme good, containing within itself all lesser goods. Both of these themes figure in Theseus' concluding speech. Now Theseus is a traditional wise man, associated with reason's proper control of sensuality not only by the victory over the Amazons, with which the poem begins, and by the victory over the Minotaur, to which the poem alludes (978–80), but also by the fundamental opposition between Athens, the city of wisdom, and Thebes, a city tainted with the evil passion of its ruler, "fulfild of ire and of iniquitee" (940). And Theseus, Chaucer tells us, has managed to serve Venus, Mars, and Diana (1682, 1814), and he has temples to all three constructed within the stadium "to doon his ryte and sacrifise" (1902–13). Palamon and Arcite and Emelye, however, each serve, and pray to, only a single deity, only a part of the whole. So according to Boethius, human wickedness breaks up the unity of the supreme good, "and whanne thei enforcen hem to gete partie of a thyng that ne hath no part, thei ne geten hem neyther thilke partie that is noon, ne the thyng al hool that thei ne desire nat" (3, pr. 9, 89–93). Surely Arcite's asking for victory and "namoore" (2420)—re-emphasized by Saturn's remark to Venus that with Arcite's victory "Mars hath his wille, his knyght hath all his boone" (2669)—epitomizes the pursuit of a partial good.

---

[44] *Troilus and Criseyde*, 5.1824; "Truth," 16.

The *Consolation*, in particular, makes brilliant sense of the paradox that the planetary gods determine exactly what the protagonists choose, for Boethius explains in his fifth book (pr. 2, 36–43) that by turning from the light of sovereign good "to lowe thingis and derke" and by yielding to their passions men "hepen and encrecen the servage which thei han joyned to hemself; and in this manere thei ben caytifs fro hir propre liberte." This Boethian paradox provides, I think, the perfect explanation for the paradox of fate and freedom in *The Knight's Tale*: the elaborate astrological machinery set in motion to impose precisely what the protagonists choose for themselves is an emblem of the captivity, the entanglement in the toils of fate, to which the protagonists, failing to recognize the true good, have brought themselves through the exercise of their own freedom.

IV

The argument that Arcite's death is just and poetically inevitable may seem at odds with the tale's conclusion, where Palamon, Arcite's virtual double, is apparently rewarded for the same mad love that causes Arcite's death and where Theseus attempts to explain the apparent injustice of Arcite's death by arguing that it is a necessary consequence of the nature of things, thus making the question of justice irrelevant. But with typical indirection, Chaucer manages to put in doubt both the extent to which Palamon's marriage is a reward and the extent to which it is undeserved, even though reward undeserved, in itself, poses a less acute philosophical problem than suffering undeserved; and more important still he makes Theseus's speech suggest, ironically and allusively, the very Boethian perspective suggested by the speeches of Palamon and Arcite in Part I,[45] a perspective which reveals the appearance of disorder and injustice in the tale as mere illusion.

The dying Arcite's praise of Palamon, in the same speech that betrays his philosophical confusion even *in extremis*, may suggest that Palamon really does deserve to win Emelye:

---

[45] On Palamon's speech see P. M. Kean, *Chaucer and the Making of English Poetry* (London: Routledge & Kegan Paul, 1972), II, 12–14.

> "To speken of a servaunt proprely,
> With alle circumstances trewely—
> That is to seyen, trouthe, honour, knyghthede,
> Wysdom, humblesse, estaat, and heigh kynrede,
> Fredom, and al that longeth to that art—
> So Juppiter have of my soule part,
> As in this world right now ne knowe I non
> So worthy to ben loved as Palamon,
> That serveth yow, and wol doon al his lyf.
> And if that evere ye shul ben a wyf,
> Foryet nat Palamon, the gentil man."
>   (2787–97)

But Arcite's praise constitutes clearer proof of Arcite's magnanimity than of Palamon's excellence of character, for there is no dramatic warrant in the tale for any of Arcite's claims. On the contrary, Palamon has betrayed Arcite to Theseus, and "hastily" (1714) at that, though swearing "by seinte charitee" and using language that cruelly echoes the biblical idea of charity as one man's laying down his life for another (1721–26). So what of "trouthe" and "fredom"? He and Arcite have reduced themselves to the level of the brutes in their quarrel over Emelye[46]—even though, as Theseus wryly notes, "she woot namoore of al this hoote fare, / By God, than woot a cokkow or an hare!" / (1809–10)—and, perverting Boethius, Palamon lamented that he could not find happiness in physical pleasure like the brutes (1315–18). So what of "wysdom"? And Palamon's "heigh kynrede" is of Thebes, that city of "ire and iniquitee." In *The Knight's Tale*, however, unlike the *Teseida*, Palamon's marriage to Emelye takes place years after the tournament, so that the passage of time, filled in the narrative only with mourning for Arcite (2967–70), leaves open the possibility of such moral improvement in Palamon that he may in fact be, as the narrator and not only his Theban cousin calls him, "gentil" (2976) in character as well as rank. The marriage, furthermore, serves Theseus' political purposes by securing the full "obeisaunce" of Thebes to Athens (2970–77), a relationship that lends itself to symbolic interpretation based on the traditional association of

---

[46] See the passages assembled by Jeffrey Helterman, "The Dehumanizing Metamorphoses of *The Knight's Tale*," *ELH*, 38 (1971), 493–511.

Athens with reason and of Thebes with passion that has informed *The Knight's Tale* from the beginning, and in his First-Mover speech Theseus advances a series of Boethian arguments to justify it. That political, symbolic, and philosophical motivation makes marriage to Emelye much more than simple reward. And as the tale several times reminds us, Emelye is in any case a mere earthly good.

The speech in which Theseus attempts to explain Arcite's death is more problematic than the marriage it arranges. It appears to offer a final statement of the tale's meaning, but because it explains Arcite's death only as a necessary part of the order of things, it never mentions issues so crucial to the tale as the freedom of the will, moral responsibility, or justice. It never illustrates the "grace" for which Theseus calls upon his audience to thank Jupiter. And the fame that Theseus urges as consolation for Arcite's early death (3047–61) Lady Philosophy has proved to be deceptive and worthless (2, pr. 7, m. 7). Indeed, although the speech is "an amalgam of phrases and ideas found in different order and context in Boethius's *De Consolatione Philosophiae*,"[47] the details have been so extensively rearranged and the context so altered that the thrust of the speech runs directly counter to that of the *Consolation*, for Theseus holds to the transience and corruption of the world whereas Boethius turns from it to the simplicity and stability of God. And this opposition between the speech and its source is most striking precisely where the correspondences are most extensive, because there the correspondences of detail throw into relief the differences of application, so that Theseus' speech becomes not simply different from the *Consolation* but conspicuously so, and yet because it is, the Boethian allusions of the speech reveal through the double vision of irony a perspective Theseus himself and the Knight do not take, one which truly resolves the appearance of injustice and disorder in the tale.

This contrast between Theseus' speech and its source in the *Consolation* emphasizes first of all how narrow the objectives of that speech are and how limited a commentary it offers, directly, on the action of the tale. After describing the First Mover, the harmonious order of the elements bound within the "faire cheyne of love" (2991), and the cycle of birth and death through which mutable things are continually renewed, Theseus concludes:

---

[47] J. A. W. Bennett, *The Knight's Tale,* 2nd ed. (London: Harrap, 1958) p. 146.

> "Thanne may men by this ordre wel discerne
> That thilke Moevere stable is and eterne.
> Wel may men knowe, but it be a fool,
> That every part dirryveth from his hool;
> For nature hath nat taken his bigynnyng
> Of no partie or cantel of a thyng,
> But of a thyng that parfit is and stable,
> Descendynge so til it be corrumpable."
> (3003–10)

This conclusion corresponds closely to Boethius' argument that the very imperfection of the world proves the existence of a higher perfection against which imperfection can be measured:

> For yif so be that perfeccioun is don awey, men may nat thinke ne say fro whennes thilke thing is that is cleped inparfyt. For the nature of thinges ne took nat hir begynnynge of thinges amenused and inparfit, but it procedith of thinges that ben alle hole and absolut, and descendith so doun into uttereste thinges and into thinges empty and withouten fruyt (3, pr. 10, 22–30).

But Boethius in this same passage turns at once from the imperfection of the world to the source and center of all things in God's perfect simplicity—"yif ther be a blisfulnesse that be freel and veyn and inparfyt, ther may no man doute that ther nys som blisfulnesse that is sad, stedefast, and parfyt" (3, pr. 10, 31–35)—while Theseus, whose objectives are narrower and more practical, instead turns back to the bottom of that chain, where it is grounded in corruption and

> speces of thynges and progressiouns
> Shullen enduren by successiouns,
> And nat eterne, withouten any lye.
> (3013–15)

Without further explanation, he presents this continual renewal of mutable nature as evidence of the First Mover's "wise purveiaunce," an "ordinaunce" "wel biset" (3011–12); but because he ignores God's "entente," what Theseus describes is fate, not providence, and in the illustrations which follow, drawn from the *Teseida* rather than the *Consolation*,[48] Theseus emphasizes not new beginnings but inevitable ends: mighty oaks die; stones wear away; rivers dry up; great towns decline; old or young, every man must die—"Ther helpeth noght, al goth that ilke weye. / Thanne may I seyn that al this thyng moot deye" (3033–34). Between these illustrations and the conclusion to which they lead, likewise drawn from the *Teseida*, Chaucer inserts four climactic lines that closely parallel a passage in Book 4, Meter 6, of the *Consolation* and point up by implication how un-Boethian Theseus' illustrations of a universe tending inevitably to death and his consequent conclusion are:

> "What maketh this but Juppiter, the kyng,
> That is prince and cause of alle thyng,
> Convertynge al unto his propre welle
> From which it is dirryved, sooth to telle?"
> (3035–38)

This "propre welle" from which everything that lives is derived and to which "Juppiter, the kyng," returns everything at its death remains so vague and unconsoling an abstraction, no obvious source of good or happiness, that when Theseus *again* turns from eternity to mutability in order to insist on the inevitability of death, he can without conspicuous self-contradiction urge only the futility of resistance:

> "And heer-agayns no creature on lyve,
> Of no degree, availleth for to stryve.
>   Thanne is it wysdom, as it thynketh me
> To maken vertu of necessitee,
> And take it weel that we may nat eschue."
> (3039–43)

[48] 12.7–8—all, that is, except for the example of great towns; Theseus' conclusion comes from 12.11. On the distinction between fate and providence, see the *Consolation*, 4, pr. 6.

Theseus himself suggests how unpersuasive such an argument must be in his references to rebellion once (3046) and *grucchyng* three times (3045, 3058, 3062) in the following lines.[49] In the passage which Theseus echoes (a broadly similar picture of mutability though emphasizing how life is sustained rather than ended) Boethius, too, insists that God brings all things back to their source, but with very different effect (4, m. 6, 40–60):

> Among thise thinges sitteth the heye makere, kyng and lord, welle and bygynnynge, lawe and wys juge to don equite, and governeth and enclyneth the brydles of thinges. And tho thinges that he stireth to gon by moevynge, he withdraweth and aresteth, and affermeth the moevable or wandrynge thinges. For yif that he ne clepide nat ayein the ryght goynge of thinges, and yif that he ne constreynede hem nat eftsones into roundnesses enclyned, the thingis that ben now contynued by stable ordenaunce, thei scholden departen from hir welle (*that is to seyn, from hir bygynnynge*), and failen (*that is to seyn, tornen into noght*). This is the comune love to alle thingis, and alle thinges axen to ben holden by the fyn of good. For elles ne myghten they nat lasten yif thei ne comen nat eftsones ayein, by love retorned, to the cause that hath yeven hem beinge (*that is to seyn, to God*).

Here the "welle" of all things is explicitly God himself, the "fyn of good" and source of all life, by which all things *seek* ("axen") to be held and to which they are returned not by compulsion but "by love." It is the very "welle of alle goodes" against which the imperfection of all earthly goods is measured in Prose 10 of Book 3 (16), the passage Theseus has echoed just before, the source of "blisfulnesse . . . sad, stedefast, and parfyt" (34–35), where in the opening words of the next meter, "ye that ben ykaught and ybounde with wikkide cheynes by the desceyvable delyt of erthly thynges enhabitynge in yowr thought" can find "reste of your labours, . . . the havene stable in pesible quiete; this allone is the open refut to wreches" (3, m. 10, 1–7).

The contrast between this final Boethian passage in Theseus' speech, with its emphasis on the destructiveness of fate, and its source in the

---

[49] Kean, II, 47.

Consolation, with its emphasis on the creativity of providence, reveals most clearly how earthbound and essentially un-Boethian that speech is. For Theseus uses those Boethian arguments not to reveal true felicity but only to arrange a wedding and thereby reinforce a political alliance, and those practical ends, not the Boethian arguments he uses to accomplish them, bring Theseus to the conclusion, "But after wo I rede us to be merye" (3068), far nearer the proverbial self-deception of "let us eat and drink for tomorrow we die" than the consolation Lady Philosophy offers Boethius. Because Theseus describes the destructiveness of fate without regard to the benevolence of providence, he omits precisely those developments of Boethius' arguments which support his reference to Jupiter's grace; and the discrepancy between his conclusion and the *Consolation's* is most evident in the impossibility of making "of sorwes two / O parfit joye, lastynge evermo" (3071–72) here, in "this foule prisoun of this lyf" (3061), where nature is "corrumpable" (3010) and Theseus himself insists that neither mighty oak nor hard stone can last.

Its narrow practicality prevents Theseus' speech from serving, *directly*, as commentary on the tale as a whole. But the Boethian passages Theseus turns to his own use, like those Palamon and Arcite pervert more simply and obviously, point to the still center from which the agitations and reversals of this world can be viewed with detached and godlike perspective. Through its context of allusion Theseus' speech provides, indirectly, the very vantage point achieved by the souls of Boccaccio's Arcita and Chaucer's Troilus:

> And ther he saugh, with ful avysement,
> The erratik sterres, herkenyng armonye
> With sownes ful of hevenyssh melodie.

> And down from thennes faste he gan avyse
> This litel spot of erthe, that with the se
> Embraced is, and fully gan despise
> This wrecched world, and held al vanite
> To respect of the pleyn felicite
> That is in hevene above; and at the laste,
> Ther he was slayn, his lokyng down he caste.

> And in hymself he lough right at the wo
> Of hem that wepten for his deth so faste;
> And dampned al oure werk that foloweth so
> The blynde lust, the which that may nat laste,
> And sholden al oure herte on heven caste.[50]

That Chaucer had already used this part of Boccaccio's narrative in his conclusion to the *Troilus* cannot explain why he did not use it in *The Knight's Tale*.[51] But since Arcite's character is neither complex nor admirable, despite the magnanimity he displays toward Palamon at the end, since his death is the direct and appropriate result of his "blinde lust," and since those final questions, "What is this world? what asketh men to have?" show that he dies confused and benighted, it is harder to see how Arcite could deserve such a vantage point than it is to see how Palamon deserved Emelye.[52] Chaucer, however, makes the failure to describe the flight of Arcite's soul a matter of character in the Knight and has the Knight call attention to the omission:

> His spirit chaunged hous and wente ther,
> As I cam nevere, I kan nat tellen wher.
> Therfore I stynte, I nam no divinistre:
> Of soules fynde I nat in this registre,
> Ne me ne list thilke opinions to telle
> Of hem, though that they writen wher they dwelle.
> Arcite is coold, ther Mars his soule gye!
> Now wol I speken forth of Emelye.
>   (2809–16)

He thereby evades the problem of merit without renouncing Boccaccio's solution and its contrast between the false beauty of this world and the

---

[50] *Troilus and Criseyde*, 5.1811–25, a virtual translation of *Teseida*, 11.1.6–3.7.
[51] Chaucer used Boccaccio's description of the temple of Venus in the *Parlement of Foules* and again in *The Knight's Tale;* see Pratt, "Chaucer's Use of the *Teseida*," p. 618.
[52] According to Lady Philosophy—2, pr. 7, 151–57—it is only the soul "that hath in itself science of gode werkes," which, "unbownden fro the prysone of the erthe, weendeth frely to the hevene [and] despiseth . . . thanne al erthly occupacioun; and, beynge in hevene rejoyseth that it is exempt fro alle erthly thynges."

true beauty of heaven. And while the implications of Theseus' speech, which Theseus himself does not admit, lead through allusion to the same contrast between earthly and heavenly goods, they do so not only more obliquely but more generally, leaving moot the question whether Arcite himself achieved such illumination. And that contrast between earthly and heavenly goods, suggested by the inconsistencies of Theseus's speech as well as by its allusions, puts in question the worth of Palamon's reward and so dissolves the last appearance of injustice and disorder in *The Knight's Tale.* If, through Arcite's death, Arcite achieves true understanding and Palamon a mere earthly good, then it must be Palamon, and not Arcite, who has it worse at tale's end. Even if Arcite's soul does not enjoy the same illumination as Arcita's, Chaucer's Boethian allusions suggest that illumination to the reader, and the speech itself insists that death will inevitably end the "parfit joye, lastynge everemo," Theseus so inconsistently promises Palamon and Emelye.

The inconclusiveness of the Knight's conclusion, like the Knight's refusal to consider the destiny of Arcite's soul, shows the same un-Boethian interest in purely earthly happiness the Knight displays in his interruption of *The Monk's Tale,*[53] and accordingly it is part of the distinctive drama of *The Canterbury Tales,* in which the tales enrich the characterization of their tellers and the characterization of the tellers enriches and complicates their tales: the limitations the Knight reveals elsewhere emphasize and confirm the limitations suggested in his tale. And *The Miller's Tale,* explicitly intended to "quite the Knyghtes tale" (I, 3128), transmuting its parallel rivalries and intricate structure into fabliau,[54] concentrates on the very *jalousie* and *teene* the Knight claims

---

[53] Cf. R. E. Kaske, "The Knight's Interruption of the *Monk's Tale," ELH,* 24 (1957), 249–68, esp. p. 266. But unless *The Knight's Tale* clearly shows the "real Boethian orientation" *The Monk's Tale* lacks, there is no philosophical discrepancy to be explained. The story of Croesus, who falls because pride makes him mistakenly trust in Fortune, is in fact the most philosophically satisfying of all those the Monk tells. Donald K. Fry, "The Ending of *The Monk's Tale," JEGP,* 71 (1972), 355–68, argues that the "modern instances" should be put last and explain the Knight's interruption, but Harry Bailly's garbled reference to the last line of the Croesus story (VII, 2781–83) would then be out of place, and it seems more natural to take the Knight's criticism of *The Monk's Tale* at face value as demonstrating, though more bluntly, the same philosophical shortsightedness that appears in the relative treatment of Palamon's and Arcite's ends in *The Knight's Tale.*

[54] The classic treatments of this relationship, to which the Miller himself draws attention, are Frost, p. 303; William C. Stokoe, Jr., "Structure and Intention in the First

Palamon was spared (3106). As the unreality of *The Knight's Tale's* conclusion prompts the Miller to tell his tale, so *The Miller's Tale* in turn demonstrates the fragility of that earthly happiness with which *The Knight's Tale* ends. And as *The Miller's Tale*, through its allusions to the Song of Songs, suggests an alternative to purely animal passion,[55] so *The Knight's Tale*, through its allusions to the *Consolation*, suggests the perspective from which the action of the tale can be understood, a perspective as much beyond the Knight's comprehension or his protagonists' as charity is beyond the Miller's.

The astrological machinery Chaucer added to *The Knight's Tale* creates the appearance of contradiction between universal order and particular disorder, between an outcome determined by the stars and one for which the protagonists themselves are responsible. But the framework of allusion to the *Consolation of Philosophy*, which Chaucer also added, turns that apparent contradiction into significant paradox: through surrender to the passions and the perverse pursuit of partial goods, Palamon and Arcite make themselves slaves of their own freedom. The paradox figures most pointedly in the elaborate correspondence between Arcite's lovesickness and his fatal injury. But though it applies most directly to Arcite, it encompasses Palamon as well, at least implicitly, and brings into common focus the equivocations of the tale's conclusion, its mythological background, the retrospective commentary of *The Miller's Tale*, and the characterization of the Knight as that is elaborated in his interruption of *The Monk's Tale*. It reveals, in short, the ordinance that underlies the rich diversity of Chaucer's vast design.

Fragment of the *Canterbury Tales*," *UTQ*, 21 (1952), 120–27; Charles A. Owen, Jr., "Chaucer's *Canterbury Tales:* Aesthetic Design in Stories of the First Day," *ES*, 35 (1954), 49–56.

[55] R. E. Kaske, "The *Canticum Canticorum* in the *Miller's Tale*," *SP*, (1962), 479–500.

Politics and the Paralysis of Poetic Imagination in *The Physician's Tale*

Sheila Delany
Simon Fraser University

THE PHYSICIAN'S TALE is generally conceded to be one of Chaucer's least interesting and least successful efforts: flat characters, a rather incompetent narrative flawed by irrelevant digressions, a plot exceedingly improbable and—unlike *The Clerk's* or *The Man of Law's Tales*—without redeeming symbolic depth. However, the failures of a great poet must interest us at least to the extent that they shed light on his creativity, and I want to propose in this paper that the intersection of Chaucer's own social views with those of his sources produced, in *The Physician's Tale,* an imaginative impasse manifested in the esthetic inferiority of the tale.

I

What stands out in *The Physician's Tale,* setting it apart from Chaucer's sources and from other medieval versions of the Virginius legend accessible to him, is the virtually complete depoliticization of a political anecdote.

The story of Virginius—who kills his daughter rather than see her coerced by legal fraud into a life of fornication—was known to the Middle Ages in Livy's history of Rome (Titus Livius, *Ab Urbe Condita* III: 44 ff.). Livy adapted it in turn from an older regional legend. Chaucer probably used Livy's history, at least as a supplement to his main source, the *Roman de la Rose* of Jean de Meun.[1] Livy's theme was the degeneration

---

[1] That Chaucer refers to Livy in the first line of *The Physician's Tale* is far from conclusive evidence of use; likewise his references to Livy as a source for the legend of

of Rome from its great republican golden age: he sets the legend of
Virginius in the mid-fifth century B.C., some 400 years in the past,
during a period of intense conflict between plebs and patriciate.[2] The
legend shows how tyrannical were the patrician rulers and how oppressed
the plebs; it also serves to justify the "Third Roman Revolution" of 449
B.C. which won important gains for the plebs. Appius Claudius, the
judge who perverts justice in the interest of lust, is a patrician and
decemvir. Virginius is a plebeian and military man. Virginia is engaged
to marry Icilius, also a plebeian and a noted champion of his class. The
other important *dramatis persona* in Livy's account is the Roman populace, who are present throughout the story. Virginia's arrest occurs in the
crowded forum; the people foil the seizure and offer bail for her; the trial
and sentence are public, as is the murder. Protesting the atrocity to
which Virginius has been forced to save his daughter's honor, the people
unite with the army to depose Appius and the rest of the decemvirate.
They demand and win restoration of the people's tribunes—plebeian
magistrates whose veto could protect the plebs against unjust patrician
legislation. They also win the right to judicial appeal, and a series of
measures is passed (the Valerian-Horatian laws) which increased plebeian
powers. Appius kills himself in prison; his accomplice goes into exile;
Roman popular liberties are restored.

Jean de Meun relied on Livy for his account of the story, but in several
ways depoliticized it. Specific social classes are not named (except that
Virginius is "bons chevaliers bien renomez");[3] the populace enter only at

---

Lucrece (*LGW*, 1683, 1873; *BD*, 1084). Bruce Harbert asserts that there is no sure
evidence of direct borrowing from Livy ("Chaucer and the Latin Classics" in *Writers and
Their Background: Chaucer*, ed. D. Brewer, London, 1974). However he does acknowledge, along with Edgar Shannon (*Sources and Analogues*), that there are some details in
Chaucer that appear only in Livy. On Livy's use of traditional material, see Ettore Pais,
Ancient Legends of Roman History (London, 1906).

[2] During the period 500–300 B.C., "plebs" meant a section of the population that
could loosely be terned "the middle classes": that is, between noble patricians and the
poor, or, as the *Oxford Companion to Classical Literature* puts it, "the Roman burgesses
other than the patricians." Their struggle, a gradual but eventually successful one, was to
win full civil rights: e.g., the right to intermarry with patricians and to hold all political
and priestly offices. Once these rights were won, the name "plebs" passed over to the
working population, the Roman masses of artisans, shopkeepers, day laborers, servants,
etc. See F. R. Cowell, *The Revolutions of Ancient Rome* (London, 1962) and P. G. Walsh,
Livy (Cambridge, 1961).

[3] "Knight" is the obvious medieval equivalent for the Latin "milites", but there is an
inconsistency between the medieval knight's privileged status as a member of the lower

the end to save Virginius from hanging; no insurrection follows, although Appius is imprisoned, his witnesses condemned to death, and the accomplice sent into exile. Nonetheless, in its context Jean's version retains a clear social thrust; for Jean, exploring the conception of justice in general and specifically its relation to wealth, contrasts a golden age of primitive justice with the social stratification and oppression of his own epoch (5345-74). Indeed the tale of Virginius immediately follows Genius's vision of a classless and stateless society in which justice is no longer required to mediate right and wrong, nor is any special judicial, legislative, or repressive apparatus necessary, for

> puis que Forfez s'en iroit,
> Joutice, de quoi serviroit?
> (5523-24)

> car se ne fust maus et pechiez,
> dom li mondes est entechiez,
> l'en n'eust onques roi veu
> ne juige en terre conneu.
> (5537-40)

Of course Jean speaks here not as a utopian socialist but as a Christian humanist: the society Genius describes is presumably not to be attained on earth but only in heaven. This is a moral vision with a political effect: to expose and denounce the perversion of social justice by the rich. To this end Genius brings in the Roman exemplum.

Though there is no hard evidence that Chaucer borrowed from Boc-

---

feudal nobility, and, on the other hand, the erstwhile exclusion of the plebs from such privileged status. Perhaps Boccaccio acknowledges this inconsistency in describing Virginius as "plebian *but* honest" ("plebs sed honestus"). Of course the really radical innovation in a medieval treatment of this legend would have been to present Virginius as a wealthy and virtuous bourgeois, Appius as a representative or ally of the feudal aristocracy. While that would have been a more accurate analogy to the political struggle recounted in Livy, it would have required crystallized class consciousness that the bourgeoisie would develop only over the next few centuries. During the high Middle Ages the upper bourgeoisie aspired to emulate aristocrats and ally with kings—not depose or expropriate them.

caccio's version of the Virginius legend in *De Claris Mulieribus* (cap. LVIII), it was from that work that Chaucer drew material for the story of Zenobia (*The Monk's Tale*), and it seems reasonable to suppose that he at least skimmed the rest of the volume. Boccaccio began to compose his text in 1361, toward the end of a period of intense political activity when, as orator, counsellor, diplomat, and elected representative, he served the Florentine city-state in its complicated municipal and international affairs. The work is close in spirit to Livy, its source, for Boccaccio—an ardent partisan of republican rights in "the good and holy Commune"—uses the legend of Virginius to advance his *haut bourgeois* republican ideals. Vittore Branca's comment about one of Boccaccio's letters could as well apply to his version of our legend: that it is "the clear reflection of intensely mediated personal experience."[4] As in Livy, class lines are sharply drawn: decemvirs versus plebs. Virginius's deed is described as one that, despite its severity, secured Roman liberties; the populace plays a prominent role throughout. After the insurrection of army and people, Virginius is chosen tribune and sentences Appius to prison, where he commits suicide. There follows a long diatribe against unjust judges and a passionate denunciation of tyrants in general for their arrogance, violence, corruption, and license. We recall that Boccaccio hated tyrannical feudal aristocrats and reproached his friend Petrarch for making his home at their courts.

Chaucer's close friend John Gower included the legend of Virginius as the penultimate exemplum in Book VII of his *Confessio Amantis*. While the verbal independence of Chaucer's text is generally acknowledged, he would certainly have had easy access to Gower's work after 1390, its publication date, and probably "knew something about its contents"

---

[4] Vittore Branca, *Boccaccio: The Man and His Works* (New York, 1976), p. 129. The phrase about the commune is Boccaccio's. For a clear outline of economic and political struggle in Florence, see also Frederic Antal, *Florentine Painting and Its Social Background: 14th and Early 15th Centuries* (London, 1948), Chapters 1 and 2. Antal notes, interestingly for my purpose here, that in the Ordinamenti di Giustizia—the constitution of 1293, in which the upper bourgeoisie won a decisive victory in obtaining political power for their guilds—"the revolutionary bourgeoisie had still proudly called themselves 'plebians' " (p. 33, n. 38). The Roman tradition remained rhetorically viable well into our own period: witness Karl Marx's comment from *The Eighteenth Brumaire:* " . . . the heroes as well as the parties and the masses of the old French Revolution performed the task of their time in Roman costume and with Roman phrases, the task of unchaining and setting up modern *bourgeois* society . . . " (his italics).

before that date.⁵ Gower used the legend to an end at once moral and political: to exhort rulers to avoid vice and its socially disruptive consequences. Book VII is a political treatise on the place of good governance in the universe—a mirror for magistrates in the broadest sense—and, as in the *Roman de la Rose*, the spokesman is Genius. As John H. Fisher shows, Gower did indeed have a political axe to grind: he was committed to the Lancastrian cause and in 1392 or 1393 changed the dedication of the *Confessio* from Richard II to Henry Bolingbroke, for Richard's intemperate financial policies had alienated many of Gower's—and Chaucer's—friends in the London business community.⁶ In the tale, Appius is referred to as "king;" Virginius urges the army to correct domestic injustice before engaging in foreign wars; the people's revolt is vindicated because they do uphold justice and law; constantly we hear the phrases "comun lawe," "comun right," "comun fere," "comun counseil." Gower's treatment of the tale is very much at home in the social-protest tradition already sketched out: its spirit is not a republican spirit, but it does reflect real partisanship in admonishing a tyrannical ruler on behalf of his citizenry.

A certain consensus appears, then, among the four authors discussed so far. Whether lust or injustice is treated as the main theme, social criticism remains a key element in the story; the latter may be conveyed in dramatic action, in authorial comment, or in both. Turning to *The Physician's Tale*, we find that only it lacks a clear political thrust. Only Chaucer systematically obliterates the traditional social content of the legend of Virginius *and* fails to replace it with explicit social commentary in his own or a narrator's voice. In so doing, I suggest, he deprives the story of convincing dramatic motivation and his characters of plausible psychological and ethical motives. I want now to examine the changes Chaucer made in the tale, along with their esthetic consequences.

II

The theme of class conflict is effaced in several ways. Virginius is a knight "of greate richesse" (VI, 4) and Appius a local governor, so that

⁵ The phrase is J. M. Manly's, cited in *Sources and Analogues*, p. 10, n. 4.

⁶ See John H. Fisher, *John Gower: Moral Philosopher and Friend of Chaucer* (New York, 1964). Also Russell Peck, *Kingship and Common Profit in Gower's* Confessio Amantis (Carbondale, Illinois, 1978).

51

they are more or less on the same social level. Icilius, Virginia's fiancé and champion of the people, is dropped from the story altogether (as in Jean), an omission which further obscures the theme of political struggle. Of course the elimination of Icilius also gives us a more saint-like and pathetic picture of Virginia. It intensifies her will to virginity, creating a more starkly moralistic counterposition to Appius' lust.[7]

The population, always so crucial to this tale, also disappears from Chaucer's story. Most of the action occurs in private, and, as in the *Roman*, the people intervene only to rescue Virginius—not one of their own class, as in Livy or Boccaccio, but one of the ruling class: Virginius must be a virtuous knight indeed to generate such loyalty among the masses. However, the absence of the populace from the body of the tale introduces some narrative puzzles. If Virginia is "strong of freendes" (VI, 135), why is there no earlier protest or intervention? And how likely is it that the people would intervene to save a knight, motivated only for "routhe and for pitee" (VI, 261), or, moreover, depose their district governor merely because "They wisten wel that he was lecherus" (VI, 266), without perceiving this crisis as an opportunity to present demands in their own behalf? Such altruism scarcely corresponds to what Chaucer could observe of "the people" in his own turbulent time. Nor does it correspond to the role played by the general populace in *The Clerk's Tale*, who are present at critical moments in the narrative and are shown to be fickle and treacherous.[8] Thus in *The Physician's Tale* the people's intervention is devoid of social motive, while their moral motive is unconvincing.

To reduce or eliminate the political dimension in a political anecdote must alter the equilibrium of a narrative. Here it increases the relative weight of the murder. In Livy, Virginia's death is provoked by an unjust

---

[7] Chaucer used a similar method in adapting the figure of Constance for *The Man of Law's Tale* from its source, the Anglo-French *Chronicle* of Nicholas Trivet: he stripped Constance of the features that make Trivet's heroine more "realistic." For Chaucer's doctrinal/symbolic purpose in *The Man of Law's Tale*, the character can, even should, be monodimensional.

[8] For Chaucer's usually unflattering view of "the people," we may also adduce *Troilus*, IV: 141–217, where it is the majority of parliament who unscrupulously vote to exchange Criseyde for Antenor, despite Hector's well-taken objection that she is no prisoner of war. Also, the assembly in *The Parliament of Fowls* offers an obvious parody of the greed of the lower orders (as well, to be sure, of the theatricality of the upper) for those who are inclined to take that scene as a social fable.

system of government and in turn provokes popular revolt. The social component in Livy lets us share the plebs' view of the murder as a desperate act by an intolerably victimized member of the oppressed class. We can derive satisfaction, too, from the redress of grievances that is achieved when that class forcefully asserts its rights. With Jean de Meun, the murder justifies Genius' denunciation of the abuse of justice by the rich. Even though Jean gives no social redress in the form of rebellion, he expresses general indignation against the wicked wealthy who provoke such extreme acts as the murder. Hence there is some legitimation of rebellion, at least to the extent that the rebellion protests tyranny.

Since Chaucer omits both the revolt and any commentary on social injustice, there is neither dramatic nor thematic justification for the atrocity. It becomes a more or less free-floating *acte gratuite*: it becomes unnecessary. We must focus, then, on moral justification: "outher deeth or shame" (VI, 214). But this choice seems shallow. Virginius could consider taking his daughter away; he could find a substitute for her, bribe his way out of the dilemma, appeal the decision to higher authority (in Livy, of course we know that the plebs could not do this; but Chaucer gives us no reason why not). How much does the father want his daughter to survive if he fails to consider these possibilities? We recall that escape with Criseyde is one of the options that Chaucer makes available to Troilus; further, that Troilus' rejection of such decisive action is presented as consistent with his general and deplorable passivity (V, 35–36). Is the killing, then, a monstrous, unnatural act, or the necessary sacrifice of a Christian martyr? The new Chaucerian context forces forward Virginius' determination to kill the girl. That determination now becomes the story's dramatic centre, displacing the social theme. But the motivation and literary consistency formerly provided in the social theme are not replaced in other material that might justify the sacrifice: praise of chastity, exemplary saints' lives, scriptural precedent, and so forth—material of the kind that allows us to see, for instance, the equally outrageous or offensive action of *The Clerk's Tale* as appropriate to Chaucer's esthetic and moral purposes (explained quite lucidly by the Clerk at the end of his tale). The original material that Chaucer does add only compounds our discomfort since it seems so irrelevant and, unlike other Chaucerian "irrelevancies," for no discernible reason.[9] The story

[9] The "digressions" are often attributed to the Physician's dubious character, as are

falls between two stools: its "realistic" (social) dimension is gone, but nothing propels it to a different level of fictional meaning.

Let me return to the list of alternatives available to Virginius. None of the possibilities that I mentioned above would be as realistic or as effective as another: Virginius could raise a popular revolt against Appius. (It is worth noting, again, that among the last-minute possibilities Troilus considers is to raise a riot in Criseyde's behalf: V, 43–46). Clearly this is his best chance to save Virginia, and if the population can be aroused after the murder, surely they could be moved to prevent it. (We might make the same objection to Livy and versions close to him, except that there the death is dramatically necessary to justify the revolt or, later, invective.) But here precisely is Chaucer's double bind. Virginia cannot be saved without mass action; her death cannot be fully meaningful nor fully avenged without mass action; Virginius is not a credible character without at least considering mass action; yet mass action is just what Chaucer excises from the legend.

In response to such criticism one could propose, as Anne Middleton has done, that all of the foregoing problems are intentionally present as part of Chaucer's artful ironic vision; that they force us to "examine, define and redefine ethical abstractions that are treated as given in his originals"; that we are not supposed to fully suspend disbelief in the work because in that margin of discomfort we contemplate "a world of wider and more emotionally complex choices than the source tale offers."[10]

---

the manifold esthetic and moral inadequacies of the tale. This approach doesn't, I believe, stand up to two objections. First: usually when a tale is a failure and intended as such (e.g., *The Squire's Tale* or *The Tale of Sir Thopas*) or when narrative inconsistencies or quirks further characterize a narrator (Wife of Bath, Prioress, Merchant) those intentions are fairly obvious: the audience reacts to the former, or in the latter case, we can pretty clearly demonstrate the relation between tale and teller. Second, there is no necessary relation between a narrator's moral character and the quality of his or her tale (Pardoner, Summoner, even Wife of Bath). Some critics have found ways of relating the digressions to a central theme, but not, in my view, convincingly. For example, Anne Middleton finds that the added material shows artists and parents functioning as "secondary creators," and that it poses the problem of who finally controls the disposition of human life; "*The Physician's Tale* and Love's Martyrs: 'Ensamples mo than ten' as a method in the *Canterbury Tales*," *ChauR* 8 (1973) 9–32. While the question is indeed a recognizable Chaucerian topos, I don't see it worked out or answered dramatically in the text—as is done, say, in *The Man of Law's Tale*—hence the material remains, to my mind, unintegrated.

[10] Middleton, p. 15.

In my view there are deficiencies in such an apologia for *The Physician's Tale*. One is that the sources do not strike me as less complex or realistic than Chaucer's version but as more so. The "given" in the sources is not "ethical abstraction" but the ongoing struggle for social justice; this, Chaucer scarcely "chips away at"—he simply ignores it. He fails to encounter the sources on their own terrain, as he would have to do to undercut that terrain—the procedure in *Troilus*, for example. Thus if the argument is that Chaucer shows the inadequacy of both Livy (because nothing justifies murder, not even revolution) and the Physician (because he passes over the atrocity too easily), then surely Chaucer's case would be far stronger if it made some connection or analogy between republican politics and the notorious rationalism of physicians.

At a certain point critics arrive at irreducible opinion. While acknowledging that some of Chaucer's best work purposely distances the reader in the interest of moral judgment, I don't believe that *The Physician's Tale* occupies that category, but rather that it is, simply, a bad piece of work no matter how we read it. Professor Middleton has compiled an extensive list of flaws and problems in the tale—she agrees it is "dull and inferior," "a dull little tale"—yet she maintains that the piece is not inartistic. I take it this means it is not an esthetic failure, but I should think such a list does amount to a statement of esthetic failure: the test of artistic quality isn't only that "the marks of making are there" but that they succeed in producing a work that is on some level coherent, that it "works" or "succeeds." The problem with *The Physician's Tale* is that we don't care enough about it to fall into the trap of suspending disbelief in the first place. If virtually every flaw and mediocrity in the tale is a deliberate distancing device, where's the good stuff—the tempting, persuasive material that we need to be distanced from? And what does the tale offer us that is better than the sources? Nothing, as far as I can see.

Another angle: any story of maladministration by a public official must objectively pose the issue of social justice. How did the corrupt official attain his position? Has he too much power? Are others complicit in the abuse? Are only individuals, or is an entire system, at fault? One scarcely needs to be a revolutionary to ask such questions: our other authors are no flaming radicals. But Chaucer, unlike the others, is unwilling to draw out the questions implicit in his plot. He deplores the corruption of Appius as an individual, but does not generalize from the incident: yet it is generalization that confers on this story its most serious interest and importance.

The last creative stalemate I wish to discuss pertains to the people. Chaucer will not show the people as collective hero, cleansing society with purgative revolt. Yet in traditional versions of the tale, the people are precisely a collective hero. This function can be demonstrated by superimposing on the tale a structural grid suggested by V. Propp's analysis of folktale,[11] as follows: I. One of the members of a family absents himself. (Virginius is away in the army.) IV. The villain makes an attempt at reconnaissance. (Appius tries to seduce Virginia.) VI. The villain attempts to deceive his victim in order to take possession of him or his belongings. (Appius initiates a false court case in which his agent claims Virginia as his abducted servant.) VIII. The villain causes harm or injury to a member of a family. (Appius is morally responsible for the murder of Virginia; he is able to consummate his plot because the plebs have no right of appeal.) IX. Misfortune or lack is made known; the hero is approached with a request or command; he is allowed to go or he is dispatched. (Virginius appeals to a mixed crowd of civilians and soldiers to defend him and themselves against the patriciate.) X. The seeker agrees to or decides upon counteraction. (Civilians and soldiers march on Rome.) XVI. The hero and the villain join in direct combat. (There is no actual war but the threat of imminent attack by the massed and armed population suffices to carry the day.) XVIII. The villain is defeated. (Appius and other decemvirs are deposed). XIX. Initial misfortune or lack is liquidated. (Virginia is not revived, as occurs in some tales, but the legislative power of the patriciate, morally the cause of her death, is eliminated in the new legislation: right of appeal—"the one real safeguard of liberty"—is stressed.) XXX. The villain is punished. (Appius is jailed and commits suicide before the trial; other decemvirs go into exile.) XXXI. The hero is married and ascends the throne. (The plebs

---

[11] See Vladimir Propp, *Morphology of the Folktale,* 2nd ed. (Austin and London: U of Texas P, 1968). Propp isolates 31 narrative functions; not all of them occur in every tale, but those which do occur appear in a definite order, and some of them are always paired or combined. I have used Livy's version as my model. Another version might add or substitute one or two minor functions. Thus Chaucer's version could be said to substitute Propp's number V ("The villain receives information about his victim") for number IV, inasmuch as in *The Physician's Tale* Appius does not try to seduce Virginia but realizes by observing her that he will be unable to do so.

eventually win the right to intermarry with patricians and to hold the highest civic offices; liberty and harmony are restored.)

In short, then, the role of the people is not merely a theme in our tale but part of its very morphology, or structure of relations. Chaucer reduces the real hero of his story, without providing another. Simultaneously, though, he cannot eliminate the people completely, nor deprecate them too far by showing them vicious or fickle, for they do after all side with the right person (and must do if injustice is not to flourish). So that "the people," in *The Physician's Tale*, occupy a fictional never-never land. They are agents of justice and moral retribution, but must not be shown to act in their own legitimate interest, must not be allowed to "go too far," above all must not emerge from the story as a genuinely sympathetic model for social action.

To glorify rebellion—the original aim of the Virginius legend—is utterly alien to Chaucer's world-view: our poet is a prosperous, socially conservative, prudent courtier and civil servant, directly dependent for his living upon the good will of kings and dukes. Whether despite or because of his position, throughout his creative life Chaucer struggled with the question of truth in art. It is curious, then, that here, where Chaucer's truth differs so sharply from that of the received tradition, the question is not raised. For Chaucer, more conservative than any of the other four writers discussed above, the challenge is to transform a political anecdote into a moral tale: to rework a tract for the times into a tract for all time. But in this case at least, the material is simply not that tractable, it is not infinitely receptive; as sculptors and wood-carvers know, the material sometimes suggests its own completed form. Remove social complexity from the legend of Virginius and you are left with insipid moralizing and trite sentimentality, a protagonist of dubious character, an unjustified crime.

Yet the social function is cryingly there *because* of its exclusion, especially once we are aware of its role in other versions. The effaced trace remains a conspicuous absence, demanding recognition. In a sense the entire text could be read as a structure of absences: not only the absence of popular insurrection but of a hero, of resistance by the main characters, of convincing motives, of an ideological or esthetic centre. In this way the text verges on a kind of pornographic or free-floating sadistic sensationalism, with the murder as its only real centre. The atypicality of the text emerges even more sharply when we compare Chaucer's procedure here with that in several other works.

Chaucer's exclusion of the social function in *The Physician's Tale* is noteworthy because we have seen him revise some sources in the same direction, others in the opposite, and in both cases succeed brilliantly. With *The Reeve's Tale* and other fabliaux, social content is deliberately heightened in order to sharpen the ironic edge of the work by exposing pretentious social ambition.[12] In *Troilus,* Chaucer adds a solid backdrop of social reality—war, parliament, the mechanics of seduction, ruling class dinners and flirtations, inconvenient conjectures about age and experience—which contributes to ironically undercutting romance convention and the courtly love ethos, and consequently to orchestrating the Christian ideology that is counterposed throughout, explicitly in the finale. In *The Clerk's Tale* Chaucer keeps the population as an important element in the story (adding to the Petrarchan source some strong vituperation against their unreliability), the better to create an allegory meaningful on the social as well as moral and doctrinal levels (people are to ruler as wife to husband and humanity to God).

So we know that Chaucer can augment the social content of his sources as a powerful instrument of exposure or commentary. But he is also able to diminish the social content of his source, or invert its social-satirical edge, with equal effect. I have already referred to *The Man of Law's Tale* as a case in point of the former. *The Nun's Priest's Tale* illustrates the latter. The thrust of Chaucer's main source here, the cycle of French tales known as the *Roman de Renart,* is social criticism: the parody of clergy, of courtly manners and the *chanson de geste,* of wealth and pomposity. In the French tale, Pinte the hen correctly interprets Chantecler's dream detail by detail, warning him of the probable time and place of Renart's attack. Her accuracy vindicates female intuitive power and a folksy, shrewd empiricism as against the fatuous husband's false assurances of normalcy. Chaucer reverses this structure: Pertelote's intuition becomes a rather vulgar (albeit endearing) pragmatism, while the real "visionary," whose elaborate, scholarly constructs are vindicated by reality, is the pedant husband Chauntecleer. Thus the weight of the story

---

[12] See. S. Delany, "Clerks and Quiting in *The Reeve's Tale,*" *Mediaeval Studies* (1967), 351–56.

is shifted from a popular/feminist/empirical viewpoint, over to the typically Chaucerian Platonic/Augustinian hierarchies.

What these samples indicate is that whether Chaucer augments or reduces the social dimension of his source, the net effect is to polarize moral issues more intensely than the source does, to dot the i's and cross the t's as it were, to provide a clearer ideological and esthetic centre for the work as a platform from which the reader may both be instructed and judge: "For oure book seith, 'Al that is writen is writen for oure doctrine,' and that is myn entente" (Retraction to *The Canterbury Tales*).

From these brief readings of several works, two corollaries may be posited. One is that social reality in art is not necessarily the hallmark of a "progressive" world-view, but may constitute a stylistic element in the service of conservatism. Second, the degree of social content, or the political stance, in a given work is not correlated to its esthetic success. *The Reeve's Tale* succeeds, as does *The Man of Law's Tale*, despite their very different levels of social reality. Most of Chaucer's works succeed, with (I deliberately avoid "despite") their social conservatism. Indeed one might suggest that Chaucer succeeds not "despite" his politics at all, but because of them, insofar as Augustinian orthodoxy gave him the certainty necessary to write effectively, laying to rest the earlier ambivalence manifest in *The House of Fame*.[13] I am reminded here of Balzac's remarks from the Preface to *La Comédie Humaine*:

> The law of the writer, by virtue of which he is a writer . . . is his judgment, whatever it may be, on human affairs, and his absolute devotion to certain principles . . . 'A writer ought to have settled opinions on morals and politics; he should regard himself as a tutor of men; for men need no masters to teach them to doubt,' says Bonald. I took these noble words as my guide long ago; they are the written law of the monarchical writer just as much as that of the democratic writer.

The immense creative energy of *The Wife of Bath's Tale* suggests that at some level Chaucer, like Balzac in contradiction to his actual social views, may have seen "the men of the future where, for the time being,

---

[13] That is the basic argument I have made in *Chaucer's House of Fame: The Poetics of Skeptical Fideism* (Chicago, 1972).

they alone were to be found," or that he at least sensed in the bourgeoisie that vitality and "brainy opportunism" lacking in the decaying feudal aristocracy.[14] Perhaps it was that visceral sympathy (sympathy for the devil, as Blake hypothesized of Milton) that produced in Dame Alice one of the most vividly powerful characters in world literature. May we speculate about *The Physician's Tale* that the relevant social reality (insurrection) was simply too dangerous to write about for a courtier with everything to lose; or that it was not a topic appropriate to Chaucer's talent? Revolt is an absolute, not to be put in its place (like an "uppity woman") with irony. It transcends rhetoric, or, as Leon Trotsky wrote of the Bolsheviks, "They were adequate to the epoch and its tasks. Curses in plenty resounded in their direction, but irony would not stick to them—it had nothing to catch hold of." One wonders if that is the real fear behind the multiple absences that constitute *The Physician's Tale*: that the tempestuous, ambitious bourgeoisie might after all prove adequate to the task, just as the plebs had done.

We do not know whether Chaucer thought, with his friend Gower and, later, the Tudor preachers, that rebels are beasts and the creatures of Satan: his silence on the rebellions of his own day is notorious. In any case, the tale at hand permits no outright denunciation of rebellion, so that Chaucer is left in a narrative, structural, and ideological conundrum: neither with the people nor against them.

If we know the "Balade de Bon Conseyl"—also known as "Truth"—we can hardly be surprised that the tradition of middle-class insurrection and republican rights evoked from Chaucer no energetic creative response. I doubt we can know what drew Chaucer to take up the story of Virginia in the first place, and am content to hazard a guess that if the project taught him something as an artist, it was the importance of choosing material more suitable to his own particular genius.

---

[14] The first phrase comes from F. Engels' letter of November 26, 1885, to Minna Kautsky. The second is from Suzanne Langer, *Feeling and Form*.

The Poet as Petitioner

J. A. Burrow
University of Bristol

Since medieval literature generally appears more impersonal than that of modern times, it is something of a paradox that medieval writers should refer to themselves by name more often than their modern successors. Whereas in recent times the author's name tends to be confined to cover and title-page, a medieval work will not infrequently find a place for it within the text itself. Quite often, too, the name will be accompanied there by further particulars about the author: occupation, age, place of residence, and so on. Where other evidence is available to check them, these particulars usually turn out to be factual ('Mandeville' is a rare exception); and it seems reasonable to suppose that other similar passages which cannot be checked against external evidence are also more likely to be fact than fiction. E. T. Donaldson adopts this position in the course of his penetrating analysis of the long 'autobiographical' passage in *Piers Plowman*, C, VI: "it seems best to assume that Langland was telling the truth about himself and not whimsically devising an elaborate fiction."[1]

In such cases it is, I think, either false historicism or undue scepticism to deny that the author is most likely "telling the truth about himself." Where this is agreed, however, a further question immediately arises. What *occasions* these autobiographical passages? In literature, as in life, there are many different reasons for speaking about oneself; and one's purpose on any particular occasion will at least partly determine the kind of truth one tells. The question of purpose is by no means a simple one—it may, for instance, be necessary to distinguish between the ostensible and the real purpose—but it cannot be avoided, if we are to

[1] E.T. Donaldson, *Piers Plowman: The C-Text and Its Poet*, 2nd ed. (London, 1966), p. 220.

understand why the author speaks of himself in the way he does. The favourite term 'autobiographical' has tended to obscure this question, because it suggests answers which are not appropriate to most of the medieval instances. Autobiography proper, after all, is a highly specialized, literary way of speaking about oneself; and, although there are no doubt many possible reasons for writing one's autobiography, the term itself suggests aims which are at any rate not basely practical. It is not *autobiography* when I give my name and address to a policeman. But in many medieval texts the reasons which lead an author to speak of himself are, precisely, practical—or at least purport to be so. What the medieval author is doing is not (in most cases) 'writing his autobiography.' Rather he is doing some practical thing such as claiming credit for his book, greeting his friends, complaining about his lot, or (as in *Piers*, C, VI) making a public confession. Most commonly of all, I think, the occasion is the presentation of a petition on the author's behalf. I shall argue here that it is this petitionary intention which lends to many 'autobiographical' passages in medieval English literature their distinctive tone and emphasis—even where, as in Chaucer and Gower, the petition is no longer meant quite seriously.

Personal petitions for the favour of the great play relatively little part in the public life of modern Western democracies; but medieval men were dependent upon the good will of those set above them; and one way for them to win that good will was to plead for it, either directly or else through an intercessor. God was the supreme source of favour and grace. Men could solicit his good will by direct prayer; or they could solicit it indirectly, either by praying the Virgin or the saints to plead their cause with God, or else by praying or paying other human beings to act as petitioners on their behalf. On earth the same pattern is repeated, both in secular and ecclesiastical courts. Men asked favours (benefices, offices, pensions) from lords and from bishops, both directly and through the intercession of courtiers or chaplains who had the ear of the great.

When seeking the favour of God or some earthly patron, an obvious prime requirement is that one should be identified—otherwise the favour might go to the wrong person. Hence the writer of any petitionary document has a strong practical incentive to register his name. There is also a natural tendency to add a few further particulars in order to support the identification. Such particulars may also perform another function, for the petitioner often introduces some account of himself and his circumstances in order to strengthen his plea. He will claim to need the favour, or to have deserved it, or both. Need is a common theme in petitions of all sorts: the petitioner needs God's grace because he is a miserable sinner, or he needs a lord's favour because he is broke. No merits can establish a claim on God's grace; but the petitioner may claim to have deserved, by his labours, the prayers of his readers for that grace; and he can certainly claim to have done enough to deserve a benefice or a pension. At the same time, he will attempt to preserve the humble tone appropriate to a man at least metaphorically on his knees.

The main purpose of this essay is to consider some passages of petitionary self-reference in the poetry of Chaucer and Gower; but before turning to these passages, which are rather complex, I shall more briefly discuss some selected examples from other medieval English writers. The most common form of petition in the literature of this period is the author's request for the reader's prayers. In the course of such requests, the author often gives his name. When this happens, a modern reader may be inclined to regard the request for prayer as itself little more than a formality—a conventional occasion for declaring authorship. In the absence of copyright laws, however, medieval writers had little direct practical interest in declaring authorship; whereas it was, for them, an eminently practical thing to be prayed for by name. Men, after all, left large sums of money in their wills in order to shorten their time in the pains of Purgatory through the prayers of beadsmen. Admittedly, not all requests for readers' prayers in medieval literature can be taken at their simple face value; but the avowed religious motive is enough to account for many of them. The very first English poet to declare his name does so in the course of just such a devout request. Four Anglo-Saxon poems are 'signed' with the name Cynewulf, spelled out in runic letters. In his essay "Cynewulf and his Poetry," Kenneth Sisam pointed out that all four signatures occur in passages which refer to the Day of Judgement, and that two of the passages (in *The Fates of the Apostles* and *Juliana*) expressly ask the reader to pray for the soul of the author—which, like all souls, faces the terror of God's judgment on that great Day.[2] Sisam quotes from *Juliana*: "I beg every man who repeats this poem to remember me *by name*

---

[2] K. Sisam, "Cynewulf and his Poetry," in *Studies in the History of Old English Literature* (Oxford, 1953), pp. 23–25. The four passages are: *The Fates of the Apostles,* 88 ff., *Juliana,* 695 ff., *Elene,* 1236 ff., and *Christ,* 779 ff.

in my need." On the subject of his 'need' the poet enlarges a little, speaking of his own sinfulness and also, in *Elene*, of his sorrowful old age. Even in this last passage, however, Cynewulf is content to speak of himself in general terms derived from the elegiac traditions of Old English verse. He evidently regards a perfectly conventional 'autobiography' as sufficient to amplify his need and move the reader to a pious response in prayer. But to ensure the efficacy of that prayer, something more particular is needed—a name. Like the number of a bank account, the name has to be right.

Recent historians have spoken of a "discovery of the individual" in the eleventh and twelfth centuries; and certainly, by about the year 1200, we find English poets speaking of themselves, on occasion, with more individual detail than any Anglo-Saxon provided. One might compare Cynewulf's epilogues with Laȝamon's prologue to his *Brut*. Laȝamon begins his prologue by naming himself, his father, and his place of residence; and he ends it by bidding the reader say prayers for himself, his father, and his (unnamed) mother.[3] In the intervening lines he describes how he conceived the work and gathered materials for its composition. The petitionary function of these lines is presumably to establish the author's claim upon the reader's good will. Whereas Cynewulf's emphasis falls upon his sad and sinful condition (need), Laȝamon stresses his diligent efforts on the reader's behalf (desert). When Laȝamon can claim to have done so much, runs the concealed argument, the reader cannot in conscience refuse him a prayer. Yet Laȝamon's claim surely also betrays some simple pride of authorship. His prologue, in fact, seems to overshoot the strict requirements of a prayer-petition in the interests of displaying writer to reader—which is not to say, however, that the petition is a mere pretext.

A poem perhaps nearly contemporary with the *Brut*, *The Owl and the Nightingale*, presents a more complex case, which anticipates, in some respects, the subtleties of the Ricardian poets. Early on in the debate between the two birds, the Nightingale proposes "Master Nichol of Guildford" as a suitably wise and discriminating judge between them. The Owl agrees: Nicholas was too fond of nightingales in his wild youth; but he has since cooled off and become mature ('ripe').[4] At the end of the

---

[3] Laȝamon's *Brut*, ed. G. L. Brook and R. F. Leslie, Vol. I, EETS 250 (1963), Cotton Caligula text, ll. 1–5 and 29–35.
[4] *The Owl and the Nightingale*, ed. E. G. Stanley (London, 1960), ll. 189–214.

long debate which follows, the Wren tells the two birds where Nicholas is to be found, at Portesham in Dorset, and adds her own word in praise of his wisdom. It is a shame, she says, that bishops give livings to unworthy recipients while allowing a man of Nicholas' calibre to live in the obscurity of a remote country parish.[5] If, as most recent scholars agree, it was Nicholas himself who wrote the poem, then he has produced a subtle and telling plea on his own behalf—a petition for preferment, in this case, addressed to some ecclesiastical patron.[6] The poet's need for such patronage is stated, without any nagging complaint, in the Wren's rapid description of the humble circumstances of his life in a Dorset village. He deserves the favours of a patron, too, by virtue of the moral qualities of wisdom and maturity which the birds affirm and the poem, by its own 'ripeness,' displays. Nicholas is equally acceptable to the solemn Owl and the joyous Nightingale because his maturity places him, as it were, at the apex of an equilateral triangle, equidistant from both. When the Owl suggests that Nicholas has simply followed a natural order of moral development from wild youth to sober age, that is no more than the Owl's version. The fact that Nicholas proves equally acceptable to the Nightingale suggests a more subtle kind of maturity. The poet is evidently not, as Montaigne says of himself in old age, "but too much settled, too heavy and too ripe." His maturity somehow incorporates, rather than supersedes, the energies of youth. Hence both birds can join with the Wren to act as intercessors on his behalf. The poet neither himself addresses the patron nor invites the reader to speak for him. His plea is conducted more insidiously, within the fiction of the poem. But it is not itself a fiction.

A full survey of passages of petitionary autobiography in Middle English literature would, I believe, reveal a rich variety of instances. Prayers and requests for intercession lead authors to register their names, either simply or (like Cynewulf) cryptically;[7] and they may add, as

---

[5] Stanley, ll. 1750–91.

[6] E. G. Stanley doubts Nicholas' authorship, pp. 20–21; but see E. J. Dobson, N&Q, 206 (1961), 373, and Kathryn Hume, *The Owl and the Nightingale: The Poem and Its Critics* (Toronto, 1975).

[7] Cryptic signatures occur in connection with prayers or requests for prayer in Thomas Usk's *Testament of Love*: see *Chaucerian and Other Pieces*, ed. W. W. Skeat (Oxford, 1897), pp. xix–xx; and in Osbern Bokenham's *Mappula Angliae*: see his *Legendys of Hooly Wummen*, ed. M. S. Serjeantson, EETS OS 206 (1938), pp. xvi–xvii. Professor E. J. Dobson has argued convincingly that the author of *Ancrene Wisse* indicates his name,

Malory does in *Morte Darthur*, some further particulars about themselves, the circumstances in which the work was composed, and so on.[8] In the later Middle English period, too, we find petitions of a different kind—pleas addressed to kings, lords, and other secular patrons. Hoccleve in England and in Scotland Dunbar depended upon favours from courts which, by the fifteenth century, regularly spoke and wrote English; and the petitionary poems which they addressed to their benefactors represent one of the high-water marks of autobiographical writing in medieval England. The detail is so rich that a modern reader may sometimes lose sight of the petitionary intention altogether. Yet when Hoccleve in his *Male Regle* asks the Lord Treasurer to pay his annuity, or when Dunbar in *To the King* ('Schir, yit remembir as of befoir') asks James IV for a benefice, these are not mere excuses for the poet to talk about himself. The self-portrait is elaborate, but it still has a practical purpose; and that purpose largely dictates its dark tones and gloomy pose.[9]

Brian of Lingen, by etymological allusion and anagram in the course of asking for his readers' prayers: *The Origins of Ancrene Wisse* (Oxford, 1976), pp. 327–68. Dobson makes the following general observation: "most commonly, in religious works and sometimes also in secular, [the author's name] is embodied in or comes in the immediate neighbourhood of a request for the readers' prayers, or else is mentioned in a direct prayer by the author himself to God for his mercy" (p. 329). For examples of the same pattern in Middle High German poetry, see Julius Schwietering, *Die Demutsformel mittelhochdeutscher Dichter* (Berlin, 1921) and 'The Origins of the Medieval Humility Formula', *PMLA*, 69 (1954), 1279–91; both reprinted in Schwietering, *Philologische Schriften*, ed. F. Ohly and M. Wehrli (Munich, 1969).

[8] *The Works of Sir Thomas Malory*, ed. E. Vinaver (Oxford, 1954), pp. 133, 623, 741, 816, and esp. 883: 'I praye you all jentylmen and jentylwymmen that redeth this book of Arthur and his knyghtes from the begynnyng to the endynge, praye for me whyle I am on lyve that God sende me good delyveraunce. And whan I am deed, I praye you all praye for my soule. For this book was ended the ninth yere of the reygne of King Edward the Fourth, by Syr Thomas Maleoré, Knyght, as Jesu helpe hym for Hys grete myght, as he is the servaunt of Jesu bothe day and nyght.' The author of *Mandeville's Travels* ends his book with a similar passage, audaciously presenting the fictional autobiography of his John Mandeville, Knight, in a petitionary context from which the reader would have expected fact: ed. M. C. Seymour (Oxford, 1967), p. 229.

[9] Dunbar's *To the King* is one of fifteen poems classified as Petitions in W. M. Mackenzie's edition, *The Poems of William Dunbar* (London, 1932). Other examples are *Remonstrance to the King, The Petition of the Gray Horse, Auld Dunbar*, and *To the Lordis of the Kingis Chalker*. Among the shorter petitionary poems of Hoccleve are his balades *To My Lord the Chancellor, To Mr. Henry Somer, Subtreasurer, To King Henry V*, and *To My Maister Carpenter:* Nos. xii, xiii, xv, and xvi in *Minor Poems*, ed. F. J. Furnivall, EETS ES 61 (1892). The melancholy description of the poet's life in the first part of Hoccleve's *Regement of Princes* leads up to the Beggar's suggestion that he should complain to Prince

In the rest of this essay, however, I want to consider certain passages from the poetry of Chaucer and Gower which are of a somewhat different character. In the passages I have chosen, the practical petitionary intention is either almost refined away or else entirely fictionalized, as it is not in Hoccleve or Dunbar. Petitionary forms, in these Ricardian poets, become detached from their original function, while retaining their power to control the way the poet portrays himself in his work. The role of petitioner is here a part which the poet plays largely for his own purposes, with a freedom from practical intention which makes possible some incongruous and, in Chaucer, comical developments.

Although not strictly speaking a dream poem, John Gower's *Confessio Amantis* follows many of the conventions of dream poetry, among them the convention stated by Professor Kane: "authors of dream-vision poems signed these by naming the dreamers after themselves."[10] Gower times and manages this signature to perfection. Towards the end of *Confessio Amantis*, after completing his confession to Genius, Amans (who corresponds to the dreamer in dream poems) writes a letter of petition and complaint to Venus and Cupid, asking to be relieved of his sufferings in love. Genius presents the letter on his behalf, and he receives a visit from the goddess:

> To grounde I fell upon mi kne,
> And preide hire forto do me grace:
> Sche caste hire chiere upon mi face,
> And as it were halvinge a game
> Sche axeth me what is mi name.
> "Ma dame," I seide, "John Gower."
> "Now John," quod sche . . . [11]

Henry and petition the Prince for his annuity to be paid more regularly: *The Regement of Princes*, ed. F. J. Furnivall, EETS ES 72 (1897), ll. 1832–1904 (cf. 4383–89). Hoccleve introduces his own name twice into this petitionary passage (1864, 1865) and nowhere else in the poem. Cf. the discussion of Gower's *Confessio Amantis* below. A collection of Anglo-Norman petitions from the time of Hoccleve is edited by M. D. Legge, *Anglo-Norman Letters and Petitions from All Souls MS. 182*, Anglo-Norman Text Society III (Oxford, 1941).

[10] George Kane, *Piers Plowman: The Evidence for Authorship* (London, 1965), p. 65. The chapter 'Signatures' gives many French examples of poets naming themselves in dream poems.

[11] *Confessio Amantis*, VIII, 2316–22, in *The English Works of John Gower*, ed. G. C. Macaulay, EETS ES 81–82 (1900–01). Charles d'Orléans names himself in a very similar

This is the first time Gower has named himself in the poem; and he does so in the time-honoured petitionary context. A great lady has received, by the hand of her confessor, a 'supplicacioun'; and before she replies to her kneeling petitioner, she must ascertain his identity. It is a familiar pattern.

Gower's petition, however, differs from those of Cynewulf, Laȝamon, Nicholas of Guildford, Hoccleve, Malory, and Dunbar, in that it is purely fictional. Doubly so, indeed. An appeal to the goddess Venus, itself necessarily fictional in a Christian poem, might mask a real appeal to a real lady; but there is no sign of such a lady in this affair. One of Gower's Latin sidenotes, opposite Book I line 60, speaks of the author "quasi in persona aliorum, quos amor alligat, fingens se . . . esse Amantem"; and the figure of Amans indeed bears all the marks of poetic fiction. He is one kind of conventional Lover—faithful, long-serving, unrewarded. It is not the real Gower who introduces the petition in Book VIII. Rather, one might say, it is the petition which introduces the real Gower. When Venus, replying to the petition, says 'Mi medicine is noght to sieke / For thee and for suche olde sieke' (VIII, 2367–68), she alludes for the first time to a fact about the narrator which is to play a significant part in the poem's closing scenes. He is *old*. The Amans who submitted his supplication had served his mistress long and unsuccessfully; but there had been no reason, even at that late stage, to suppose that he faced any but the usual lover's obstacles.[12] Once Venus has drawn attention to his age, however, 'Gower' realises that his passion is worse than hopeless:

> "Ma dame," I seide, "be your leve,
> Ye witen wel, and so wot I,

---

context in his *Songe en Complainte*. Like Gower, Charles represents himself as submitting a letter of petition to Cupid and Venus, asking to be relieved of his sufferings in love: 'Supplie presentement, / Humblement, / Charles, le duc d'Orlians, / Qui a esté longuement, / Ligement, / L'un de voz obeissans . . .', *Songe en Complainte* 179–84 (cf. 251–53), ed. P. Champion, *Poésies*, CFMA, Vol. 1 (Paris, 1971). The equivalent English passage is ll. 2718–23 in *The English Poems of Charles of Orleans*, ed. R. Steele and M. Day, EETS OS 215 and 220 (1941 and 1946, repr. 1970).

[12] *Pace* Donald Schueler, "The Age of the Lover in Gower's *Confessio Amantis*," *MÆ*, 36 (1967), 152–58. The passages Schueler cites are indeed consistent with the idea of an elderly Amans; but they could only establish that idea in the mind of a reader already (as Schueler implausibly suggests) thinking of the real Gower.

That I am unbehovely
Your Court fro this day forth to serve"
(VIII, 2882–85)

Gower was himself old at the time of writing (see VIII, 3120–31), and he portrays the renunciation of love with real feeling; yet there can be no question of reading these closing scenes in any strict autobiographical sense. The autobiographical details of name and age which the petition introduces do not point outwards into real life; rather they point forwards to the end of the poem—towards the 'beau retret' of which Venus speaks (VIII, 2416). The incongruity of a love petition from such an 'unbehovely' servant of Venus helps to prepare Gower's poem for its powerful moral conclusion. In Chaucer, as we shall see, a similar incongruity is turned to different, comic effect.

Chaucer made surprisingly little use of his art for practical purposes of petition. He must have depended more than Gower on the favour of the great. We may see it as a testimony to his sense of the dignity of his art that he did not more often write like Hoccleve; or perhaps his salary was paid more regularly. Only three of his poems directly betray any impurity of intention: *Fortune, The Complaint of Chaucer to his Purse,* and *Lenvoy to Scogan.* In *Fortune*, a stilted philosophical dialogue between Le Pleintif and Fortune leads abruptly to an envoy in which Fortune prays the King's three uncles or Richard himself to relieve the poet's distress. In the *Complaint*, a rather silly pseudo-amorous complaint to his purse is followed, in the envoy, by a solemn address and 'supplication' (Chaucer uses the same word as Gower) to the new king, Henry IV. The uncertain and uneven character of both these poems suggests that Chaucer was not quite happy—as a poet, at least—in the role of humble petitioner to the great. At any rate, *Scogan* is a much better poem.

Lenvoy to Scogan presents its petition in the last of its seven stanzas:

Scogan, that knelest at the stremes hed
Of grace, of alle honour and worthynesse,
In th'ende of which strem I am dul as ded,
Forgete in solytarie wildernesse,—
Yet, Scogan, thenke on Tullius kyndenesse;

> Mynne thy frend, there it may fructyfye!
> Far-wel, and loke thow never eft Love dyffye.[13]

Nobility, honour, and favour flow down from a high source—in this case the king, the very 'fount of honour', and his court. All three manuscripts write 'Windsor' against line 43 and 'Greenwich' against line 45. The stream is not only a 'stream of honour'[14] but also the River Thames—a touch of transfigured geography which anticipates Spenser and Milton. Both literally and metaphorically, Chaucer is downstream of his friend. Scogan, a member of Richard II's household, may not himself be a source of favour; but the gracefully posed image of the courtier 'kneeling at the stream's head' serves to remind him that he is well placed to put in a word for his friend: "Mynne thy frend, there it may fructyfye." The petition is unspecific, but presumably Scogan was expected to understand what he could do. And the words of the poem are addressed, steadily and unmistakably, to *him*. His name occurs no less than seven times in the poem's forty-nine lines, twice in the petitionary last stanza quoted above. Invoking Cicero's *De Amicitia*, Chaucer bases his claim to Scogan's good offices on the fact of their friendship; and he takes every opportunity to evoke his own unhappy circumstances. The weather is frighteningly bad (1–14); he is grey-haired and overweight (27, 31), too old for love (26–28), and no longer ambitious for his poetry (37–40); and he is living alone, dull and forgotten, in a part of the world which, as he describes it (45–46), is scarcely better than Nicholas of Guildford's obscure parish in Dorset.

Yet anyone who had not read *Scogan* would get a quite incomplete idea of it from my description so far. *Scogan* presents a real petition, and it does not neglect the perennial topics of the petitioner: his claim upon favours and his need for them. Yet here, much more than in the *Brut* or the *Owl*, the autobiographical writing tends to leave its petitionary occasion behind. Chaucer is writing a letter to a friend, and he addresses Scogan in a tone of ease and familiarity. Scogan may be on his knees, we feel, but Chaucer is not—certainly not to Scogan. Although the poem

---

[13] Ll. 43–49, in *Works*, ed. F. N. Robinson (1957).

[14] The phrase is Dr. Johnson's, speaking of Cardinal Wolsey: "Turned by his nod the stream of honour flows, / His smile alone security bestows" (*Vanity of Human Wishes*, 102–03, pointed out to me by my colleague David Hopkins).

does not neglect the realities of human lordship and dependence, it in fact gives greater prominence to the fictive lordship of Venus and Cupid; and in relation to that court, Chaucer and Scogan are both at an equal disadvantage. Like Gower in *Confessio Amantis*, they are both too old to expect any favours from the God of Love. If anything, it is Chaucer who is better placed than Scogan here; for he at least has not committed the blasphemy of giving up his mistress, like a rented house, on a quarter-day. Hence the poet can claim a certain superiority over his friend and benefactor. One must do full justice to Chaucer's diplomatic touch in this matter. His claim to be somewhat less out of favour with Cupid and Venus than the rebellious Scogan could not offend the latter, because it is obviously just a friendly joke: "Lo, olde Grisel lyst to ryme and playe!" Indeed, one might say that the playful fantasy actually strengthens Chaucer's petition, for it helps him to avoid that nagging tone of humble complaint which can so easily irritate potential benefactors. However, when 'petitionary autobiography' becomes as subtle as this, it begins to seem irrelevant to insist upon the practical intention. The display of personality in *Scogan*, indeed, is so absorbing that many readers hardly notice the petition when it is finally presented.

In Chaucer's longer works there are (leaving aside the *Retraction*) three main passages in which he refers to himself (twice by name) and to his circumstances and writings: *The House of Fame*, 605 ff., the Prologue to *The Legend of Good Women*, G, 234 ff., and the Introduction to *The Man of Law's Tale*, 45 ff. Although the last does not belong to the present subject, we may note in passing that it does involve something not unlike a petition. Its formal model seems to be the bill of complaint; and this, like the bill of petition, is a public, non-literary form. Chaucer employs it in a playful and extravagant fashion. One of his creations, the Man of Law, makes a public complaint against his own creator, alleging that he has irresponsibly used up all the good stories. Autobiographical details are therefore given a most peculiar twist. The same thing happens, we shall see, in *The House of Fame* and *The Legend of Good Women*, both of which distort the pattern of petition in a fashion just as fictive and outrageous.

Chaucer's vision of Cupid in the Prologue to *The Legend of Good Women* presents the God of Love as a king, accompanied by Queen Alceste and followed by a train of ladies forming part of his 'court' (G, 328). Chaucer portrays the lordship of Cupid quite realistically: like Theseus in *The*

Knight's Tale, he bears the heavy responsibility of deciding difficult cases.[15] As Queen Alceste reminds him:

> [H]e that kyng or lord is naturel,
> Hym oughte nat be tyraunt and crewel,
> As is a fermour, to don the harm he can.
> He moste thynke it is his lige man,
> And that hym oweth, of verray duetee,
> Shewen his peple pleyn benygnete,
> And wel to heren here excusacyouns,
> And here compleyntes and petyciouns,
> In duewe tyme, whan they shal it profre.
> (G, 356–64)

Alceste's terms 'compleynt', 'petycioun' and 'excusacyoun' precisely indicate what is going on in the central scene between Cupid, Chaucer, and Alceste. After the poet has identified himself (though not by name, G, 240), Cupid indignantly and scornfully rehearses the complaints and accusations which have been made against Chaucer in his court (see G, 326–39). Like Scogan, Chaucer has uttered heresy (G, 256) against the God of Love—in this case, by translating the *Roman de la Rose* and telling the story of Criseyde's infidelity. Cupid threatens vengeance on his renegade liegeman, to which Alceste responds with what is in effect a petition for clemency, suggesting 'excusacyouns' for the two offending works. When the decision is delegated to the Queen, Chaucer drops to his knees (G, 445) and addresses to her his own plea of excuse. After responding at first rather sharply—"Love ne wol nat counterpletyd be"—Alceste releases the poet with a light penalty.

This summary will have shown how Chaucer's references to himself and his writings occur, in the Prologue to *The Legend*, as part of a quite elaborately developed court scene of complaint and petition. The scene is, of course, entirely fictive in itself; and the fiction does not, as in *The Owl and the Nightingale*, serve a serious petitionary purpose. At most, Chaucer is asking the ladies in his audience to forgive him for his portrait

---

[15] Cupid is a god as well as a lord, Chaucer a penitent as well as a petitioner; but as we have already seen, a god (heavenly lord) and a lord (earthly god) would stand in much the same relation to their dependents.

of Criseyde—and that half-jokingly, 'halvinge a game.' Yet the petitionary context, fictive and humorous though it is, largely determines what Chaucer says about himself. The role of petitioner is itself inimical to any heroics. Like Gower in *Confessio Amantis*, Chaucer is discovered on his knees to a higher power; and it would be hard for any poet, from that humble posture, to make lofty claims for himself or his art. Furthermore, Chaucer represents himself as cutting an incongruous figure in the court of Love. Like Gower, again, he is an 'old fole' (G, 262, 315). His days of love are over (G, 400–01).[16] When the God of Love passes him on to Alceste, we may be reminded of his own words to Scogan:

> He wol nat with his arwes been ywroken
> On the, ne me, ne noon of oure figure.
> (26–27)

Cupid does not so much forgive Chaucer as dismiss him from consideration, treating him, as Alceste advises him to, as a lion treats a troublesome fly: "Hym deyneth nat to wreke hym on a flye." (G, 381).

Chaucer's account of his own work as a poet takes on, in this extravagant petitionary context, a very peculiar character. Cupid's hostile description seems unfair; but the 'excusacyouns' offered by Alceste and later by the poet himself only make things worse. Like the Man of Law, Alceste implies that Chaucer writes more than is good for him. He translates to order and "taketh non hede of what matere he take," not caring—perhaps not even noticing—what he writes. When Alceste speaks of his 'innocence,' consequently, she is sacrificing a good deal of the petitioner's dignity in order to win him a reprieve—as friends at court no doubt often did. Chaucer's own plea to Alceste does little to restore his standing. His excuses are admittedly not ridiculous, as is his apology to the ladies at the end of *Troilus* (V, 1772–85); but they do not carry conviction:

> a trewe man, withoute drede,

[16] All three allusions to the dreamer's age are absent from the F version of the *Prologue*, where he sometimes speaks like a conventional lover: F, 50–59, 84–96, 249–77.

> Hath nat to parte with a theves dede.
> (G, 454–55)

And so on. Alceste's brisk rejoinder, "Lat be thyn arguynge," saves her protégé from further abasement.

There is a passage in *Troilus* which describes a type of humour very characteristic of Chaucer's work. Pandarus is doing his best to amuse Criseyde:

> And he gan at hymself to jape faste,
> And seyde, "Nece, I have so gret a pyne
> For love, that everich other day I faste—"
> And gan his beste japes forth to caste,
> And made hire so to laughe at his folye,
> That she for laughter wende for to dye.
> (II, 1164–69)

Like Pandarus, Chaucer takes special pleasure in 'japing at himself'; and the role of humble petitioner offered a variety of opportunities for comedy of this self-depreciating sort. In the Prologue to *The Legend*, as in *Confessio Amantis*, the poet represents himself pleading for a favour which he is unlikely to receive from an unsympathetic patron; in *The House of Fame* he is shown reluctantly enjoying a favour which he did not want from a patron who is only too sympathetic.

The best-known of all Chaucer's autobiographical passages, the description of his life as a customs official, forms part of a comically distorted pattern of petition in the second book of *The House of Fame*. The first requirement for such a pattern is the presence of an exalted source of patronage, capable of dispensing grace and favour. In *The House of Fame*, this role is played by Jupiter. 'Thorgh hys grace' (661), Jupiter decides to grant Geoffrey the reward or 'guerdon' which the poet has for so long failed to receive from Cupid and Venus:

> And thus this god, thorgh his merite,
> Wol with som maner thing the quyte.
> (669–70)

In contrast to the god, the poet—addressed 'by his name' at line 558 and identified as 'Geoffrey' at line 729—cuts a comically undignified figure. In *The Legend of Good Women* he was compared to a fly and a worm (G, 244, 381); here, rigid with fear in the claws of the giant eagle, he is compared to a lark (546; cf. *Troilus* III, 1191–92). When the eagle explains his mission, he portrays the poet as a humble but deserving case for favourable treatment. He deserves a guerdon because he has laboured long and selflessly as a writer in praise of love; and he needs it because he leads such an obscure and dully bookish life. The eagle's double portrait of the poet as a comically indefatigable writer (614–40) and reader (641–60) combines the fantasy of Chaucer as a servant of the servants of Love with the realities of Chaucer as a servant of the servants of the King—ill-rewarded, by implication, in both capacities. It is the perfect portrait of a petitioner.

But, unlike the dreamer in the *Legend*, the dreamer here is *not* a petitioner. He is apparently quite happy among his books (there is even a hint of discreet self-indulgence in line 660); and he receives Jupiter's unsolicited favours with a distinct lack of enthusiasm. 'Can you believe this?' 'No'; 'Can you see any towns?' 'No'; 'Do you want to learn about the stars?' 'Certainly not'. He is too old to learn astronomy; his eyes are not good enough to look at the stars; and so on. It is, by common consent, one of Chaucer's 'best japes'—to portray himself as not only an unlikely, but also an unwilling recipient of the favours of the great. The theme of petition is, as it were, inverted in this most extravagant variation.

Confessio Amantis, Scogan, The Legend of Good Women and *The House of Fame* thus all display a certain playfulness on the part of the Ricardian poet in his role of petitioner. Forms of autobiographical utterance which originally had, and could still have, serious and practical functions tend in their work to shed those functions, either completely or in part. When these poets represent themselves as dependent upon the favours of the great, they most often write 'halvinge a game'—half (at least) in jest. Yet their work presents an image of the writer which is still recognizably shaped and coloured by those circumstances of petitionary dependence in which their medieval predecessors and successors so often appeared before their readers.

The Order of *The Canterbury Tales*

Larry D. Benson
Harvard University

THE ORDER OF *The Canterbury Tales*—how an editor should arrange the Blocks of tales—is the oldest and one of the most vexing problems in Chaucerian scholarship. It bothered Chaucer's earliest printer: William Caxton printed the tales in one order in his first edition and another in his second, though neither was satisfactory and Wynkyn de Worde used yet a third arrangement when he reprinted Caxton's second edition. The problem faced by Caxton and his successor bothered even the scribe of our earliest surviving mss, the Ellesmere and the Hengwrt. When he wrote the Ellesmere he had no difficulties; he wrote the tales continuously and confidently in the order familiar to us from the editions of Robinson and others. However, when he wrote the Hengwrt MS., he had no orderly exemplar or guide to the order of the tales. He had instead a set of fragments. They were fragments of one or more mss that had an orderly arrangement (as shown in Section VIII below), but once the ms(s) had been broken up, there was no way of telling exactly what the order had been, and the scribe had to arrange the fragments as best he could. This often happened in the manuscript history of *The Canterbury Tales*. Chaucer had not organized his tales into numbered books (as in Gower's *Confessio Amantis*), nor days (as in the *Decameron*), nor apparently had he jotted down numbers for the tales (as did some later scribes of *The Canterbury Tales*), and when the work was broken into fragments to facilitate copying, as seems often to have been the practice, confusion about the proper order frequently resulted.

Such confusion, along with rearrangements to accommodate scribal errors, the development of a variety of spurious links and, sometimes, mere carelessness, produced what seems to be a bewildering variety of competing arrangements of the tales in the mss—perhaps as many as twenty-seven in all—that confront the editor of *The Canterbury Tales* with the problem of which of these arrangements, if any, represents Chaucer's intention.[1] The mss seem so confusing that it is often said that they can be of no help at all in determining the proper order of the tales, and there is perhaps almost as much a sense of relief as of characteristic gusto in Furnivall's enthusiastic acceptance of the "Bradshaw shift": "A happy hit! and it sets us free to alter the arrangement of any or all the MSS, to move up or down any *Group* of tales, whenever internal evidence probability, or presumption requires it."[2]

The still flourishing debate over the order of *The Canterbury Tales*, which has now narrowed to arguments for or against the "Ellesmere order" and the "Bradshaw shift," has been carried on pretty much free of any necessity to consult the mss, and proponents on both sides argue almost purely on the basis of literary analysis. Though Skeat years ago and E. T. Donaldson more recently argued vigorously for the importance of the manuscript evidence, the debate has continued to be conducted on purely literary grounds mainly because Manly and Rickert's great study seems to have demonstrated that the mss indeed have no authority in this matter.[3] They made a full study of the manuscript arrangements of the

---

[1] See E. T. Donaldson, "The Ordering of the Canterbury Tales," in *Essays in Honor of Francis Lee Utley* ed. Jerome Mandel and Bruce A. Rosenberg (New Brunswick: Rutgers UP, 1971), p. 195; for a survey of the literature see, in addition to Donaldson, the thorough discussion in Robert A. Pratt, "The Order of the *Canterbury Tales*," *PMLA*, 66 (1951), 1141–67. See also Edward S. Cohen, "The Sequence of the *Canterbury Tales*," *ChauR*, 9 (1974–75), 190–95, who proposes a new order; George R. Kaiser, "In Defense of the Bradshaw Shift," *ChauR*, 12 (1977–78), 191–201, offers fresh arguments in favor of the B^1–B^2 arrangement; Charles A. Owen Jr., *Pilgrimage and Story Telling in the Canterbury Tales* (Norman: U of Oklahoma P, 1977), reiterates and expands his arguments for arranging the tales on the basis of a round trip to and from Canterbury; Donald R. Howard, *The Idea of the Canterbury Tales* (Berkeley and Los Angeles: U of California P, 1976), esp. pp. 212–16, provides arguments for the Ellesmere order.

[2] F. J. Furnivall, *Temporary Preface*, Chaucer Society, Second Series, 3 (London, 1868), pp. 9, 20–22.

[3] Skeat adopted the Chaucer Society order for his edition, though he objected to the position assigned to C; *The Works of Geoffrey Chaucer* (Oxford: Clarendon, 1894–97) III, 434. He later argued for a return to the mss and rejected the Bradshaw shift for a scholarly edition, though he apparently believed that for a school text it was acceptable; *The Evolution of the Canterbury Tales*, Chaucer Society, Second Series, 38 (London, 1907), p. 31. See J. M. Manly and Edith Rickert, eds., *The Text of the Canterbury Tales on the Basis of All Known Manuscripts* (Chicago: U of Chicago P, 1940), II, 475–94. Further references to Manly and Rickert are parenthetically cited in the text by volume and page number; all quotations from *The Canterbury Tales* are from this edition.

tales, presented the data in detail (II, 475–94), and concluded that only two facts could be established:

> One is that none of the extant MSS exhibits an arrangement which with any probability can be assigned to Chaucer. The other is that very soon after Chaucer's death several separate attempts were made at gathering the tales that Chaucer was known or reported to have written. (II, 489)

One hesitates to disagree with scholars from whom every student of *The Canterbury Tales* has learned so much. Yet, in this case, the evidence that Manly and Rickert so carefully gathered and presented does not support their conclusions. The mss show that there were at most two orders as the text came to the earliest scribes; all the other orders in the mss are scribal rearrangements or distortions of these two orders. One of these original orders is that familiar order of the Ellesmere MS. (I use the Chaucer Society letters to indicate the Blocks of tales):

$$A\ B^1\ D\ E\ F\ C\ B^2\ G\ H\ I$$

The other differs only in the place of Block G:

$$A\ B^1\ D\ E\ F\ G\ C\ B^2\ H\ I$$

The two orders are obviously related and, after a re-examination of the manuscript evidence presented by Manly and Rickert, I shall argue that both orders can indeed be assigned to Chaucer and that the order of the tales in the Ellesmere MS. (and others) represents Chaucer's own final arrangement.

The re-examination of the manuscript evidence will be, I must admit, a tedious business, for which I apologize at the outset. Yet the problem merits such scrutiny. If the mss do indeed show only a variety of different orders, none of which is Chaucer's, we remain dependent purely on "internal evidence, probability, or presumption," and we must recognize that the most likely explanation for the situation in the mss is that Chaucer himself had never decided on a plan for his work. On the other hand, if the mss testify, as I hope to show, to but two orders, so similar that they must have been invented by the same person, the only question that remains is: was that person Chaucer?

I am sure it was. To attribute the invention to anyone else (a scribe or literary executor) requires a long series of strained assumptions, and in this matter, as in most, Occam's razor must be applied: the fewer assumptions necessary to account for the facts, the more probable the validity of that account.

I shall therefore try to avoid elaborate speculation and depend instead on the evidence of the mss (drawing almost entirely on Manly and Rickert for that evidence; one assumption I do make—and this seems safe enough—is that their analyses of the contents of the mss are generally correct). I shall not even speculate on the plans Chaucer had for his work in the year of his death, when, as many students of this problem assume, he was still working on the tales and, interrupted by death or illness, left them lying in disorder in his chest or on his desk. Speculation about that matter, at least, is not necessary, since we have Chaucer's own word, in the *Retraction*, that, unfinished as *The Canterbury Tales* obviously is, he was finished with it. We have, in short, not a work in progress to which Chaucer intended to return and would have, had not death or illness prevented this, but rather Chaucer's final version, as it was when he decided his work on it was ended.

Critics of an earlier generation could ignore this because they doubted that Chaucer could have written the *Retraction* or *The Parson's Tale* itself. Manly and Rickert showed that "The textual evidence is overwhelming for including the PsT among the CT, and there can be no doubt that Chaucer was the author of both PsP and PsT" (II, 454); likewise, the *Retraction* was "in the ancestor of all the MSS of PsT" (II, 471). This, Manly and Rickert argue, does not dispose of the question of whether Chaucer actually wrote the *Retraction* and whether it belongs in *The Canterbury Tales*. They raise doubts about Chaucer's authorship and about the sincerity of the *Retraction* ("or was the repentance only a pretence?" II, 472). Few critics today would question its sincerity and I know of no one who would still question its authenticity, which even Manly and Rickert reluctantly accept.

The second question—whether the *Retraction* might have been a death-bed repentance not intended for inclusion in *The Canterbury Tales*—arises partly because *The Parson's Tale* and *Retraction* seemed to Manly and Rickert "a strange substitute for the jolly ending of the CT which the Host's words in Pro 796–801 encouraged us to expect" (II, 472) and partly because

> 'The tales of Caunterbury' occupy an undistinguished position in the shambling enumerations of the 'endytynges of wordly vanitees,' neither leading off as the most important nor closing the list as a climax. The reference to them suggests that they were already published and unfortunately beyond the control of the penitent. (II, 472)

The suggestion of previous publication is indeed there, though other explanations may be possible. This, however, does not affect the significance of the *Retraction*. If it was indeed written separately from *The Canterbury Tales*, we have a strong possibility that the work was already in circulation; if, as the mss testify, the *Retraction* belongs where it stands in *The Canterbury Tales*, then we have Chaucer's word he has finished his work. In either case, we have the work in what Chaucer regarded as its final state; unfinished, unrevised, and imperfect as *The Canterbury Tales* may be, Chaucer was finished with it.

At least he was when he wrote the *Retraction*. Boccaccio likewise repented for having written his *Decameron*, but he spent the last painful months of his life in Certaldo carefully recopying this work.[4] Chaucer rejected earthly love at the end of the *Troilus* but that did not prevent his returning to that theme in his later works, and *The Complaint of Chaucer to His Purse* shows his wit still sparkling and his literary powers undiminished at the very end of his life. Who knows? Reassured by a reconfirmation of his pension and reinforced by a daily pitcher of wine, Chaucer may well have been ready to return to his great work, perhaps even to make some of the changes in order that some scholars believe he was working toward when he stopped. But there is no indication that he ever did so. We are left with what, at least at that moment when he decided to end his work with *The Parson's Tale*, Chaucer regarded as his final draft.

---

[4] See Vittore Branca, ed., Giovanni Boccaccio, *Tutte le opere* (Brescia: La Scuola, 1974), pp. 46–47. .

That, at least, is what the text tells us, and it is to the mss that transmit this text that I must now turn.

I. The Type a Order

The mss of *The Canterbury Tales*, as Manly wrote, "are not so chaotic as usually assumed."[5] Manly and Rickert, basing their work on an earlier study by Robert L. Campbell, found that of the fifty-seven mss that contain enough of *The Canterbury Tales* to indicate an order, forty-seven can be classed into only four general types of arrangement (each with subclasses and distortions), which they labelled Types a, b, c, and d in more or less chronological order.[6] The mss belonging to each group are listed and analyzed in the charts following p. 494 of Volume II of their edition (and reproduced as an appendix to this article). On those charts the notation is very detailed; for the sake of clarity in what follows I employ (in most cases) the simpler notation Manly and Rickert used in Volume I for their analyses of individual manuscripts, ignoring the links unless they are important to the order itself.[7]

Chart I contains the order known to us from the Ellesmere MS., Type a. Manly and Rickert distinguish between the order in El and Gg and that in the next seven mss on Chart I, since El and Gg lack the Nun's Priest's Endlink contained in those other mss. The distinction is valid, but it is useful to refer to them as a single group (as Manly and Rickert often do, referring to the El-a order), since they derive ultimately from the same ancestor, and so I shall usually refer to the order simply as Type a. The order is:

a: A B^1 D E F C B^2 G H I

[5] J. M. Manly, ed., *The Canterbury Tales* (New York: Holt, 1928), p. 78.

[6] See Robert L. Campbell, "Extra-textual Data for a Classification of the Manuscripts of the Canterbury Tales," Diss. U of Chicago 1927, for the work on which these charts, revised for inclusion in the Manly-Rickert edition, were based.

[7] For the abbreviations used in the following discussion, see Manly-Rickert I, xix–xxiii and II, 474.

Manly and Rickert's Chart I shows that the order appears in nine mss (some with omissions). It appears with distortions in three others: Bo² (regular through Th, then follow only Me and SN), Ad³ (SN, Ck, and CY out of place), and Ha⁵ (lacks GP and Ck, then regular through C, with the rest lost).

Three of the mss listed on Chart I should be removed. Bo¹ and Ph², as Manly and Rickert note in their discussion of the manuscripts (I, 59, 422), were based on a common exemplar that embodied a composite order; it follows Type a̰ through block D, and then follows the Type d̰ order. Likewise, Ad² properly belongs with Type d̰. The text of this ms is closely related to that of Ht, which Manly and Rickert believe was based on the same exemplar (I, 37). It contains only (in this order) Kt Mi Su Ph Pd Cl Sh Pr Mel, which is, with many omissions, the order of Ht, which shows the same sequence Ph-Pd-Cl-Sh-Pr. Ad² therefore properly belongs with Ht as a variation of the Type d̰ order.

Even with the removal of these three mss, Type a̰ includes a dozen mss. In contrast to the other orders that we shall examine, texts with the Type a̰ order show no genetic relationship. The Ellesmere MS. is not consistently related to the mss of Textual Group a̰, all of which have the Type a order, nor is Gg related to the foregoing (it is "independent of the other major mss" in about half of its text; I, 175–76); nor are the other constant Textual Groups that embody this order, A̰d³ and Ḛn³, genetically related to one another nor to the other mss with the Type a̰ order, save for the "Mixed" Bo² (I, 67).

Each of the other orders is associated with a single scribal tradition. We have already seen examples of this in the cases of Ad², which has the same deviant order as its exemplar, Ht, and MSS. Bo¹ and Ph², which share a common exemplar and deviant order. As Manly and Rickert show in detail (II, 482–86), the Type c̰ order appears only in mss of Textual Group c̰, the Type b̰ only in mss of Textual Group b̰ (and mss of mixed descent), and Type d̰ only in mss of Group d̰ (and again mss of mixed descent). This is not surprising since, as we shall see, the Types b̰, c̰, and d̰ orders are all scribal rearrangements.

II. MS. Harley 7334 (Ha⁴) and the Type c̰ Order

Ha⁴ is the ms that Manly and Rickert regard as next in time after the

Ellesmere and Hengwrt MSS. It has an order similar to that in the Type a mss, differing only in that it contains *The Tale of Gamelyn* ("X" in the notation below) and the Man of Law's Endlink, with the Summoner as the interruptor (represented by "su"), and it has G before rather than after C-B²:

Ha⁴: A X B¹ su D E F G C B² H I

Apparently *The Tale of Gamelyn* was not in the exemplar used by the scribe; at the end of *The Cook's Tale* "in a director's scribble is 'Icy commencera le fable de Gamelyn' . . . It is clear that, as no more of CkT could be found, Gam was inserted according to the direction." (I, 223).

Probably *Gamelyn* was inserted in this position because that was its usual position in the Type c order, which Manly and Rickert believe was the first of the non-Type a orders. The c order was probably known to the director of Ha⁴, since the scribe of Ha⁴ also wrote the Corpus Christi MS. (Cp), the earliest surviving representative of Type c. The ancestor of Type c had exactly the same order as Ha⁴, though it differed in many details, the most important of which which is the identity of the speaker in the Man of Law's Endlink; in Ha⁴ the obstreperous speaker who interrupts the Host and Parson is the Summoner, whereas in the ancestor of Type c it was the Squire (the Endlink with this reading is represented by "sq"):

√c: A X B¹ sq D E F G C B² H I

A scribe-editor accommodated the order to this erroneous reading by detaching *The Squire's Tale* from its usual position in Block F and moving it forward to follow the Endlink, thus creating the model for those mss on Chart IV that embody the Type c order:

c: A X B¹ sq Sq D E Fk G C B² H I

It is possible that the reading "Squyer" in the Man of Law's Endlink is a deliberate error. The originator of the c̲ order may have found *The Squire's Tale* misplaced in his exemplar and changed the reading from "Summoner" (or "Shipman") to accommodate the misplaced tale. Whichever error was involved, the Type c̲ order is a scribal accommodation to that error, and all three mss in which it appears belong to the same scribal tradition.

III. Rearrangment for Error in the Squire–Franklin Link (Type d̲)

The Squire's and *Franklin's Tales* are explicitly linked in the Type a̲ order ("In feith squyer, thou hast thee wel yquit . . . quod the frankeleyn" vv. 673–75). In the Type c̲ order, when *The Squire's Tale* was moved forward to accommodate the order of the tales to the error in the Man of Law's Endlink, the Squire-Franklin Link was omitted (in the Lansdowne MS. a spurious Squire-Wife of Bath Link was added). Apparently in at least one ms with this rearrangement (Manly and Rickert regard the c̲ and d̲ orders as genetically related; II, 485–86) or, possibly, in an independent accommodation to the reading "Squier," in the Man of Law's Endlink—when *The Squire's Tale* was moved forward the Squire-Franklin Link was retained with, however, the erroneous reading "Marchaunt" for "Frankeleyn" (vv. 675, 696, 699). This, like the reading "Squyer," may have been a deliberate error in order to accommodate a misplaced *Merchant's Tale* (which in the c̲ order has lost its connecting links). However that may be, the ancestor of Type d̲ had this shape ("2" represents the Sq-Fk Link with the erroneous reading "Marchaunt"):

$$\sqrt{\underline{d}}: A\ X\ B^1\ sq\ Sq\ 2\ D\ E\ Fk\ G\ C\ B^2\ H\ I$$

The Prologue of *The Merchant's Tale* (IV, 1243–44), in which the Merchant says he has been married only two months, would have been in contradiction with this erroneously modified link, in which the speaker, now the Merchant, complains about the failings of his (presumably legitimate) son, and this contradiction would perhaps have prevented moving *The Merchant's Tale* to a position immediately following the altered link. However, that prologue is found in none of the Type c mss and in only one (Ry¹) of the mss with the Type d arrangement. Whether by accident or design, the Prologue was omitted from the ancestor of this rearrangement, and it was possible to move *The Merchant's Tale* forward to the position immediately following the erroneously modified link:

d: A X B¹ sq Sq 2 Me D Cl Fk G C B² H I

The pure Type d order is found in nine mss (Chart V), ten if we add Ry¹, which differs from the other d mss in links (there are a variety of spurious or altered links in this order; II, 483) but which has the same arrangement of tales. Of these, all but Bw, Dl, and Ry¹ are genetically related. Bw is a "copy of an upper d* type" ms, though a careless copy with missing parts picked up from a variety of sources (I, 56); Dl is "regularly a d* ms, though badly contaminated" (I, 111). Dl and Bw thus do have a genetic relation to the other mss in this group, though more distant than that among the mss in Textual Group d. Ry¹ is a ms "picked up from many sources" (I, 478). Apparently among the mss drawn on by the scribe or exemplar of Ry¹ was a ms with the d order, since the tales are numbered (I, 479); traces of numeration appear in Cp, a c ms, and in Fi (I, 166), Mm (I, 368), Pw (I, 412), Ph³ (I, 431), and Sl¹ (I, 507), all of which belong to Type d.

The next four mss on Chart V form a distorted subgroup, characterized by the movement of *The Franklin's Tale* forward to follow *The Merchant's Tale*, to which it is joined by a spurious adaptation of the Merchant-Squire Link. That link—which consists of the Host's comment on the lecherous May (beginning, "Ey goddes mercy seyde our hoost tho / Now swich a wyf god kepe me fro") and his address to the Squire (beginning: "Squyer com neer if youre will be / And sey som what of loue")—was left behind when *The Merchant's Tale* was moved forward. The Host's prayer to be kept from such a wife now seemed to apply to Griselda, and he now seemed to be calling for a tale from the Squire (whose tale had also been moved forward). The solution that appears in most Type d mss is a spurious adaptation of the link (represented by "3" in Chart V): the Host's comment on *The Merchant's Tale* was reduced to only lines E, 2427–32 (with additions that turn it into a rime royal stanza), in which the Host complains about his own wife and in this reduced version therefore seems to be drawing a contrast between her failings and Griselda's virtues; the Host's words to the Squire (F, 1–5) were then changed to fit the Franklin: "Sire Frankeleyn cometh neer ȝif it ȝoure wille be / And say vs a tale as ȝe are a gentilman" (III, 481–82).[8] The result was a neat transition from *The Clerk's* to *The Franklin's Tale.*

The following mss show what may have been an earlier solution to the problem (III, 480). The whole of the Host's comment on *The Merchant's Tale* is retained but modified by generalizing its application: "swich a wyf" is changed to "all euel wyves" (v. 2420), "Lo whiche" to "ffor many" (v. 2421), and "by this marchauntes tale" to "by mony ensaumples" (v. 2425). The Host's words to the Squire were then changed in a manner similar to what we have already seen. (This Me-Fk link is represented by "4" On Chart V). This link appears in Pw and Mm, joining *The Clerk's* and *Franklin's Tales*, but in the ancestor of the following mss, perhaps because the Host's comments still seemed to fit *The Merchant's Tale* (or because those comments were carried forward with the tale), the whole unit was moved forward and *The Franklin's* now follows *The Merchant's Tale*:

```
Fi  : A    X  B¹     sq Sq 2  Me 3    Fk D Cl G C B² H I
Ii  : A    X  B¹     sq Sq 2  Me 4    Fk D Cl G C B² H I
Ht  : A  B¹ ck X     sq Sq 2  Me 4    Fk D   G C Cl B² H I
Ra² : A       B¹     sq Sq 2  Me ...     X D Cl G C B² H I
```

(The hiatus in the notation of Ra² indicates lost leaves; I, 457). Ad² properly belongs with this group, since, as noted in Section I, it was copied from Ht (I, 37) and has, with many omissions, the same order. The fragmentary Pl and the Hengwrt MS., to be discussed later, are also related to this group.

Apparently Fi and Ii reflect the original distortion of the d̲ order

---

[8] The use of the word "gentilman" for the Franklin is noteworthy, since the old argument over the Franklin's social status still continues. D. W. Robertson, for example, adds a citation from Shakespeare in support of his previously published argument that the Franklin is of non-gentle birth; *Essays in Medieval Culture* (Princeton: Princeton UP, 1980), p. 273. The mss show that some fifteenth-century scribes regarded the Franklin as a gentleman.

(placing of Fk before D) represented in these mss even though Fi has the link "3" rather than "4." It looks as if in an ancestor of Ht and Ra² the leaves containing *The Cook's Tale* and *Gamelyn* were out of place. In Ra² they show up after *The Franklin's Tale*; otherwise the order of this ms is the same as that of Fi and Ii. In Ht they show up after B¹; otherwise the order is also the same as in Fi and Ii, but with the misplacement of *The Clerk's Tale,* a misplacement that also shows up in Ad².

Ra², like Ad², is related to Ht; though of mixed textual derivation, it is through the SqT "steadily with Ht" (I, 458). Ht itself is mixed but "in the main related to four mss, Ra², Hg, Ad², and a d̲ ms, perhaps nearest to Ph³" (I, 252). Ii is likewise related to Ht; though textually "Ii is a b̲* MS, usually very near the top of the line" (I, 296), in the crucial passage for the order Ii seems to draw on "the same source as Ht: e.g., CkT, the adapted Sq-Fk and Me-Sq links" (I, 297). There is therefore a genetic relation, though not always close, between all the texts in this group, with the exception of Fi, which is a unique ms, "exceedingly corrupt and imperfect" (I, 163). It apparently owes its order to the use of one or more models; some of the tales are numbered, though the numeration reflects the c̲ order rather than the d̲ : " It may perhaps be suggested that these numbers represent an earlier attempt at arrangement according to Type c̲ (cf. Cp), in which the numbers would be correct, and that the tales were later shifted around without erasing the numbers" (I, 166).

The last four mss on Chart V are very closely related. Together they form constant Textual Group P̰w. They all show the d̲ order with, as in some mss on Chart II, considerable distortion due to the break-up of Block B²:

```
Pw  : A X Sh Pr        B¹ sq Sq2 Me D Cl Fk      G C Th Mel Mk NP    H I
Mm  : A X Sh Pr Mk     B¹ sq Sq2 Me D Cl Fk NP G C Th Mel            H I
Gl  : A X Sh Pr Mk     B¹ sq Sq2 Me D SN Pd H         Th Mel    NP** Fk I
Ph³ : Kt X Sh Pr Mk NP B¹ sq Sq2 Me D Cl         G C Th Mel         Fk I
```

(The asterisks in the notation of Gl represent a repetition of *The Shipman's* and *Prioress' Tales,* which were copied twice). The order in all four mss is confused, but it is clear that the confusion began with an ancestor that had the usual Type d̲ order (II, 484).

Type d̲ is the largest of Manly and Rickert's four groups, since it contains some eighteen mss. Yet the Type d̲ order clearly arose from scribal accommodation to errors, and it is clearly related to the scribal tradition of Textual Group d̰. The Type d̲ order is found in five mss that are not members of that textual group, but all are of mixed derivation so far as their texts are concerned and all, except for Fi, are related, at least in part, to the d̰ or d̰* Textual Groups. Though this makes for a more complicated situation than that in Type c̲, we have no examples of several different Textual Groups embodying this order, as was the case with Type a̲, and it seems clear that, as Manly and Rickert conclude (II, 485–86), this order, like that of c̲, is connected closely with one scribal tradition, that of Textual Group d̰. The type is thus, like Type c̲, scribal in origin and in transmission.

IV. Rearrangement for Errors in ML Endlink
and Sq-Fk Link without *Gamelyn* (Type b̲)

Those mss listed in Manly and Rickert's Chart II (Type b̲ and Smaller Groups) derive from an ancestor similar to that of Type d̲, though it lacked *The Tale of Gamelyn:*

√b̲: A B¹ sq Sq 2 D E Fk G C B² H I

That ancestor thus contained the same two errors as the ancestor of d̲: "Squyer" for "Shipman" in the Man of Law's Endlink (though some Type b̲ mss, like some Type d̲, read "Summoner" here) and "Marchaunt" for "Frankeleyn" in the Squire-Franklin Link. As Chart II shows, the first five mss lack that link and have the Merchant's Prologue instead (noted as "Sq L-Me"), whereas the next four mss have that link and lack the prologue ("Sq-2-Me"). Perhaps the ancestor of Type b̲ contained both the modified link and the prologue, which appear together in none of the surviving mss, presumably because they so obviously contradict one another. One can at least theorize that the ancestor of this group did have both the link and the prologue and that the scribes who used that examplar resolved the contradiction by omitting one or the other.

The resemblances between Types b̲ and d̲ are such that it is tempting to assume a genetic relation between them. Manly was once convinced that was indeed the case and derived Types b̲, c̲, and d̲ from a common ancestor.[9] That possibility is rejected in the Manly-Rickert edition (II, 485–86). Though an immediate common ancestor is the simplest explanation for the resemblances between Types b̲ and d̲, it is not a necessary assumption, since it is not unlikely that two or more scribes would react in the same way to the same error (in this case the spuriously produced Sq-Me Link). Whether because of a common immediate ancestor or because of independent accommodation to the erroneous link, Type b̲ shows the same rearrangement (though lacking *Gamelyn*) as we have seen in Type d̲:

b̲: A B^1 sq Sq 2 Me D Cl Fk G C B^2 H I

Chart II shows a total of seven mss with this arrangement (the first five mss plus Ln and Py, even though they read "Summoner" rather than "Squier" in the Man of Law's Endlink and have the Sq-Me link rather than the Prologue to *The Merchant's Tale*). Not all these mss are textually related. The first four constitute Textual Group b̲ and are genetically related. Ha^3 is a ms of mixed descent, though it is related to Textual Group b̲* through most of its text (I, 211). Py is another mixed ms, "the most difficult of al the MSS to place" though it may have been derived from a ms "akin to Hg" (I, 441). Ln is also of mixed descent; it is, as Manly and Rickert note, an "example of visible editing" (I, 311), "with clear directions, apparently written by more than one supervisor, not only for its present arrangement but for a rearrangement of the tales according to a different type of order, which must have resulted from a careful comparison with the other MSS" (I, 332). Its order, like that of the other mss of mixed descent, seems thus to be due to imitation, to the use of some model or plan of the Type b̲ arrangement.

Ln, though not related textually to the Type b̲ mss with which it shares its order, is genetically related to the next two mss on Chart II, Ra^3 and Tc^1, with which it shares a common ancestor through the first

---

[9] *Canterbury Tales* (1928), pp. 79–81.

part of *The Merchant's Tale* (I, 464); to which point these mss are of the Type b order:

Ra³ : A B¹ su Sq 2 Me Cl D   C   H   Th Mel NP Ph Sh Pr Fk I
Tc¹ : A B¹ sq Sq 2 Me Cl D G C NP H   Th Mel Mk   Sh Pr Fk I

The orders of the two mss are quite different from that of b after *The Merchant's Tale* and so constitute a small group to themselves, notable for the break up of Block B² and the placing of Cl and Fk, though this is a development of the Type b order scribally transmitted in the common ancestor of Ln-Ra³-Tc¹ (I, 524) rather than an independent rearrangement .

Two other mss form the second of the smaller classes listed in Manly and Rickert's Chart II (each is defective in the beginning, though I use "A" for the fragmentary first Blocks, and each is incomplete):

Mc : A B¹ su Sq Cl Sh Pr Th Mel Mk D NP H G
Ra¹ : A B¹ sq Sq Cl Sh Pr Th Mel Mk D NP H

Even though one reads "Summoner" and the other "Squyre" in the Man of Law's Endlink, the two mss are closely related (Mc may be the examplar of Ra¹; I, 357). Mc is "an obviously picked up MS," which seems to have been modelled on some manuscript in which at least the beginning was based on the b order, perhaps something similar to that in the beginning of Ra³ and Tc¹, though with the loss of *The Merchant's Tale*.

Each of these smaller groups is composed of genetically related mss, and each is derived, by scribal distortion, from Type b. Type b itself, as we have seen, is composed of mss that are related to the same scribal tradition, with the exception of Ln (which is related to the smaller group Ra³-Tc¹) and Py, a ms of mixed origin.

V. The ancestors of Ha⁴-b-c-d and of Type a

All the mss on Charts II, IV, and V embody either the "pure" forms of Types b, c, and d or a distortion of, or a subclass derived from, one of these Types. Each of these Types, as we have seen, is a rearrangement of an ancestor that had an arrangement similar to Ha⁴. The immediate ancestor of c and d had exactly the same arrangement:

√c-d: A X B¹ Endlink D E F G C B² H I

Ha⁴ itself was based on an exemplar that lacked *The Tale of Gamelyn*, which was also lacking from the ancestor of the Type b mss:

√Ha⁴-b: A B¹ Endlink D E F G C B² H I

Since *Gamelyn* is clearly spurious, the ultimate ancestor of c and d must have had the same shape as that of Ha⁴ and b, to which the spurious tale may have been added for the same reason it seems to have been added in Ha⁴, as a sort of substitute for the missing conclusion of *The Cook's Tale*. Whatever the explanation for the presence of *Gamelyn*, it is clear that all these scribal orders are ultimately dependent on an ancestor that differed from the Type a order only in the inclusion of the Man of Law's Endlink and the placing of Block G.

Those mss with Type a must also derive from a single ancestor. As we have noted, this group of mss differs from the other Types in that the Type a order appears in a great variety of scribal traditions—in Textual Group a, in El, in Gg, and in Textual Groups Ad³ (Ad³-Ha⁵) and En³ (En³-Ad¹), none of which has a genetic relation to any of the others. Whereas we could postulate one ancestor to account for the transmission of both text and order in each of the non-Type a arrangements, we would have to assume five ancestors to account for both the texts and the arrangement in the mss with the Type a order.

It is, of course, impossible that five different scribe-editors, working with five unorganized piles of tales, would have by chance hit upon exactly the same arrangement. One can imagine a series of scribes reacting in the same way to an error in a link in an already ordered set of tales; Manly and Rickert thus may be correct in assuming that the c-d orders and order b were independently produced by scribes resolving the same errors in the same way. However, one can not imagine that even two, much less five, scribes working with disordered piles of tales and links with no indication of how the Blocks of tales should be organized—no hint, that is, that B^1 should follow A, that C should follow F, and so forth—could have produced exactly the same arrangement. All Type a mss must, so far as their order is concerned, depend on an ultimate common ancestor, as Manly and Rickert conclude (II, 480).

Thus, all forty-seven mss listed on Manly and Rickert's Charts I, II, IV, and V derive ultimately from one of two ancestors, which, so far as the ordering of the Blocks is concerned, differ only in the position of G:

$$\sqrt{}\text{Type a} : A\ B^1\ D\ E\ F\ \quad C\ B^2\ G\ H\ I$$
$$\sqrt{}\text{All others} : A\ B^1\ D\ E\ F\ G\ C\ B^2\ \quad H\ I$$

The two orders are obviously related to one another, since it is nearly impossible that two scribe-editors, working independently, would have hit upon two arrangements that differ so little. However, before we consider that relation, we must examine the mss on Chart III.

VI. The Anomolous mss

Manly and Rickert were convinced that the mss show that "very soon after Chaucer's death several different attempts were made at gathering and arranging the tales that Chaucer was known or was reported to have written." None of the evidence examined thus far provides any support for that belief. If there were such evidence, one would expect to find it among the anomolous mss listed in Chart III. With the possible but unlikely exceptions of Selden and Holkham, none of the mss listed in Chart III provides any such evidence. The scribes who produced these anomolous orders were working not with piles of disorganized tales but with fragments of mss that embodied one or more of the orders already discussed.

Ha⁴ is listed in Chart III but, as we have noted, its order is based on that of the ultimate ancestor of all the non-Type a orders, expanded by the addition of *The Tale of Gamelyn*. Ld¹ is closely related to Ha⁴:

Ld¹: A X D Cl B¹ Me F G C B² H I

B¹ and D-Cl are transposed; the order is, as Manly and Rickert note, "as in Ha⁴ but with B¹ misplaced" (I, 311).

Two other mss listed among the anomolies show the same order as Ld¹ in the beginning portion (underlined):

Ch: <u>A X D Cl</u> C B² H Fk B¹ Me Sq Plowman's Tale G I
To: <u>A X D Cl</u> Me Sq Ph Fk Sh Pr Pd B¹ Th Mel Mk NP G H I

Manly and Rickert hold that the agreement of Ch and To with Ld¹ and with one another is accidental, and they find no significance in the fact that these three mss agree with Hg in placing D after A and before B¹ (since Hg lacks X; I, 87). However that may be, the confused order of Ch is clearly because its texts were "picked up from many sources" (I, 87), and it is just as clear, from the sequences A-X, Me-Sq, C-B²-H, that its sources were fragments of ordered mss. The order of Ch is indeed "wild" but, as Manly and Rickert show, the wildness is due to the circumstances of its production. The same is true of To: "MS To shows many signs of amateurish work and apparently came from various fragmentary sources" (I, 538). The sequences A-X, Me-Sq, and Th-Mel-Mk-NP-G-H-I show that this scribe, like the scribe of Ch, was working with fragments of ordered mss.

The apparently anomolous Ps likewise shows traces of an established order:

Ps: A B¹ Cl D Me F C B² G H (incomplete)

The Clerk's Tale is transposed with Block D; otherwise, the order is, as Manly and Rickert note, that of Type a̱ (I,400). The placing of *The Clerk's Tale* before Block D also appears in Ra³, Tc¹, and Se, "but this agreement is purely accidental" (I, 400). Perhaps the scribe himself was responsible for the confusion, since Ha¹, which used the same exemplar (I, 401), though it contains only five tales, arranges them in a manner that suggests the correct Type a̱ order (I, 190).

Nl shows clear affinities with the Type ḇ order, with a break-up of Blocks G, C, and B², and with *The Tale of Beryn* (the portions showing the ḇ order are underlined):

Nl: A̱ Ḇ¹ S̱q̱ 2̱ M̱e̱ D Cl Fk S̱Ṉ Pr Ph Sh Th Pd CY Beryn M̱e̱ḻ M̱ḵ ṈP̱ H̱ I̱

The Cook's Tale is missing and part of SuT follows *Beryn*, though this is not noted above, and the Man of Law's Endlink has dropped out. Otherwise, we have the ordinary ḇ order through *The Second Nun's Tale* and again at the end, beginning with *Melibee*. The distortion, as in most of the anomolous mss, is due to its "mixed" character, "having picked up tales from at least three sources" (I, 389). Whatever may be the explanation for its irregular order, it is clear that Nl, like the other five anomolous mss thus far examined, represents a disarrangement of an established order rather than an attempt to create a new order. The scribes of these mss were working not with piles of disordered tales but with fragments of ordered mss.

Caxton's second edition (Cx²) is also listed among the anomolous mss on Chart III, but it too was based on an ordered ms, and it provides a nice illustration of how easily an order can be rearranged in response to clues in the links. Caxton's first edition has the "pure" ḇ order, with the Merchant's Prologue but without the spuriously modified link ("2") connecting *The Squire's* and *Merchant's Tales:*

Cx¹: A B¹ sq Sq Me D Cl Fk G C B² H I

For his second edition Caxton obtained the genuine Squire-Franklin Link. He therefore moved *The Franklin's Tale* up to follow *The Squire's Tale* and, perhaps finding no other position for it, put *The Merchant's Tale* immediately before *The Squire's Tale:*

Cx^2: A B^1 Me sq Sq Fk D Cl G C B^2 H I

Wynkyn de Worde recognized the awkwardness of this arrangement, and he moved the Me-Sq-Fk sequence to the position immediately following *The Clerk's Tale* and thus inadvertently came to the order that was embodied in the ancestor of Type b and the other scribal orders (though with "sq" misplaced).

Wynkyn de Worde: A B^1 D E sq F G C B^2 H I

The Selden MS. is, compared to the other mss examined thus far, much more disorderly, and it shows fewer traces of the ordinary arrangements. This ms is celebrated as the only ms to have the correct reading "Shipman" in the Man of Law's Endlink ("sh" in the notation below) and, to accommodate that reading, the scribe of Se (or that of an exemplar) joined B^1 and B^2, thus almost achieving the "Bradshaw Shift" (but not quite, since D still comes before B^2):

Se: A Cl D Me Sq B^1 sh B^2 G C Fk H I

There is an intriguing resemblance between the Selden and the Paris MS. (Ps), which also has the sequence A–Cl–D–Me–Sq and which, as we have noted, is a disarranged version of the a–El order. Manly and Rickert regard the resemblance as accidental (I, 400). Even so, the sequences D–Me–Sq and B^2–G seem to show traces of the a order; the Selden also contains part of the spurious Squire-Wife of Bath Link found in the Lansdowne MS. (La); it has the spurious Canon's Yeoman-Physician Link common in mss with the d order. It is clearly based on fragments of ordered mss. There is the possibility that the sequence B^1-sh-B^2 was in one of those fragments. If so, while Se itself results from a scribe working with fragments of ordered mss, the fragment containing B^1-sh-B^2 may show the prior existence, surviving only in this trace, of an alternate order quite different from those examined thus far. But that remains only a possibility, and not a very likely one at that.

It is difficult to say whether the Holkham MS. has any real order. It starts well enough with A, but mere chaos follows:

Hk: A G H Fk Sq B^1 WB E Fr Su Sh Pr Th Mel (incomplete)

This is the only ms in which Block D is broken up, and only the sequences G-H and B^1-WB resemble any of the other mss. If we could assume a misplacement of leaves in some exemplar to account for the transposition of *The Friar's* and *Summoner's Tales* with Block E, we would have the usual B^1-D-E sequence of Type a, which the G-H sequence also implies. Yet we have no way of knowing that was the case, and the Holkham MS. may indeed show the work of a scribe who in effect had a pile of disordered fascicles which he arranged to suit himself. However, Holkham, like Selden, is late (1440–50) and shows us not a scribe at work creating a new order but one who simply tried "to form from such sources as happened to be accessible to him a good collection of the Canterbury stories, perhaps using as his basis a somewhat battered and disarranged MS" (I, 287), and "with no attempt at orderly arrangement" (II, 487).

Neither the Holkham MS. nor the Selden offers any support for the idea that shortly after Chaucer's death several attempts were made to create an order for *The Canterbury Tales*. Only the sequence B^1–sh–B^2 in Se hints at the possibility of the existence of an alternate order, and that but faintly. What mss such as Se and Hk more clearly show is that for some fifteenth-century scribes and their readers the order was less important than it seems to us. Certainly they offer no evidence to contradict the conclusion that emerged from the examination of the other forty-seven mss. The same is true even of those mss not listed on Manly and Rickert's charts. Those fragmentary mss in which any order can be discerned (Ha^1, Ox, Ph^1, Pl, and Si, the others being single or unconnected tales and fragments of tales) are all related to the ordinary Types of order.[10] Leaving aside the Hengwrt for later discussion and with the possible but doubtful exception of Se and the insignificant exception of Hk, all sixty-two mss of *The Canterbury Tales* containing two or more connected tales clearly derive from one of but two ancestors, which differed in order only in the placing of Block G.

VII. The Relation of the Two Orders

I have tried to avoid speculating about the relation of the two orders on which the arrangements of the tales in the existing mss are based, though clearly some explanation is needed for the near identity of the two. The most simple explanation is that which has been offered in the past to explain the place of G in the scribal orders: the leaves containing G were accidentally misplaced in the process of copying the ancestor of the scribal orders. This is certainly possible; we have seen a number of examples of misplaced Blocks in the mss discussed above.[11]

Despite the simplicity of that explanation, it leaves another problem unresolved: the ancestor of the non-Type a orders also contained the Man of Law's Endlink, and one must account for that. It could be argued that both the a and non-Type a ancestors are the result of errors. That is, both derive from an ultimate ancestor with the shape of a but with the Endlink:

A B^1 Endlink D E F C B^2 G H I

When √a was copied, the Endlink was lost, and when the non-Type a ancestor was copied the leaves containing G were displaced. Or, though I

---

[10] Ha^1 has "Type a suggested" for its five tales (I, 190); Ox is "Type b" (I, 397); Ph^1 consists of two fragments, C-B^2 and I, the C-B^2 sequence suggesting one of the usual orders, perhaps a since textually the ms is "very close to Gg" (I, 416); Pl is "undoubtedly Type d" (I, 448); Si, which contains Cl-D, with the note "Vide supra" indicating *The Clerk's Tale* should follow D, has the Type a order (I, 502). The other mss with more than one tale are: Ct, SN and Pr "almost certainly copied from Cx^2" (I, 83); Ll^1 *Kt* and *Cl* "possibly copied from En^2" (I, 407); Pp, *Mel* and **Pars** (I, 407); Ra^4 *Cl* and *Pr* (I, 473).

[11] Eleanor P. Hammond, "On the Order of the Canterbury Tales: Caxton's Two Editions," *MP*, 3 (1905), 162, for examples from other English works.

think no one has ever argued for the superiority of the G-C sequence, one could argue that the non-Type a order is correct and that a derived from that with two errors, the loss of the Endlink and the displacement of G. In either case, one has to assume two errors rather than one.

Other difficulties arise when we look more closely at the two orders. For example, Manly and Rickert's textual analysis shows the possibility that the Manciple's prologue "was lacking in the ancestor of the MSS which usually form b*–cd*" (II, 445), the textual tradition of the non-Type a mss, whereas it was present in the ancestor of the Type a mss. There are, moreover, a number of passages which circulated in two forms, one an early the other a later revised version. They are perhaps not so numerous as Rickert believed (II, 495–518). However, one clear instance is the Physician-Pardoner Link, which exists in an early version in Ha^4 and in a later version in El and most other mss (II, 325–28). The Wife of Bath's Prologue may be another example; five passages, absent from most non-Type a mss, were added in the ancestor of Textual Group a and that of El and of Gg (II, 192–93). Yet another may be *The Monk's Tale*, which has revisions in the "Modern Instances" in the Type a mss, which are lacking in the ancestor of Textual Groups b, c, and d; these "Modern Instances" occur at the end of the tale in the Type a mss rather than in the middle, between Zenobia and Nero, as in the others (II, 397, 406–09). The Type a mss have a "long form" of the Monk-Nun's Priest Link, whereas many non-Type a mss have a "short form" in which the Host rather than the Knight was the original interrupter (II, 410–11). The Type a mss have the "Host Stanza" at the end of *The Clerk's Tale*, whereas most non-Type a mss do not (II, 265), and most Type a mss (though not El and Gg) have the Nun's Priest's Endlink, lacking in almost all non-Type a mss (II, 422–23).

The differences between the Type a and non-Type a mss thus extend to more than placing of Block G. Perhaps not all these differences are due to actual revision, and which is the earlier and which the later version cannot be determined in all cases. Most critics regard the placing of the "Modern Instances" in the Type a mss as due to scribal error; Brusendorf has argued vigorously that it represents Chaucer's final intention, and E. T. Donaldson prints them in the Type a position in his edition.[12]

---

[12] Aage Brusendorf, *The Chaucer Tradition* (London: Oxford UP, 1925), pp. 77–78; E. T. Donaldson, *Chaucer's Poetry: An Anthology for the Modern Reader*, 2nd ed. (New York: Ronald, 1975).

Brusendorf also argued that the "Host Stanza" was not an early composition marked for cancellation but a later addition.[13] Though Manly and Rickert note that "Strangely enough, it is preserved almost solely in MSS containing the latest work," they judge its status to be "the same as that of ML Endlink—a bit of Chaucerian work but rejected because of change of plan" (II, 265).

The "Host Stanza" is the only case in which El and Gg contain what Manly and Rickert believe is an early feature; the rest of the Type a mss contain the Nun's Priest Endlink, the only other feature which Manly and Rickert, with most other scholars, regard as an earlier version to appear in the Type a mss. In all other cases, including those involving actual revision rather than possible additions or cancellations (Physician-Pardoner Link, Nun's Priest's Prologue, the text of the "Modern Instances"), the Type a mss invariably have what Manly and Rickert believe are the later versions.

The most probable explanation for this and for the circulation of differing versions of the same link or tale, though there is no manuscript evidence for their separate circulation (I, 37–38), is that two distinct versions of *The Canterbury Tales* survived. One is an earlier version, perhaps derived from a working draft (or, possibly, actual publication), in which the order was: A B^1 Endlink D E F G C B^2, perhaps breaking off at this point, since not only was the Manciple's Prologue lacking in the ancestor of Ha^4 and b*–cd* (and hence of the non-Type a orders), "the comparative simplicity of the MS relations" shows that *The Manciple's Tale* itself "had not been widely circulated" (II, 449). In the second, final version the Man of Law's Endlink was cancelled, H and I were presumably added, and the position of G was changed: A B^1 D E F C B^2 G H I.[14]

---

[13] *Chaucer Tradition*, p. 76.

[14] The absence of the Man of Law's Endlink from Type a seems to indicate it was cancelled. Its references to the previous tale clearly fit the Melibee rather than the tale of Custance; see Furnivall, *The Academy*, No. 1223 (12 Oct 1895), 297, and Frederick Tupper, "The Bearings of the Shipman's Prologue," *JEGP*, 33 (1934), esp. pp. 354–55; on the early history of the Endlink see R. A. Pratt, "The Development of the Wife of Bath," in *Studies in Honor of Professor Albert Croll Baugh* (Philadelphia: U of Pennsylvania P, 1961), and his "The Order" (note 1 above), esp. pp. 354–55. Some scribes omit the line "That I shal waken al this compaignye" (v. 1187) and substitute "Ne of arte ne of astrologye" (Manly-Rickert III, 231), which does contain what seems to be a reference to the extended astrological passages in the new *Man of Law's Tale*. Moreover, as perhaps these scribes realized, the promise to "waken al this compaignye" is inappropriate in tone; it is one thing for a churlish character to object to a long and heavily learned

Skeat, who believed Chaucer himself was responsible for the non-Type a orders, explained that the position of G was changed in order to bring the reference to Boughton under Blee (G, 556) closer to the reference to Bobbe-up-and-doun under the Blee in the Manciple's Prologue (H, 2–3).[15] If indeed there was an earlier version of *The Canterbury Tales* and that version did lack the Manciple's Prologue, Skeat's theory provides a plausible explanation both of how G could have occupied the place it had in the earlier version (no problem about two references to Blee) and of why it was moved in the later.

The assumption that there was an earlier version seems to me the best explanation for the G-C-B² arrangement in the non-Type a orders, since such an assumption can also account for the several other features that set the Type a mss apart from the others. The problem of the order of *The Canterbury Tales*, however, is not much affected even if the idea of an early version is rejected. If one chooses to assume that the order of the Blocks in the non-Type a orders resulted from an accidental misplacement of leaves, then all non-Type a orders ultimately derived from Type a, which then would be the original order attested by all the mss. If, on the other hand, one accepts the idea of an early version, revised to produce Type a, that order becomes the final arrangement. In either case, all mss testify to the superior authority of Type a.

VIII. The Hengwrt Manuscript

I have reserved an examination of the Hengwrt MS. until this point, since the most recent discussion of the order of *The Canterbury Tales*, by N. F. Blake, uses the Hengwrt MS. as a basis for an argument completely different from that outlined above.[16] A friend of mine, to whom I showed an early draft of this paper, observed that what I said seemed well

---

discourse that has apparently put some of the company to sleep and quite another matter for such a character to object so boisterously to a pious tale of Christian suffering. The Man of Law's Endlink is tactless as an epilogue to the tale of Custance and so, though it was allowed to stand temporarily in the early version, Chaucer finally cancelled it. He was sometimes careless about small details, but his sense of tact was infallible.

[15] Skeat, *The Evolution* (note 3 above), p. 22.

[16] "The Relationships between the Hengwrt and Ellesmere Manuscripts of the *Canterbury Tales*," *Essays and Studies*, 32 (1979), 1–18. The friend to whom I refer in the next sentence is Father Laurence Shook who, while not necessarily agreeing with all I say in this article, kindly read it in two earlier drafts and offered valuable advice.

enough but he wondered if one could not construct a case for the Hengwrt MS. as the best witness to the order of the tales, with the Ellesmere order as the derivative. This is what Blake has argued—that all orders are scribal, that the Hengwrt order was invented by its director, and that the Ellesmere was based on Hengwrt. The Hengwrt MS. and Blake's argument thus deserve special consideration.

The Hengwrt MS. is generally regarded as the earliest ms of *The Canterbury Tales* (the fragments Ad^4 and Me may be earlier; Manly and Rickert put both around 1400; I, 48, 361), and its text is believed to be close to Chaucer's own. Because it has a confused arrangement, Hg is often taken as proof that Chaucer's own ms was left in disorder and that it came to the scribe (or his director) as a mere pile of tales and links, which the scribe attempted, with only partial success, to arrange in some rational order. Hg thus seems to offer an illustration of the situation that Manly and Rickert believed existed shortly after Chaucer's death and thus seems to be the earliest attempt to put the tales into order. As we shall see, this is not the case.

The process by which the Hg scribe produced his work has been well described by Manly and Rickert (I, 270–75) and, more recently, by A. I. Doyle and Malcolm B. Parkes.[17] The ms, they explain, consists of five parts, written at differing stages in its production. Part III (Mk–NP–H) was accidentally misplaced in binding. With that part restored to its original position between IV (B^1 to Mel) and V (Block I), the order is:

Hg: A D B^1 Sq 2 Me 4 Fk SN Cl C B^2 H I

Even though the Man of Law's Endlink is missing, the sequence of B^1-Sq-2-Me is that familiar from the b and d orders, as is the last part of the ms, with the C-B^2-H-I sequence characteristic of all non–Type a orders. As customary in the d order (and about half the b mss), Hg joins *The Squire's* and *Merchant's Tales* with a spurious adaptation of the Squire-Franklin Link (the "2" in the above notation). The "4" in the above notation is the spurious modification of the Merchant-Squire link,

---

[17] "A Palaeographical Introduction," *The Canterbury Tales: A Facsimile and Transcription of the Hengwrt Manuscript*, ed. Paul G. Ruggiers (Norman: U of Oklahoma P, 1959), pp. xix–l.

which was discussed in relation to mss Ht and Ii in Section III above.
This spuriously adapted link appears in six mss in all: Hg, Ht, Ii, Pw, Mm, and Pl (III, 418). In Pw and Mm *The Franklin's Tale* is in the position it usually has in the $\underline{d}$ order, perhaps because the tales were numbered in the ancestor of $\underset{\sim}{Pw}$ (traces of the numeration appear in Pw; I, 412). In that ancestor B^2 was disarranged, and it is interesting to note that the Hg scribe apparently got B^2 in separate parts (he had it through Mel at the first stage of his work, later, as noted above, got Mk and NP along with H).

More significant is the fact that three other mss that have that link (including the fragmentary Pl, which has only *The Merchant's* and *Franklin's Tales*) embody an order very similar to that in this section of Hg. That order also appears in Fi (which instead of the spuriously modified link has the equally spurious two-stanza link—"3"—characteristic of Type $\underline{d}$). It was also apparently in Ra^2, though the pages containing *The Merchant's* and *Franklin's Tales* have been lost (I, 455–56), and presumably it is reflected in Ad^2 which, though with many omissions, shows the same order as Ht:

```
Fi   :  A     X  B¹ sq Sq 2  Me   3  Fk D  Cl SN  CY C       B² H I
Ii   :  A     X  B¹ sq Sq 2  Me   4  Fk D  Cl SN  CY C       B² H I
Ra²  :  A        B¹ sq Sq 2  Me   ... X D  Cl SN  CY C       B² H I
Ht   :  A     X  B¹ sq Sq 2  Me   4  Fk D     SN  CY C  Cl   B² H I
Ad²  :  Aᵇᶜ      B¹                     Su                C Cl  B²ᵃᵇᵈ
Pl   :                       Me   4  Fk
Hg   :  A     D  B¹    Sq 2  Me   4  Fk        SN       Cl C    B² H I
```

D and Cl are out of place. Otherwise, the order of Hg is, with omissions (X, sq, CY), that of the modified $\underline{d}$ order in Fi-Ii-Ra²-Ht-Ad²-Pl. Ht, it might be noted, also has Cl out of place. Like all the other mss in this group, Hg lacks the Merchant's Prologue.

That the order in Hg is not accidental, due to the scribe's coming upon the spuriously modified links "2" and "4" and organizing his disorderly pile of tales to fit them, is shown by the fact that he did not at first have these links. Doyle and Parkes explain that Part IV (B^1 to Mel) was written first, with spaces left for the links (including the Man of Law's

Endlink, which the scribe never got). Next he got the fragment containing *The Monk's, Nun's Priest's,* and *Manciple's Tales;* at about the same time he got and wrote in (using the same ink as for these three tales) the spuriously modified links. When the scribe next got Part V, *The Parson's Prologue and Tale,* he realized it came last but—as shown by the erasure over which "Manciple" is written—he had some initial doubts about which tale should precede the Parson's Prologue. Finally, when he got Parts I (Block A) and II (Block D), he knew A came first but either did not know where to put D or, having already written Part IV, could not put it where it properly belonged and therefore simply placed it after the unfinished *Cook's Tale.*

If Doyle and Parkes are right in their analysis of the making of the Hengwrt MS., it seems clear that the Hg scribe did get his work in bits and pieces, did not know what the overall plan of *The Canterbury Tales* should be, and did have to decide on his own where some of the tales (those of Block D) should go. Yet that was the only problem he had. It was obvious that Part I, beginning with the General Prologue should come first, that Part V, with *The Parson's Prologue and Tale,* should come last, and the links supplied the order for Parts III and IV and showed they should be joined to Part V. In other words, the scribe (or director) of Hg was not faced with the task of creating an order for an unorganized pile of tales and links; he had, rather, fragments of one or more already ordered mss, and his task was to put those fragments back together. The fact that he did not at first have the links in part IV but did have the texts suggests the possibility that at least in this part of his ms, the scribe was working in the same way as those scribes who produced the "mixed" mss in the b and d orders; that is, he got his text from one source (or sources) and got his order, including the necessary links, from another ms that supplied a pattern to be followed in arranging the tales. This could be the explanation for the fact that the order of Hengwrt reflects a rather late distortion of the non-Type a order, whereas its texts are generally thought to be close to Chaucer's own and usually contain what are thought to be the latest revisions.

N. F. Blake, in the article to which I alluded at the beginning of this section, rejects Doyle and Parkes' analysis of the production of the Hengwrt MS. He argues that the scribe must have received all the material at once rather than in stages, that he received Chaucer's own copies in complete disorder, and that the scribe's director devised the order of Hg, most obvious in Part IV (MLT to Mel), for which the director himself composed the links that establish the Sq-Me-Fk sequence. Hg thus is the earliest order of *The Canterbury Tales* and the source for the other orders, such as those in El and Ha[4]. The director of El based his order on Hg, adapting the links the Hg director had composed in order to change the Sq-Me-Fk sequence in Hg to the more familiar E-F order.

The idea that the director of Hg is the author of these links is essential to Blake's argument; if El contains the authentic versions and Hg spurious adaptations, the links in Hg and the order they serve are derivitive from some previously established order rather than the creation of the Hg director. In the Ellesmere MS. the Squire-Franklin link begins:

> In feith Squier / thow hast thee wel yquit
> And gentilly / I preise wel thy wit
> Quod the Frankeleyn / considerynge thy yowthe

The last line is a regular pentameter ("considerynge" is trisyllabic in Chaucer's verse; cf. *Womanly Noblesse,* 18). In the Hengwrt version, the last line has only nine syllables:

> Quod the Marchant / considerynge thy yowthe

Later, at line 696, the Ellesmere again has a pentameter:

> What Frankeleyn / pardee sire wel thou woost

Again the Hengwrt version lacks a syllable:

> What Marchant / pardee sire wel thow woost

Three lines later, in line 699, Ellesmere reads:

> That knowe I wel sire / quod the Frankeleyn

This time Hengwrt adds a syllable to the Ellesmere pentameter:

> That knowe I wel sire / quod the Marchant certeyn

Fifteenth-century versifiers did not always aim at, or achieve, exact pentameters in every line, but it is beyond probability that the original composer would have missed all three times, whereas a later scribe adapting these lines would have hit on a regular pentameter every time. Nor is it clear how he would have happened to hit upon the Franklin, whom this link fits so very well, to replace the Merchant, to whom it has no very clear relation.

In the Squire's Prologue there are again metrical difficulties, but the Hengwrt version contains difficulties in sense as well. In the Ellesmere MS. the opening lines read:

> Squier com neer / if it youre wille be
> And sey somwhat of loue / for certes ye
> Konnen ther on / as muche as any man

In the Hengwrt MS., where these lines are used as a prologue to *The Franklin's Tale*, they read:

> Sire Frankelyen / com neer / if it youre wille be
> And sey vs a tale / for certes ye
> Konnen ther on / as muche as any man

The change of "sey somwhat of loue" to "sey vs a tale" leaves "ther on" without a reference. One might argue that it refers to an understood "telling of tales," but this would not save the lines from being reduced to near meaninglessness.

There can be no doubt that the Hg versions are adaptations of the versions that appear in El. Moreover, these spuriously modified links are an integral part of an order derived by scribal distortion from a Type d ancestor. Hg then, far from being the earliest order we have, is, so far as its order goes, a derivative considerably removed from the ancestor of all the non-Type a orders. The only other explanation for the presence of these links and the distorted order in Hg is that offered by Blake and, more extensively, by Germaine Dempster: the adapted links and the order originate in Hg, which influenced the order of El and Ha[4], as Blake holds, and, as Dempster argues, Hg itself was the ancestor of Type c, Type d, and the later distortions of Type d. Since all these mss contain materials and arrangements that differ from Hg and from one another, a most complicated series of events must be postulated to maintain this theory.

First, as Dempster argues, the Hg scribe must have received Chaucer's own copies of the links and tales, and his work "represents the very first editorial attempt at arranging the tales."[18] The adaptation of the links could have been part of the editorial work; one need not assume that the Hg director composed them. One does have to assume that the El scribe got another completely disarranged set of copies of Chaucer's tales and links. Where they came from is not clear; they could not have been the ones Hg used; nor could they have come from Chaucer's own desk, for we know that Chaucer was very particular about the copying of his mss (as, for example, in the lines to Adam Scrivener), and if El and Hg both had access to Chaucer's own copies they would in effect have been using the same exemplar. Nor does it seem likely that the tales and links circulated separately; if that were the case we would expect separate tales and links to show up in the mss; they do not.[19]

Nevertheless, one must assume, the El director somehow got his own pile of unorganized copies, which he then put into his own order, improving upon Hg, which he used as a model. The scribe of Ha^4, who came next, used the El order, but he was associated professionally with the Hg scribe, and he studied what Hg had done very carefully. He took the Sq-M Link from Hg, but he readapted it back into the Sq-Fk Link, since he preferred the D-E-F order to the Sq-Me-Fk sequence in Hg. But he was much taken with Hg's sequence C-B^2-H-I, which Dempster insists *"does not reflect an antecedent of any kind"* (her italics), and he adopted this rather than the order in the Ellesmere.[20] The scribes who wrote the ancestors of Type c, Type d, and of the later distortions of Type

---

[18] Germaine Dempster, "The Fifteenth-Century Editors of the *Canterbury Tales* and the Problem of the Tale Order," *PMLA*, 64 (1949), 1133.

[19] See note 10 above for mss containing more than one tale. Individual tales do show up, but only the pious tales, frequently in collections of religious verse: Ds^2, *MLT*; Ee, *MLT*; Hl^1 *PrT*; Hl^2, *PrT*; Hl^3, *PrT*; Hl^4, *ClT*; Hn, *MkT*; Kk, *PrT*; Ll^2, *ParsT*; Np, *ClT*; Sl^3, *Mel*; St, *Mel*. The other *CT* do not show up as separate pieces. Ad^4 has vv. 478–528 of *GP* "apparently written from memory" (I, 48). Do has vv. 298–368 of *GP* (it is a single leaf; I, 48). Me has fragments of *NPP/NPT*; originally Me had "the couplet inserted after 4060 by a Ln Nl Ry^1 . . . Like Dd Ln Nl, it omitted 4353–56" (I, 361), and it seems therefore to be a fragment of a complete ms of *The Canterbury Tales*.

[20] Dempster (note 18 above), p. 1132.

d̲ all worked in the same shop, and each of them followed the same procedure as that used by the scribe of Ha⁴. Although each had a perfectly acceptable order at hand, each felt obligated to consult Hg, whose owner would not allow it to go to the shop, so that most consulted it only briefly and could not use its text, though none could have "failed to recognize the superiority of the Hg text over those available in the c̲d̲ shop."²¹ Though each scribe in turn consulted Hg, if only briefly, and though each was moved to change his order accordingly, none adopted the whole Hg order and each changed his own order in a different way.

Anything is possible; Manly and Rickert believe that at least one scribe did study the problem of order (I, 332), but that a whole group of scribes used the technique of modern scholarship, recognized a superior text when they saw it, and devised their own orders only after carefully comparing mss and weighing alternatives, and—most modern of all— never reached any agreement, seems to me, to say the least, improbable.

Yet so improbable a series of events must be hypothesized to maintain the theory that the director of Hg invented its order, since one must somehow explain the similarities of Hg to the c̲ and d̲ orders, including the distortion of d̲ that appears in mss such as Ht, which share the spurious Merchant-Franklin Link and the order Sq-2-Me-4-Fk that appears in Hg but not in c̲ and the other d̲ mss. The only possible explanation for this is much simpler: the director of Hg, like the scribes and directors of the other mss with distorted orders, was working not with a mere pile of tales and links but with fragments of ordered ms(s); the links and arrangement of the tales in Part IV show that in this section the scribe was using as his model a fragment of a ms that embodied the arrangement that appears in Fi-Ii-Ra²-Ht and is implied in the fragmentary Ad² and Pl.

It follows that the ancestor of the non-Type a̲ mss, the Type d̲ order that was derived from it (and the Type c̲ before that, if Manly and Rickert are right in deriving d̲ from c̲), and the distortion of d̲ that appears in Hg were all in existence before Hg was written. The scribal rearrangements of the non-Type a̲ ancestor could, of course, have developed rather rapidly. Nevertheless, if Hg is as early as is generally believed, *The*

---

²¹ Dempster, p. 1124; see also the same author's, "A Chapter of the Manuscript History of the *Canterbury Tales*: The Ancestor of Group *d*; the Origin of Its Texts, Tale-order, and Spurious Links," *PMLA*, 63 (1948), 469.

Canterbury Tales must have been in circulation very early indeed, perhaps even in Chaucer's own lifetime.[22]

This is not impossible. The only reason for thinking that *The Canterbury Tales* did not circulate in Chaucer's lifetime is the assumption that Chaucer was not finished with the work and therefore would not allow it to circulate. We have in the *Retraction* Chaucer's own word that he was finished with them, and Manly and Rickert note that the reference to *The Canterbury Tales* seems to imply that they were indeed in circulation (perhaps in the earlier version reflected in the non-Type a ancestor). The *Envoy to Bukton,* usually dated in 1396, seems clearly to imply that Chaucer's friend had access to a copy ("The Wyf of Bathe I pray yow that ye rede"). Moreover, Manly and Rickert date the very earliest mss of *The Canterbury Tales* at around 1400. These are Ad[4], which contains a copy of Chaucer's *Boethius,* his poem *Truth,* and the portrait of the Parson from the General Prologue (vv. 478–528), apparently reproduced from memory (I, 48–49). The fragments of the Nun's Priest's Link and Tale in the Merthyr MS. may be almost as old; Manly and Rickert date this ms at "c. 1400?" (I, 361). Finally, John Lydgate shows a close knowledge of *The Canterbury Tales* even in his earliest works. He quotes from *The Canterbury Tales* in *The Churl and the Bird,* which Schirmer dates "before 1397," and again in *The Complaint of the Black Knight* (*Complaint of a Lover's Life*) and *The Temple of Glass,* both of which Schirmer dates 1400–03, and in the latter Lydgate refers to characters from *The Canterbury Tales*—"good women" such as Custance, Griselda, and Dorigen—in a manner that shows that he expects his audience to recognize them.[23]

---

[22] For the problem of dating, see Doyle and Parkes (note 17 above), pp. xx–xxi.

[23] Derek Pearsall, *John Lydgate* (London: Routledge and Kegan Paul, 1970), pp. 53, 221, n. 8, on echoes of *CT*, I, 1838; IV, 1637; IX, 163–74 in *The Churl and the Bird,* which Walter F. Schirmer, *John Lydgate: A Study in the Culture of the XV Century,* tr. Ann E. Keep (London: Methuen, 1952), p. 23 n. 4, dates before 1397; J. Schick, ed., *The Temple of Glas,* EETS, ES 60 (1891), p. cxii, dates it c. 1398. *The Complaint of a Lover's Life* mentions "Arcite" and "Palamone" in v. 368 and Pearsall (p. 85) notes an echo of *CT*, IV, 2220 in vv. 54–55; John Norton-Smith, ed., *John Lydgate: Poems* (Oxford: Clarendon, 1966), notes echoes of *CT*, I, 1493–96 (p. 163); I, 2062 (p. 165); VII, 675 (p. 168); IX, 105 (p. 172); V, 1038 (p. 173). Schirmer (p. 37) follows Schick (p. cxii) in dating the poem 1400–02. For the references to characters from *The Canterbury Tales* in the *Temple of Glass* see vv. 75, 102–10, 137–42, 184–85, 409–10. Schirmer (p. 37) following Schick (p. cxii), dates this poem 1400–03. Both Pearsall and Norton-Smith emphasize the difficulty of dating Lydgate's early poems; there is no firm evidence for the dates Schirmer and Schick assign for these works, which may have been written at any time between 1398 and 1412 or even later.

However, the dating of Lydgate's poems is very problematical; all three of the poems in which Lydgate quotes *The Canterbury Tales* may be later than Schirmer believed. Likewise, one might explain Chaucer's urging Bukton to read the "Wyf of Bath" by assuming that Bukton had access to Chaucer's own copy or perhaps to a copy of only the Wife of Bath's Prologue, even though the mss show no evidence that it ever circulated separately. Separate circulation might also be invoked to account for the fragments preserved in MSS. Ad^4 and Me, though again there is no evidence of separate circulation. The alternate explanation, that the memorizer of Ad^4 and the scribe of Me had access to Chaucer's own copy, begins to imply considerable access to that copy. Finally, Manly and Rickert may have been wrong in assigning so early a possible date to Ad^4 and Me. It seems to me most probable that *The Canterbury Tales* were in circulation before 1400, but that remains a probability rather than a certainty. However, given the fact that our earliest complete mss of *The Canterbury Tales*, the Ellesmere and Hengwrt, are both dependent on previously established orders, we can be certain that the work was in circulation if not before Chaucer's death, then immediately afterwards.

IX. The Author of the Type a Order

As we have seen, the mss offer no support for Manly and Rickert's belief that shortly after Chaucer's death there were a number of different attempts to put *The Canterbury Tales* into some order. Their second conclusion was that none of the orders could be attributed to Chaucer. The b, c, and d and their associated smaller groups and derivatives they rightly rejected as scribal. The Type a order they rejected on the basis of what were then widely held assumptions about Chaucer's literary realism.[24] They felt that Chaucer could not have been responsible for an order that contained temporal and geographical contradictions.

Despite the literary objections that have been raised, which we must shortly consider, we should note that the Type a order is an arrangement

---

[24] See for example J. S. P. Tatlock, "The Canterbury Tales in 1400," *PMLA*, 50 (1935), who put the case flatly: Chaucer was a "realist" with a "highly realistic plan" (p. 121); thus the order H-I cannot be correct, because "There is a lack of reality in putting two tales in the last two miles before Canterbury, and no "thropes ende' is known between it and Harbledown" (p. 123). The circularity of such reasoning is obvious.

of considerable artistic merit. Even those who would reject its authority would move but one Block, adopting the "Bradshaw shift" and placing B^2 immediately after B^1 and the Man of Law's Endlink. It is difficult to believe that anyone other than Chaucer could have made so satisfactory an arrangement. The scribes, as we have seen, were willing to tamper with the order, but the mss show no instance of a scribe changing the order of the tales on the basis of anything other than the most obvious clues in the links—"seyde the Squyer" and such. Most scribes were apparently interested only in smooth transitions from one tale to another, and they were not above making such transitions by adding spurious links or changing readings when this seemed necessary. No scribe was ever influenced by internal evidence within the tales—allusions by one speaker to another tale, or geographical allusions to the Canterbury Road, which apparently no one ever noticed until the nineteenth century. Blocks D and B^2 are for modern critics, as we shall see, the most troublesome, since the geographical allusions seem to show that B^2 should come before D. Yet no scribe was troubled by this; the WB Pro comes before the Mk Pro in only five mss, more or less by accident each time (Mc, Ra^1, Mm, Gl and Ph^3), and the sequence $C-B^2$ is almost invariable. On the other hand, Blocks D, E, and F are, from the standpoint of internal allusions, the most tightly linked of all the Blocks. Yet this is the sequence that is broken up in all the scribal rearrangements. *The Merchant's Tale* clearly alludes to the Wife of Bath's Prologue in terms that make it obvious the Wife has already had her say (vv. 1685–87); yet no scribe hesitated to follow the d̲ and b̲ orders, in which *The Merchant's Tale* precedes that of the Wife of Bath.

The creator of the Type a̲ order had an intimate knowledge of the contents of the tales, by which he knew that D, E, and F came in that order. Moreover, he had a sophisticated literary sense that enabled him to get the right order even when there were no clear signals: he knew that B^1 followed A, that C followed F, and that G came before H. This is not the sort of accomplishment that one associates with scribes or their directors. Even Caxton, an editor of considerable literary attainments, did not recognize the error in his ordering of the tales, though it was simple enough that Wynkyn de Worde could easily correct it. If we assume that some one other than Chaucer invented the Type a̲ order, we must assume the existence of an unknown literary prodigy who has left no other traces of his genius. So improbable an assumption is unnecessary; it is much more reasonable to assume that the Type a order was the work of the author of *The Canterbury Tales*, Geoffrey Chaucer.

There is even one slight bit of external evidence for Chaucer's invention of the order of the tales. The scribe of O[1] says in his *explicit* that the work was "compiled" by Geoffrey Chaucer. The force of the word "compiled" has only recently been made clear by A. I. Doyle and Malcolm B. Parkes, in an article in which they argue persuasively that *The Canterbury Tales* belong to the genre of the *compilatio:*

> The *compilatio* was developed as a genre in legal and academic circles during the course of the thirteenth century to make inherited material excerpted from the writing of established *auctores* accessible in a more systematic and convenient form. In theory the compiler added no material of his own but was free to arrange; he imposed a new *ordinatio* on the materials that he extracted from the works of others. The value of a *compilatio* depended on the wealth of the *auctoritees* employed, but its utility depended on the ways in which the *auctoritees* were arranged. The *ordinatio* of the Ellesmere manuscript interprets *The Canterbury Tales* as a *compilatio* in that it emphasizes the roles of the tales as repositories of *auctoritates*—sententiae and aphorisms on different topics which are indicated by marginal headings.[25]

At least some of the glosses that give *The Canterbury Tales* the appearance of a *compilatio* are due to Chaucer himself (III, 527), and the scribe of O[1] in his *explicit* tells us that Chaucer himself was the compiler:

> Heere is ended the book of the tales of Caunterbury compiled by Geffrey Chaucer of whos soule Iesu Crist have mercy. Amen.

Here we have the direct testimony of one of the earliest scribes of the tales, if not the earliest, that Chaucer was not only the "maker" of the book but the one who "compiled" it, who gave it its *ordinatio*.

The testimony of this scribe, the evidence of the mss, and the

---

[25]"The Production of Copies of the *Canterbury Tales* and *Confessio Amantis*," in *Medieval Scribes, Manuscripts and Libraries: Essays Presented to N. R. Ker*, ed. M. B. Parkes and Andrew G. Watson (London: Scolar Press, 1978), p. 190.

improbability that anyone other than Chaucer could have invented the Type a order make a strong case for this as Chaucer's own arrangement. In order to argue that someone other than Chaucer put the tales in this order one would have to assume that the testimony of the *Retraction* can be ignored, that Chaucer left his work unfinished, and that his disorderly manuscript came into the hands of some otherwise unknown literary prodigy who invented the order but concealed his work and allowed his scribe to believe that the work had actually been "compiled" as well as composed by Geoffrey Chaucer.

One would be forced to adopt such a series of conjectures only if there were some very convincing evidence against Chaucer's authorship of the order. Manly and Rickert were convinced there was such evidence:

> It was long ago pointed out that Chaucer cannot have been responsible for placing the tales forming Block B^2 after those forming Block D, for in B^2 line 3116 reads "Lo Rouchestre stant heer faste by," whereas in D, 645–48 the Summoner promises to tell two or three stories of friars before they come to "Sittingbourne," which lies some eleven miles beyond Rochester. Moreover, it is incredible that after placing the telling of the Manciple's short tale in the morning (cf. H, 15–17) Chaucer should represent the hour of the day at the close of it as four in the afternoon, (I, 1–5). We may therefore dismiss the El-a arrangement as non-Chaucerian. (II, 475)

Manly and Rickert's argument on the basis of time has carried little weight with critics, and few today would question the authenticity of the opening line of the Parson's Prologue ("By that the Maunciple had his tale ended"). Indeed, if one were to take Chaucer's references to time as attempts at representing a consistent chronology, he would have to conclude that *The Canterbury Tales* ended the day before they began; in the Man of Law's Prologue, when Harry Bailly makes his elaborate astronomical calculation of the time of the day, Chaucer tells us the day is April eighteenth; in the Parson's Prologue, where again the time of the day is calculated by astronomical means, the astronomical situation that is described "can apply only to April 17 or earlier."[26] This is not a

---

[26] Sigmund Eisner, "Chaucer's Use of Nicholas of Lynn's Calendar," *Essays and*

problem, since most critics today accept, as they must, the fact that Chaucer was not bothered by such inconsistencies, and neither are most readers.

The geographical references are another matter. The confused order of the references to Rochester and Sittingbourne has weighed very heavily in the judgment of editors and critics; the Type a-Ellesmere order has been rejected solely on the basis of these confused geographical references.[27] If the Summoner had only mentioned some place other than "Sittingbourne," the whole argument over the order of *The Canterbury Tales* might never have begun.

Should a single place name carry this much weight? Perhaps so, if we could be sure that geographical accuracy mattered as much to Chaucer as it did to his nineteenth-century readers, such as A. P. Stanley, who complained indignantly that Chaucer's geographical errors were almost as bad as Shakespeare's.[28] Not quite: Shakespeare sets Act II, scene ii, of *Richard III* in London. Richard determines that the young Prince, who is in Ludlow, should be fetched "forthwith from Ludlow / Hither to London" (vv. 128–29). Twenty lines later Shakespeare has forgotten that the scene is set in London and that the little Prince is in Ludlow, and Richard appoints messengers "that strait shall poste to London" (v. 150), who forthwith set out "by thy direction / toward London then" (vv. 161–62), though they are already there. Then, in scene iv of this same act, Shakespeare confuses the stopping places on the road to London:

> Last night I heard they lay at Stony Stratford
> And at Northampton they do rest tonight:
> Tomorrow, or next day, they will be heere.
>
> (4–6)[29]

Studies, 29 (1976), 21; cf. J. D. North, "Kalenderes Enlumyned Ben They," *RES*, 80 (1969), 422–26.

[27] Stanley B. Greenfield, "Sittingbourne and the Order of the *Canterbury Tales*," *MLR*, 48 (1953), 51–52, argues that "we ben almost at town" at the end of *The Summoner's Tale* need not refer to Sittingbourne, but this solution to the problem has not won general acceptance.

[28] Arthur P. Stanley, *Historical Memorials of Canterbury* (London: John Murray, 1855), p. 169: "The stages of the journey" are "so roughly calculated as to introduce into the geography, though on a small scale, incongruities as great as those which disfigure the 'Winter's Tale' and 'Two Gentlemen from Verona.' "

[29] *The Tragedy of Richard the Third*, ed. Horace Howard Furness, Jr., A New

One would have thought that Stony Stratford would have sounded familiar enough that Shakespeare would have remembered it is closer to London than Northampton. Chaucer did better than that; he did not believe there was a sea coast in Bohemia and, though he too confused the stopping places on the London road, his errors are separated by thousands of lines rather than occurring in two consecutive verses. Yet it is not at all certain that such things mattered to Chaucer any more than they did to Shakespeare.

Even if we assume that Chaucer, unlike his distinguished successor, did indeed care about geographical accuracy, it is difficult to give much weight to one faulty reference when there are so many other minor errors in *The Canterbury Tales* as we now have them: Chaucer confuses the number of pilgrims in the General Prologue and fails to provide a description of, or even a clear reference to, the Nun's Priest; the Man of Law announces that he will tell a tale in prose when he actually tells one in rime royal; the Second Nun refers to herself in the masculine gender; the Shipman is assigned a tale that is obviously told by a woman; and the geographical references in B^2 and D are confused.

Scholars and editors explain all these errors, except the last, on the assumption that *The Canterbury Tales* underwent a considerable revision at an earlier stage of its composition. It is assumed that the Man of Law once did tell a tale in prose, the *Melibee*, but that he was later given the tale of Constance; hence his reference to speaking in prose. *The Second Nun's Tale*, it is assumed, was written to be told by a man (hence the masculine reference) and then later assigned to the Second Nun.[30] *The Shipman's Tale* was likewise once assigned to another teller, the Wife of Bath, and then later reassigned to the Shipman without the necessary revision of the gender of the narrator. Probably *The Nun's Priest's Tale* was written well after *The Canterbury Tales* were begun, and this accounts for the failure to provide for him in the General Prologue. All these errors, it

---

Variorum Edition (Philadelphia: Lippincott, 1908); see the discussion in the note on pp. 182–85. Many editors formerly reversed the references to Stony Stratford and Northampton to correct the error; e.g., the edition of A. H. Thompson (London: Methuen, 1903). Contemporary editors accept the text as it stands; see G. Blakemore Evans, ed., *The Riverside Shakespeare* (Boston: Houghton Mifflin, 1974). I owe this reference to my colleague, Professor Evans.

[30] Robert A. Pratt offers an alternate explanation in the note to v. 62 of the Second Nun's Prologue in his edition, *The Tales of Canterbury* (Boston: Houghton Mifflin, 1974).

is usually assumed, would have been corrected had Chaucer lived (or cared) to make a final revision of his work.

The same explanation must surely apply to the error in geography, which the majority of readers (as opposed to scholars) find much less bothersome than most of the others listed above. As Eleanor P. Hammond objected long ago, if we are to give the temporal and geographical allusions the weight which they had with many nineteenth-century scholars:

> We must assume that, although the feminine pronouns of the Shipman's Tale, the promise of the Man of Law to speak in prose, the Second Nun's terming herself 'unworthy son of Eve,' etc., were inconsistencies to be filled out later, the time and place allusions are all correct and final; that Chaucer could not, for instance, have planned his Monk and Nun's Priest as a separate piece of work, with a partially written head-link placing his Monk at Rochester, the most important stage of the journey, and then have connected that bit with B^2 without revision.[31]

Hammond's suggestion is an intriguing one, since we know that B^2 was formed late in the composition of the tales (after the *Melibeus* and *The Shipman's Tale* were reassigned), and it does seem prone to breaking up (as in Pw and associated mss). One wonders if Manly might have been correct in his suggestion that the inconsistencies in B^2 show that Chaucer was moving away from the Bradshaw shift rather than toward it.[32]

That, however, is a question that cannot be settled. As Skeat wrote about the confusion in geography, "The simplest, and I believe the only true way, is to admit the fact and leave it. I do not doubt that Chaucer could have set it right, but if we are to go by the evidence, it is obvious that Chaucer never even attempted it."[33] At the very least, it seems to me clear that this one error, one of several that show *The Canterbury Tales* were never carefully revised, is not of sufficient weight to negate the evidence of the mss.

The evidence seems to me very strong indeed. We have Chaucer's own words in the *Retraction*, which clearly indicate that he had finished working on *The Canterbury Tales*. The mss show that from the very

---

[31] E. P. Hammond (note 11 above), p. 165.
[32] Manly, *Canterbury Tales* (1928), pp. 77–78.
[33] Skeat, *The Evolution* (note 3 above), p. 30.

beginning the work circulated in but two orders, both of which can be attributed to Chaucer; one may be an early version, in which case the Type a-Ellesmere order is the final arrangement, or it may be derived from the Type a by scribal error, the accidental misplacement of the leaves containing G, in which case Type a is the only order attested by the mss. This order was in circulation very early indeed, perhaps even in Chaucer's own lifetime if Manly and Rickert's dating of the fragments in Ad^2 and Me are correct, and the earliest scribe states that *The Canterbury Tales* was "compiled by Geoffrey Chaucer." The evidence for Chaucer's authorship of the Type a order as it appears in mss such as the Ellesmere is overwhelming. The only argument against this is based on the assumption that Chaucer *could* not have confused the geographical order of Rochester and Sittingbourne; certainly he *ought* not to have done so; he ought to have left us a more nearly perfect, revised and polished work. But, as Skeat insisted with some asperity, "I submit this ought to be final; and that, instead of considering what Chaucer ought to have done we have rather to consider what he actually did."[34] What Chaucer actually did was to leave us the Type a-Ellesmere order, imperfect and blemished though it be. I submit this ought to— though I fear it will not—be final.

---

[34] Skeat, *The Evolution*, p. 31.

ORDER of TALES

CHART I

MSS OF TYPE a, PURE AND MIXED

El	Pro-Kt-L-Ml-L-Re-L-Ck	L-ML	WB-L-Fr-L-Su	L-Cl-b-L-Me-L-L-Sq-L-Fk	Ph-L-Pd Sh-L-Pr-L-Th-L-Mel-L-Mk-L-NP	SN-L-CY L-Mc L-Ps R
Gg	Pro-Kt-L-Ml-L-Re-L-..	L-ML	WB...Fr...Su	..Cl-b...Me.....Sq...Fk	Ph...Pd Sh...Pr-L-Th...Mel-L-Mk...NP	SN-L-CY L-Mc L-Ps..
Dd	Pro-Kt-L-Ml-L-Re-L-Ck	L-ML	WB-L-Fr-L-Su	L-Cl-b-L-Me-L-L-Sq...Fk	Ph-L-Pd Sh...Pr...Th-L-Mel-L-Mk-L-NP-L	SN-L-CY ....
En[1]	Pro-Kt-L-Ml-L-Re-L-Ck	L-ML	WB-L-Fr-L-Su	L-Cl-b-L-Me-L-L-Sq-L-Fk	Ph-L-Pd Sh-L-Pr-L-Th-L-Mel-L-Mk-L-NP-L	SN-L-CY L-Mc L-Ps R
Ds	Pro-Kt-L-Ml-L-Re-L-Ck	L-ML	WB-L-Fr-L-Su	L-Cl-b-L-Me-L-L-Sq-L-Fk	Ph-L-Pd Sh-L-Pr-L-Th-L-Mel-L-Mk-L-NP-L	SN-L-CY L-Mc L-Ps R
Cn	Pro-Kt-L-Ml-L-Re-L-Ck	L-ML	WB-L-Fr-L-Su	L-Cl-b-L-Me-L-L-Sq-L-Fk	Ph-L-Pd Sh-L-Pr-L-Th-L-Mel-L-Mk-L-NP-L-c	SN-L-CY L-Mc L-Ps R
Ma	Pro-Kt-L-Ml-L-Re-L-Ck	L-ML	WB-L-Fr-L-Su	L-Cl-b-L-Me-L-L-Sq-L-Fk	Ph-L-Pd Sh-L-Pr-L-Th-L-Mel-L-Mk-L-NP-L-c	SN-L-CY L-Mc L-Ps R
En[3]	Pro-Kt-L-Ml-L-Re-L-Ck	L-ML	WB-L-Fr-L-Su	L-Cl-b-L-Me-L-L-Sq-L-Fk	Ph-L-Pd Sh-L-Pr-L-Th-L-Mel-L-Mk-L-NP-L-c	SN-L-CY L-Mc L-Ps R
Ad[1]	Pro-Kt-L-Ml-L-Re-L-Ck	L-ML	WB-L-Fr-L-Su	L-Cl-b-L-Me-L-L-Sq-L-Fk	Ph-L-Pd Sh-L-Pr-L-Th-L-Mel-L-Mk-L-NP-L-c	SN-L-CY L-Mc L-Ps R
Bo[2]	Pro-Kt-L-Ml-L-Re-L-Ck[1]	L-ML	WB-L-Fr-L-Su	L-Cl-b-L-Me-L-L-Sq...Fk	Ph-L-Pd Sh-L-Pr-L-Th-L-	Mc SN ******
Ad[3]	Pro-Kt-L-Ml-L-Re	L-ML	WB-L-Fr-L-Su	SN L-Cl-L-L-Me-L-L-Sq-L-Fk	Ph-L-Pd Sh...Pr-L-Th-L-Mel-L-Mk-L-NP	L-Mc L-Ck L-CY L-Ps..
He[5]	...Kt-L-Ml-L-Re	L-ML	WB-L-Fr-L-Su	SN L-Cl-L-Me-L-L-Sq-L-Fk-j-Ph-L-Pd	[end of MS lost]	
Ad[2]	...Kt-L-Ml...........	L-ML	..........Su	Ph-L-Pd L-Cl............	Sh-L-Pr........Mel [rest of MS lost]	
Bo[1]	Pro-Kt-L-Ml-L-Re	L-ML.	WB-L-Fr-L-Su	L-Cl	Fk	SN-L-CY-f-Ph-L-Pd-e-Sh-L-Pr-L-Th-L-u-Mel-L-Mk-L-NP L-Mc L-Ps R
Ph[2]	Pro-Kt-L-Ml Re	ML	WB-L-Fr-L-Su	L-Cl	Fk	SN-L-CY-f-Ph-L-Pd-e-Sh-L-Pr-L-Th-L-u-Mel-L-Mk-L-NP L-Mc L-Ps..

Symbols:

L—	Link joined to tale following	***	MS left incomplete	f	14-line CY-Ph Link
-L	Link joined to tale preceding	b	7-line Cl Endlink	j	6-line Fk-Ph Link (CY-Ph Link edited)
-L-	Link joined both ways	c	6-line continuation of NP Endlink	u	4-line addition to Th-Mel Link
....	Passage lacking by loss of leaves	e	12-line Pd-Sh Link	CK[J]	40 spurious lines to complete CKT

The charts were made by Robert Campbell in 1929, and slightly revised later.

Reprinted from *The Text of The Canterbury Tales*, by John M. Manly and Edith Rickert, by permission of The University of Chicago Press. © 1940 by John Matthews Manly.

MSS OF TYPE b AND OTHER SMALL GROUPS

```
He   ... Kt-L-Mi-L-Re-L-Ck       L-ML-sq-Sq  L-Me  WB-L-Fr-L-Su  L-Cl-b  Fk  SN                Pr-L-Th-L-Mel-L-Mk-L-NP    L-Mc  L-Ps..
Ne   Pro-Kt-L-Mi-L-Re-L-Ck       L-ML-sq-Sq  L-Me  WB-L-Fr-L-Su  L-Cl-b  Fk  SN-L-CY           Sh-L-Pr-L-Th-L-Mel-L-Mk-L-NP L-Mc  L-Ps R
Cx¹  Pro-Kt-L-Mi-L-Re-L-Ck       L-ML-sq-Sq  L-Me  WB-L-Fr-L-Su  L-Cl-b  Fk  SN-L-CY           Sh-L-Pr-L-Th-L-Mel-L-Mk-L-NP Ph    L-Ps R
Tc²  Pro-Kt-L-Mi-L-Re-L-Ck       L-ML-sq-Sq  L-Me  WB-L-Fr-L-Su  L-Cl  Pd b  Fk SN             Sh-L-                        Mel-L-Mel-L-Mk-L-NP L-Mc L-Ps R
Ha³  Pro-Kt-L-Mi-L-Re-L-Ck       L-ML-sq-Sq  L-Me  ....Fr-L-Su  L-Cl-b  Fk  SN-L-CY            Ph                           Pr-L-Th-L-Mel-L-Mk-L-NP L-Ps..

Ln   Pro-Kt-L-Mi-L-Re-L-Ck       L-ML-su Sq-2-Me   WB-L-Fr-L-Su  L-Cl-b  Fk  SN-L-CY  Ph-L-Pd  Sh-L-Pr-L-Th-L-Mel-L-Mk-L-NP L-Mc  L-Ps..
Py   Pro-Kt-L-Mi-L-Re-L-Ck       L-ML-su Sq-2-Me   WB-L-Fr-L-Su  L-Cl-b  Fk  SN-L-CY   Ph-L-Pd Sh-L-Pr-L-Th-L-Mel-L-Mk-L-NP L-Mc  L-Ps..
Ra³  Pro-Kt-L-Mi-L-Re..Ck        L-ML-su Sq-2-Me   L-Cl WB-L-Fr-L-Su         SN-L-CY-f-Ph-L-Pd *L Sh-L-Pr-L-Th-L-Mel-L-Mk-L-NP Sh-L-Pr Fk L-Ps R
Tc¹  Pro-Kt-L-Mi-L-Re-L-Ck       L-ML-sq-Sq-2-Me   L-Cl WB-L-Fr-L-Su         SN Pd L-Mc Th-L-Mel NP Ph                      Sh-L-Pr Fk L-Ps..

Mc   ........L-Re-L-Ck-p         L-ML-su Sq                      L-Cl  Sh-L-Pr-L-Th             -L-Mel-L-Mk  WB-L-Fr-L-Su  L-NP L-Mc SN-L-CY [MS left incomplete]
Ra¹  ... Kt-L-Mi-L-Re-L-Ck-p     L-ML-sq-Sq                      L-Cl  Sh-L-Pr-L-Th             -L-Mel-L-Mk  WB-L-Fr-L-Su  ...NP L-Mc [MS left incomplete]
```

CHART III

ANOMALOUS MSS, EARLY AND LATER

```
Hg'  Pro-Kt-L-Mi-L-Re-L-Ck           WB-L-Fr-L-Su     L-Mk-L-NP  L-Mc   L-ML  Sq-2-Me-L-4-Fk  SN    L-Cl-b Ph-L-Pd  Sh-L-Pr-L-Th-L-Mel  L-Ps..[present order]
Ha⁴  Pro-Kt-L-Mi-L-Re-L-Ck           WB-L-Fr-L-Su     L-ML  Sq-2-Me-L-4-Fk Sq  L-Me  L-Cl-b  Ph-L-Pd      Sh-L-Pr-L-Th-L-Mel-L-Mk-L-NP  L-Mc  L-Ps..[original order]
Ch   Pro-Kt-L-Mi-L-Re-L-Ck X         L-ML-su WB-L-Fr-L-Su L-Cl-L-Me-L-L-Sq • Fk  3N-L-CY Ph-L-Pd Sh-L-Fr-L-Th-L-Mel-L-Mk-L-NP  L-Ps R
Ld¹  Pro-Kt-L-Mi-L-Re-L-Ck X         WB-L-Fr-L-Su     L-Cl-b  Ph-L-Pd Sh-L-Pr-L-Th-L-Mel-L-Mk-L-NP-L  L-Me Fk  L-ML  L-Me-L-L-Sq² SN-L-CY L-Ps..
To   Pro-Kt-L-Mi...L-Re-L-Ck X       WB-L-Fr-L-Su     L-Cl L-ML...Me-L-L-Sq-L-Fk SN-L-CY..Ph..Pd/Sh-L-Pr-L-Th-L-Mel...Mk-L-NP L-Mc
Hk   ... Kt-L-Mi-L-Re SN-L-CY L-Me Fk Sq ML  L-Cl 5-L-Me-L-L-Sq Ph Fk Sh-L-Pr *Pd L-ML L-Th-L-Mel-L-Mk-L-NP SN-L-CY Mc L-Ps R
Ps   Pro-Kt-L-Mi-L-Re L-ML  L-Cl L-Me L-ML Sq-L-Fk Ph-L-Pd Sh-L-Pr-L-Th-L-*  L-WL L-Pr-L-Th...Mel [rest of MS lost or incomplete]
Se   Pro-Kt-L-Mi-L-Re-L-Ck         L-Cl-b WB-L-Fr-L-Su L-Me-L-L-Sq-l* L-ML-sh-Sh-L-Pr-L-Th-L-Mel-L-Mk-L-NP SN-L-CY-f-Ph-L-Pd Fk L-Mk-L-NP L-Ps R
Nl   Pro-Kt-L-Mi-L-Re*....         ML Sq-2-Me WB-L-Fr-L-Su L-Cl 3-g*-Fk SN Pr Ph Sh Th-L-u¹ Pd L-CY² Su¹ Mel-L-Mk-L-NP Mc L-Ps..
Cx²  Pro-Kt-L-Mi-L-Re-L-Ck         L-ML  L-Me sq-Sq-L-Fk WB-L-Fr-L-Su L-Cl-b Sh-L-Pr-L-Th-L-Mel-L-Mk-L-NP-L L-Ps R
```

Symbols

2	Sq-Fk Link reading "marchaunt"	1*	First 8 lines of spurious Sq-WB Link, from La
3	Short form of Me Endlink	p	4-line ending to Ck
4	Sq Headlink reading "frankeleyn"	r	Genuine lines of SuT end 2158, 4-line ending added
5	Sq Headlink reading "marchaunt"	s	4-line Th Headlink
b	7-line Cl Endlink	u¹	2-line addition to Th-Mel Link
f	14-line CY-Ph Link	sh	ML Endlink reading "shipman"
g	7-line Fk Headlink	sq	ML Endlink reading "squyer"
g*	Lines 6-7 of g omitted in Nl, which has F 7-8	su	ML Endlink reading "somnour"

CY²	CY followed by Tale of Beryn
*L	Cl-Me Link preceded by F 675-99 (deleted)
-L-*	Ps lacks Mel but has heading for it.
*Pd	Lines C 287-88 written and deleted before PdT
Re*	A 4228-4422 and B 1-916 missing
Sq²	Sq followed by Plowman's Prologue and Tale (in later hand)
Sq*	Leaves out F 617-1223
Su¹	Lines D 2159-2294 follow Beryn
X	Gamelyn

Reprinted from *The Text of The Canterbury Tales*, by John M. Manly and Edith Rickert, by permission of The University of Chicago Press. © 1940 by John Matthews Manly.

CHART IV

MSS OF TYPE c

```
Cp    Pro-Kt-L-Ml-L-Re-L-Ck    X  L-ML-sq-Sq     WB-L-Fr-L-Su L-Cl Me Fk SN-L-CY      Ph-L-Pd   Sh-L-Pr-L-Th-L-Mel-L-Mk-L-NP L-Mc L-Ps..
Sl²   Pro-Kt-L-Ml-L-Re-L-Ck    X  L-ML-sq-Sq     WB-L-Fr-L-Su L-Cl Me Fk SN           Ph-L-Pd   Sh-L-Pr-L-Th-L-Mel-L-Mk-L-NP L-Mc ***
La    Pro-Kt-L-Ml-L-Re-L-Ck-k-X  L-ML-sq-Sq-l-WB-L-Fr-L-Su L-Cl Me Fk SN-L-CY-m-Ph-L-Pd-n-Sh-L-Th-L-Mel-L-Mk-L-NP L-Mc L-Ps R
```

CHART V

TYPE d, PURE AND DISTORTED

```
Lc    Pro-Kt-L-Ml-L-Re-L-Ck-a-X    L-ML-sq-Sq...Me        WB-L-Fr-L-Su       L-Cl    3-g-Fk   SN-L-CY-f-Ph-L-Pd-e-Sh-L-Pr-L-Th-L-   Mel    Mk-L-NP       L-Mc L-Ps R
Mg    Pro-Kt-L-Ml-L-Re-L-Ck-a-X    L-ML...Sq-2-Me         WB-L-Fr-L-Su       L-Cl    3-g-Fk   SN-L-CY-f-Ph-L-Pd-e-Sh-L-Pr-L-Th-L-   Mel    Mk-L-NP       L-Mc L-Ps..
Ha²   Pro-Kt-L-Ml-L-Re-L-....X     L-ML-sq-Sq-2-Me        WB-L-Fr-L-Su       L-Cl-b  3-g-Fk   SN-L-CY...Ph-L-Pd-e-Sh-L-Pr-L-Th-L-   Mel-L-Mk-L-NP       L-Mc L-Ps R
Sl¹   Pro-Kt-L-Ml-L-Re-L-Ck-a-X    L-ML-sq-Sq-2-Me        WB-L-Fr-L-Su-r     L-Cl    3-g-Fk   SN-L-CY-f-Ph-L-Pd-e-Sh-L-Pr           -L-Mk-L-NP          L-Mc L-Ps R
En²   ...Kt-L-Ml-L-Re...Ck-a-X     L-ML-sq-Sq-2-Me        WB...Fr...Su       L-Cl    ...Fk    SN-L-CY-f-....Pd-e-Sh-L-Pr...Th...    Mel...Mk-L-NP       ...  L-Mc R
Bw    Pro-Kt-L-Ml-L-Re-L-Ck-a-X    L-ML-sq-Sq-2-Me-d-WB-L-Fr-L-Su-r L-Cl-b   3-g-Fk   SN-L-CY-f-Ph-L-Pd-e-Sh-L-Pr-L-Th-L-            Mel-L-Mk-L-NP       L-Mc ***
Ry²   Pro-Kt-L-Ml-L-Re-L-Ck-a-X    L-ML-sq-Sq-2-Me-d-WB-L-Fr-L-Su-r L-Cl     3-g-Fk   SN-L-CY-f-Ph-L-Pd-e-Sh-L-Pr-L-Th-L-            Mel-L-Mk-L-NP       Mc  L-Ps R
Ld²   Pro-Kt-L-Ml-L-Re-L-Ck-a-X    L-ML-sq-Sq-2-Me-L-ML   WB........          ..Cl    3-g-Fk   SN-L-CY-f-Ph-L-Pd-e-Sh-L-Pr-L-Th-..   ............       ...  L-Ps R
Dl    Pro-Kt-L-Ml-L-Re-L-Ck        X sq-Sq-2-Me-L-ML-su   L¹-L-Sq L-Me WB-L-Fr-L-Su L-Cl     Fk       SN-L-CY-f-Ph-L-Pd              Sh-L-Pr-L-Th-L-u-Mel-L-Mk-L-NP  Mc  L-Ps R
Ry¹   Pro-Kt-L-Ml-L-Re-L-Ck-a-X    L-ML-sq-Sq-2-Me-3-g-Fk WB-L-Fr-L-Su       L-Cl    3-g-Fk    SN-L-CY-f-Ph-L-Pd                     Sh-L-Pr-L-Th-L-Mel-L-Mk-L-NP  L-Mc L-Ps..
Fl    Pro-Kt-L-Ml-L-Re-L-Ck-a-X    L-ML-sq-Sq-2-Me-L-4-Fk WB-L-Fr-L-Su       L-Cl             SN-L-CY-f-Ph-L-Pd-e-Sh-L-Pr-L-Th-L-    Mel-L-Mk-L-NP       L-Mc L-Ps R
Il    Pro-Kt-L-Ml-L-Re-L-Ck-a-X    L-ML-sq-Sq-2-Me-L-4-Fk WB-L-Fr-L-Su                        SN-L-CY-f-Ph-L-Pd-e-Sh-L-Pr-L-Th-L-   -L-Mk-L-NP           L-Mc L-Ps R
Ht    Pro-Kt-L-Ml-L-Re L-ML L-Ck-a-X sq-Sq-2-Me*.........X WB-L-Fr-L-Su                       SN-L-CY-f-Ph-L-Pd L-Cl e-Sh-L-Pr-L-Th-L- Mel-L-Mk-L-NP     L-Mc L-Ps R
Ra²   Pro-Kt-L-Ml...Re L-ML-sq*-Sq-2-Me*.                   X WB-L-Fr-L-Su-r                   L-Cl SN-L-CY-f-Ph-L-Pd-e-Sh-L-Pr-L-Th-L- Mel-L-Mk...L-NP  L-Mc L-Ps R
Pw    Pro-Kt-L-Ml-L-Re-L-Ck-a-X e-Sh-L-Pr L-ML-sq-Sq-2-Me WB-L-Fr-L-Su-r     L-Cl L¹-4-Fk  SN-L-CY-f-Ph-L-Pd L-Th-L-                  Mel-L-Mk-L-NP      L-Mc L-Ps R
Mm    Pro-Kt-L-Ml-L-Re-L-Ck-a-X e-Sh-L-Pr L-MK L-ML-sq-Sq-2-Me WB-L-Fr-L-Su SN Pd L-Mc Th-L-Mel NP Ph Sh-L-Pr-L Fk                     L-Th-L-Mel         L-Mc L-Ps R²
Gl    Pro-Kt-L-Ml-L-Re-L-Ck-a-X e-Sh-L-Pr L-Mk-L-NP L-ML-sq-Sq*.Me WB-L-Fr-L-Su-r L-Cl SN-L-CY-f-Ph-L-Pd L-Th-L-Mel L-Fk                                    ...  L-Ps..
Ph³   ...Kt...............X e-Sh-L-Pr L-Mk-L-NP L-ML-sq-Sq*.Me WB-L-Fr-L-Su-r L-Cl SN-L-CY-f-Ph-L-Pd L-Th-L-Mel L-Fk
```

Symbols

```
2     Sq-Fk Link reading "marchaunt"          g   7-line Fk Headlink                  Me*  For contents of lost leaves see
3     Short form Me Endlink (E 2427-32)       k   4-line Ck-X Link                         description of Ra².
4     Sq Headlink reading "frankeleyn"        l   12-line Sq-WB Link                  Sq*  For contents of lost leaves see
a     2-line Ck-X Link                        m   16-line CY-Ph Link                       description of Ph³.
b     7-line Pd-Sh Link                       n   6-line Pd-Sh Link                   sq   ML Endlink reading "squyer"
c     7-line Cl Endlink                       r   Genuine lines of SuT end 2158,      sq*  ML Endlink reading "squyer" over erasure
d     16-line Me-WB Link                          4-line ending added                 su   ML Endlink reading "somnour"
e     12-line Pd-Sh Link                      u   4-line addition to Th-Mel Link      R²   L-Cl and L-CY added after R
f     14-line CY-Ph Link                      L¹  Me Endlink, regular                 X    Ganelyn
```

120

Reviews

DAVID AERS, *Chaucer. Langland and the Creative Imagination*. London and Boston: Routledge & Kegan Paul, 1980. Pp. xii, 236. $25.00.

Although I admired David Aers' book for its scholarly breadth and marvelled sometimes at his ingenious arguments, as I read through it I found myself increasingly unsettled by the intrusion of the author's personal biases, by his unwillingness to countenance the common assumptions of the age of Langland and Chaucer, and by his use of jargon and other ill-chosen expressions. In the first paragraph, Professor Aers promises to "show how due attention to the writers' contexts is necessary in the attempt to grasp the specific meaning and resonance of their poetry" (Preface, ix), but I have seldom found literary criticism which so consistently wrenches works out of their milieu and imposes on them the personal and societal tastes of the critic.

Aers devotes the first three chapters to *Piers Plowman*, drawing to some extent on his previous book, *Piers Plowman and Christian Allegory* (London, 1975), but concentrating in these chapters on the way he sees Langland undermining his own seeming acceptance of orthodox church doctrine in poem by the force of his imaginative presentation of realistic characters and situations. As Aers puts it, "Langland's imaginative receptivity to conflicts and social movement pushes the total context beyond the perceptual bounds of his traditional model" (p. 15). Langland may disapprove of rebellion, says Aers, but his portrayal of the oppression of the peasants and the economic inequities of his time shows that he sympathized with their discontent. Aers sees in the ending of *Piers Plowman* Langland's almost involuntary despair of the institutional church's being an instrument for realizing his ideals. Aers establishes in these chapters the principal method of the book: illustrating how Langland and Chaucer paid lip-service to orthodoxy and established hierarchy, but at the same time showed the inadequacy of these institutionalized values almost in spite of themselves, by the power of their art. He is only moderately successful in credibly applying this method to *Piers Plowman* (preoccupied as he is with what he judges to be the irredeemable corruption of medieval institutions), but he is even less successful in doing so in the chapters on Chaucer.

The latter half of the book is devoted to analyses of several of Chaucer's characters, notably Criseyde, the Wife of Bath, the Pardoner, and the Parson. He sees Chaucer explaining the personalities of the first three primarily by reference to the interaction of social forces around them, rather than by emphasis on their personal responsibility for their actions. He is particularly at pains to demonstrate Chaucer's presentation of these characters in such a way as to make us aware of how inescapably oppressed they are by the manipulative pressures of medieval social institutions. In explicating the characterizations of Criseyde and the Wife of Bath, Aers waxes exceedingly indignant at the "male domination and egotistic predatoriness" by which he sees them being victimized and dehumanized, and he asserts that this victimization constitutes the primary perspective from which Chaucer meant them to be viewed. Strangely enough, however, he holds the Parson, for whom he has great distaste, personally responsible for the severity (and even perverseness) of his sermon at the end of *The Canterbury Tales*. In fact, Aers seems to think that Chaucer's principal purpose in the *Tales* was to exonerate many of the rascals he portrayed by showing how they were formed by their society, while undermining the portraits of those whom he has traditionally been thought to idealize (e.g., the Knight, the Clerk, and the Parson). Aers is convinced that so enlightened a man and so subtle an artist as Chaucer could not really have tolerated the military exploits of the Knight (and of Theseus in his tale) nor the doctrinaire stances of the Clerk and the Parson. However, in so uncompromisingly rejecting the "elitism" of those in political and religious power referred to in Chaucer's works, Aers seems to me to establish just as indefensible a kind of elitism by assuming the superiority of his modern moral sensitivity and his behavioristic convictions over the common ideologies and assumptions of the Middle Ages.

The difficulties of Aers' approach are capsulated in his comments on three of Chaucer's endings: those to *Troilus and Criseyde*, *The Knight's Tale*, and *The Canterbury Tales* as a whole (i.e., *The Parson's Tale* and the *Retraction*). In each case Aers denies any depth or positive significance to the ending, and contends that even if Chaucer temporarily lapsed into a conventional and uncritical ("unreflexive" is Aers' special word) point of view, the very strength of his imaginative insight which has preceded it invalidates the "weak" ending. The most important and vital element of Chaucer's work is its "complex moral thought" (p. 139), and an ending which is characterized by "a simple and unreflexive assertiveness" which fits "conventional didactic and moralistic formulations" (pp. 139, 140) simply has no force in comparison with the more analytic portions of Chaucer's work. Aers is certainly correct in claiming support from such critics as Monica McAlpine, Judson Allen, and Alfred David in his dealing with the difficulties created by Chaucer's allowing endings which embrace some kind of absolute perspective on human affairs; but to dismiss them (as Aers does in discussing *The Parson's Tale*) as "most superficial in [their] assumptions about the modes and scope of human cognition" and "altogether . . . hopelessly crude . . . for moral thought" is to ignore the even more complex possibility that Chaucer tried to embrace *both* a kind of *joie de vivre* in this world and something of the commonly accepted metaphysics of his day. If the mere introduction of the concept of an absolute point of reference is to be deemed invalid by the fact that it does not mesh with the relativity of human experience which Chaucer so masterfully depicts, then the philosopher-critic may be charged with his own kind of negation of complexity. It seems to me that Aers' position goes further toward the over-simplification of human thought and experience than does the acceptance of a Chaucer who, as much as he enjoys the variety of human interactions, and as sensitive as he is to the effect of human folly, nevertheless feels compelled in the final analysis to submit his depiction of his fellow-creatures to a more-than-human judgment. We should resist the temptation to make Chaucer over in our own image, even when yielding to it would make our job as critics easier and perhaps more personally satisfying.

Aers' superciliousness toward the Middle Ages is exacerbated by his adoption of a kind of arbitrary jargon which obscures rather than enlightens. It is never quite clear, for example, why he felt it necessary to use the word "reflexive" (and its derivatives) to describe the kind of self-critical and analytical attitude which he admires in Chaucer and Langland, and the lack of which he excoriates in some of their characters (see pp. 81–83, 93, 96, *et passim*). The word is not only unhelpful, but actually misleading; one associates it with "reflex actions," which are automatic and unthinking, the very opposite of what Aers wishes to be associated with it in the book. Similarly arbitrary, arcane, or inaccurate are his uses of "de-sublimate" (pp. 83, 85, 90), "foreground" as a verb (pp. 83, 84, 85, 92, 189 *et passim*), and "focalize" (pp. 90, 109). He overuses the words "mediate" and "meditate" so much that they lose their force and become vague in their meaning (pp. 35, 37, 51, 115; 98, 104, 147; *et passim*). Other instances of obfuscation through wording or syntax may be illustrated by the following: "Chaucer's works contain many examples of the de-sublimization of reified discourse, retrieving the specific human speakers who have become occluded . . ." (p. 88); "Now the standard practices of medieval exegesis included the sustained pulverization and fragmentation of Biblical texts . . ." (p. 86); "The poet's imagination has presented a vision where the official means of grace and authoritative instruction is irrelevant to the serious pursuit of social practices informed by the kind of moral consciousness Piers reflects in his puzzled questions to 'hunger' " (p. 52).

It may seem ungracious to have cited all of these examples of infelicitous style, but cumulatively they add to the impression that Aers was more interested in a highly personal and somewhat esoteric commentary than he was in objective criticism or calm analytical discussion. It may be legitimate to reinterpret a former age in the light of one's own time, but one should not try to present that interpretation as what writers of the former age *really* meant. If one age is to throw light upon another, each must first be described and tolerated on its own terms; and we must be particularly careful not to assume that the judgments of our own time have some kind of absolute value. I think Professor Aers has violated this important principle.

ELTON D. HIGGS
University of Michigan, Dearborn

C. DAVID BENSON, *The History of Troy in Middle English Literature: Guido delle Colonne's* Historia destructionis Troiae *in Medieval England*. Woodbridge, Suffolk: D. S. Brewer; Totowa, New Jersey: Rowman and Littlefield, 1980. Pp. vii, 174. $29.50

In one respect, the title of David Benson's study of medieval versions of the story of Troy is deceptively broad, though its subtitle helps to clarify the limits of his subject. Here, the student of Troy literature will not find a work comparable to George Cary's magisterial *Medieval Alexander*, but neither will he find anything more than passing reference to *The Seege of Troye, The Prose Siege of Troy*, or Caxton's *Recuyell of the Historyes of Troye*, all of them interesting ME works in their own right and perhaps more interesting because they clearly show the influence of two other, less well-known traditions of the story of Troy: one having its origin in the late classical *Excidium Troiae* and the other embodied in Raoul Lefevre's late medieval hodgepodge omnium-gatherum of mythological lore. Nor will the student of Troy literature find more than a footnote allusion to the two lengthy fragments which fill gaps in Scots mss of Lydgate's *Troy Book*, though both are translations from Guido. The study's primary subject is the three lengthy and complete ME translations of the *Historia destructionis Troiae:* the alliterative *Destruction of Troy* (entitled by its first editors *The 'Gest Hystoriale' of the Destruction of Troy*, the *Laud Troy Book*, and Lydgate's *Troy Book*. Benson's title, however, points where he wishes, for it is his purpose to consider each of these poems, as well as their common source, from an historiographical point of view—not as works the historical accuracy of which may be evaluated, nor as imaginative visions of putative historical events, but as the work of authors whose intent is far more historical than literary.

The first of the book's three sections is an attempt to place Guido's *Historia* in a medieval tradition of the writing of history and also to examine its essential characteristics, especially what Benson sees as that work's "most remarkable quality: Guido's deep pessimism concerning man's ability to shape or even comprehend his own destiny." In the second section, the heart of the book, Benson discusses at length each of the three ME poems in order to describe the way in which each poet finds a "solution" to the problem of "serving two disciplines," history and poetry. For Benson, the *Destruction of Troy* is "history as poetry," the *Laud Troy Book* "history as romance," and Lydgate is "history as learned rhetoric." The book's final section contains critical analyses of Chaucer's *Troilus and Criseyde* and Henryson's *Testament of Cresseid* in relation to "the historical context" which Guido's *Historia* may provide. These essays are only loosely related to the book's primary concern and even more loosely related to each other. One cannot help but wonder why, especially since both pieces have appeared elsewhere in substantially the same form, the author and publisher saw fit to include them here, for the same space might more profitably have been given over to a look at other, less well-known works and other influential traditions of the story of Troy.

The weakness of Benson's study is the very rigor with which he keeps to his thesis and neglects to consider works in relation to any other context. In his discussion of the ME poems, Benson stresses the poets' "struggle . . . to turn history into verse, to be both historian and poet" and their sense of the "contradiction of serving two disciplines;" however, in doing so, he surely exaggerates the late medieval sense of the distinction between history and fiction. The *Laud Troy Book,* for example, asserts in its prologue that the deeds of its hero, Hector of Troy, are a fitter subject of "romance" than those of any other hero, and it lists fifteen heroes of romance, some historical (Charlemagne, Roland, Richard the Lion-Hearted) and some fictional (Gawain, Percival, Havelock, Wade), without any sign of a distinction between them. This lack of a sense of the difference between history and fiction is most likely shared by the three ME poets (even Lydgate, though perhaps to a lesser degree) and by the audiences of the poems. At the same time, Benson is surely right in emphasizing the fidelity with which the ME poets render the details of Guido's narrative and the radical differences between the translations themselves.

The study's narrow focus is even more confining in its treatment of the common source of the ME poems. Basing his discussion upon the work of William J. Brandt and Paul Archambault among others, Benson locates Guido's *Historia* with the tradition of aristocratic chronicle and asserts Guido's firm grasp of the fundamental principles of that tradition, in particular its dedication to surface representation of events without any attempt to place those events in any framework of meaning. Yet, in a way which loosely contradicts his argument, Benson is forced to admit to Guido's unsatisfactory performance as a chronicler, especially his "extradordinary shallowness as a war reporter" as compared with other historians, such as Froissart. Moreover, though he takes care not to invoke any literary context or associations, Benson points out the pessimism which informs Guido's view of men and events, a conceptual framework which suggests that the *Historia* might profitably be studied as a kind of collective "tragedie" in which both Trojans and Greeks fall "out of heigh degree / Into myserie, and end[en] wrecchedly. . . . whan that Fortune list to flee . . . " Because of his dedication to the pursuit of

Guido as historian, Benson fails to inquire adequately into Guido's use of his own source, Benoit de Sainte-Maure's *Roman de Troie*. It is true that Guido adapts as he translates, but the source of almost everything Benson identifies as being characteristic of Guido has its origin in Benoit, even Guido's claims to translate from his source with absolute fidelity and the rhetorical laments against the implacable will of Fortune which are the most important vehicles of Guido's pessimism. This failure to take into account Guido's use of Benoit becomes downright misleading in Benson's essay on *Troilus and Criseyde*. In it, he argues that the origin of Chaucer's narrator and a major influence on Chaucer's pessimism lies in Guido's rhetorical intrusions, yet almost all of these set pieces in which Guido speaks in his own (or narrator's) voice have their source in the *Roman*, a work which Chaucer's borrowings suggest he knew far better than he knew Guido. Guido's *Historia* and the three ME poems are, first and foremost, translations. As such, each demands comparison with its immediate source and also with other works within related narrative traditions, whether we judge those traditions to be historical or fictional. To limit comparisons to a single narrative tradition, however instructive such comparisons may be, is to ignore a significant stock of evidence and thereby to limit the significance of the conclusions that can be drawn. Benson is most successful and enlightening when, as in his discussions of the three ME poems, he allows himself freer rein and least successful when he isolates a single historiographical tradition and, eschewing comparisons with literary works and examinations of literary conventions, restricts himself to that single focus. After all, even the ME poets' protestations of historical accuracy and of fidelity to their source, upon which Benson relies so heavily for evidence of intention, are themselves both translations of that source's protestations and also examples of a literary convention.

So far, I have dwelt upon the limitations of Benson's work, but I must take care not to mislead concerning the book's real worth as an introduction to three woefully undervalued ME poems. Benson's description of each poem's distinctive character and its especial virtues is clear, just, and enlightening. His enthusiasm for the poems, expressed at times in a style which verges on the rollicking, is genuine and, one hopes, contagious. All students of ME literature and of the story of Troy, in particular those just beginning to hitch oxen to their plows, owe him a debt of gratitude.

That many scholarly books have priced themselves beyond the means of an individual's pocket is now a reviewer's *topos*. It is an even greater pity that the price of this modest, useful book should be so high that most of us, in these times of shrinking acquisitions budgets, will be forced to hesitate and to consider carefully the best use of what money is available before recommending it to our own university libraries for purchase.

McKAY SUNDWALL
East Carolina University

JULIETTE DE CALUWÉ-DOR, trans., *Geoffroy Chaucer: Les Contes de Cantorbéry*, Ière partie. Gand, Belgique: Editions Scientifiques E. Story-Scientia, 1977. Pp. v, 147. 290 BF.

Studies of the treasures of medieval French literature by English-speaking critics have appeared in such large numbers during the last several decades that it would be perfectly easy to compile a respectable bibliography of such studies on practically any major author or significant literary genre of the period. In striking, and really rather surprising contrast, the record of published studies by French critics of the poetry of medieval English authors, even of such luminaries as Chaucer, Langland, and the *Gawain*-poet, is, over the same period, virtually a blank, even the traditional philological investigations conducted by German, and more recently Japanese scholars, having been eschewed by their French counterparts. There are certainly many and varied reasons for this seeming neglect. French in the later Middle Ages was the richest, most prestigious, and most influential of the vernacular literatures. Blest with vast resources in their home territory, French scholars have not, like their north-American colleagues, been pressed to colonize, but could happily cultivate their own garden. Cognizance of the seminal role played by medieval French literature in forming the literary fashions of the age may have led these same scholars casually to relegate certain foreign authors to an unfairly dependent and imitative role, and to view Chaucer, for example, as standing in relation to the authors of the *Roman de la Rose*, to

Machaut, Deschamps, Froissart, and the other love allegorists, as Hartmann von Aue stands in relation to Chrétien de Troyes and the French Arthurian romancers. But one is also tempted to suspect that, at the level of engagement which might prompt some creative response to his genius, Chaucer is simply not well understood in France, his subtle shifts in register, and the other devices which create his characteristically complex, ironic vision tending to inhibit full and sympathetic appreciation of his artistry.

Professor Caluwé-Dor, in offering her translations of the General Prologue, and *The Knight's, Miller's,* and *Nun's Priest's Tales,* sets out to alleviate the problem of Chaucer's inaccessibility to French readers, while acknowledging and making some deliberate concessions to the ultimately insurmountable difficulties of her task. What she presents is a "traduction juxtalinéaire," a line-by-line prose translation of F. N. Robinson's edition meant to be used in conjunction with Chaucer's English text, and directed at researchers seeking guidance in understanding the precise sense of Chaucer's words and phrases. No attempt is made to reproduce the English author's poetic effects, and while Chaucer's lines are generally translated with conciseness and elegance, those qualities are frequently sacrificed to achieve the most precise possible rendering of the literal sense of his verse. We know exactly the terms, consequently, on which Professor Caluwé-Dor's translation offers itself for evaluation, and my overall impression of her work is that it achieves her objectives with a creditable degree of accuracy. She has made good use of Robinson's notes, and has been quite scrupulous in establishing and faithfully reproducing the sense of those passages which create difficulties for English readers. The sureness of her touch in these matters is aided by her familiarity with other editions and translations of Chaucer's work, and with a range of general Chaucer scholarship.

Despite this evident care, a few errors have slipped through. Robinson's glossary, which in all fairness must be admitted capable of frustrating and baffling even his English-speaking readers, records only "sick" and "ill" under the entry *sik,* and "sigh" only under the entry *syken,* with no cross-referencing, and this probably accounts for "he gan to sike" (I, 1540) being translated "il se sentit mal" rather than "il commença de soupir." A negative sense which inexplicably crept into the translation of "And wilnest to darreyne hire by bataille" (I, 1609) has produced a reading opposite to that indicated in Chaucer's text, "Et que tu ne prétends pas la gagner par bataille." At lines 1658 and 1699 in *KnT* Chaucerian *bores* are mistakenly interpreted as "bears" (*ours*) rather than "boars" (*sangliers*). That the knights wounded in the tournament organized by Theseus "buvaient . . . de la sauge" (*sage*) is a rather desperate rendering of "and eek save / They dronken," *save* being explained by Robinson as a decoction of herbs, Latin *sapa*. The antecedent of the relative *that* in "that loved hem so weel" (I, 3063) is Arcite, and the 3rd pers. pl. pron. refers to Palamon and Emilie, so that the clause should be translated "qui les aimait tant," and not "allors qu'ils l'aiment tant." The line "But natheless she ferde as she wolde deye" becomes nonsensical if *wolde* is assigned volitional rather than merely future implication: "Néanmoins elle fit mine de vouloir mourir" (I, 3606). The phrase "the verray hogges" (VII, 3385) means "même les cochons," not "les vrais cochons," which suggests contrast with some spectral *cochons contrefaits*.

In a few instances an error protracts itself over a more extended passage. Lines 1199–1200 of *The Knight's Tale*, recounting Proëtheus' visit to the underworld, are without warrant made conditional. Later in the same tale (I, 2605–06) a wrong inference causes confusion about the general import of the scene:

> Ther shyveren shaftes upon sheeldes thikke;
> He feeleth thurgh the herte-spoon the prikke.
>
> (Les hampes tremblèrent sur les épais boucliers;
> Chacun ressentit un pincement à l'estomac.)

The meaning of *shyveren* here is of course not *tremblent* but *se brisent en morceaux*. If "shake" is understood, then presumably the situation is conceived in the sense that lances are rattled against the knights' own shields (as expressing, or creating, nervous excitement prior to the actual engagement?), and they are then depicted as experiencing 'butterflies in the stomach,' a far cry from the actual fate of the unfortunate combatant described, who having failed to parry the point of his opponent's lance, feels himself pierced below his breastbone. Chaucer's deliberately paratactic and sometimes elliptical style in passages of this sort contributes to the difficulty here, as it does in a similar passage in the description of Mars' temple (I, 2005–08):

> The sleere of hymself yet saugh I ther,—
> His herte-blood hath bathed al his heer;
> The nayl ydryven in the shode anyght;
> The colde deeth, with mouth gapyng upright.

The author confronts us here with a montage of three grisly vignettes to add to those already presented. The translator interprets the details which establish the latter two scenes as simply parenthetic extension of the first:

> (J'y ai aussi vu un suicidé;
> Le sang de son coeur avait baigné ses cheveux;
> Il s'était enfoncé un clou dans la tempe durant la nuit;
> [Il avait] la froideur de la mort et la bouche ouverte.)

If committing suicide by driving a nail through one's own temple is not totally beyond the bounds of possibility, it is certainly bizarre enough to constitute an argument in favor of any alternative reading feasible within the dictates of the author's normal rhetorical practice.

English idiom is responsible for two misreadings in the General Prologue, and perhaps for some problems with a difficult expression in *The Knight's Tale*. "For blankmanger, that made he with the beste" (I, 387) means "with the best cooks," not "the best ingredients," as is suggested by "Car dans le blanc-manger il mettait ce qu'il y avait de meilleur." "Al speke he never so rudeliche and large" (I, 734) means "however vulgarly and loosely he [i.e., the man whose tale the poet records] may speak," not "even if he [i.e., the poet] never speaks that vulgarly and loosely as a rule," the sense implied by "Même s'il ne parle jamais aussi grossièrement ni aussi librement d'habitude." I am not sure what a French reader might make of "Sois le bienvenu, o Mai beau et frais, / Car j'espère pouvoir trover quelques feuilles," as a translation of "Welcome be thou, faire, fresshe May, / In hope that I som grene gete may" (I, 1512). Robinson notes that Manly saw here some reference to the controversy of "the flower and the leaf." Fisher sees it as "possibly an allusion to some sort of Maying custom." Arcite's hope to "get some green" may rather express his desire that the circumstances of his life, particularly those affecting his relationship to Emilie, might change for the better, and that such a change is to be looked for in the spring, which is the lover's season. The green he seeks, that is to say, is probably the symbolic green of *Le Songe vert*, and I do not suppose he is to be understood as foraging for spring foliage.

Puns pose particular difficulties for the translator wishing to provide a faithful literal rendering of the text to be translated, since they offer two (or more) literal meanings which can seldom be captured idiomatically in a language other than the punster's own. Professor Caluwé-Dor's method of handling this difficulty is to provide a literal translation of one possible meaning and to indicate the presence of word play in a note. Thus, in addition to "Elle tendait fort posément la main pour prendre son repas" as a translation of "Ful semely after hir mete she raughte" (I, 136), she offers "très décement elle rotait après son dîner," acknowledging with a sensible degree of caution the possibility of a pun on *raughte*. Similarly, the possibility of a *jeu de mots* in "This Somonour bar to hym a stif burdoun" (I, 673) is hinted in a note on *bourdon*, but the likelihood is weakened when *bourdon* is qualified as *solide* rather than, say, *raide*, a word which would have helped confirm the pun in about as idiomatic a way as Chaucer's *stif*.

English scholarship has perhaps been overly zealous in beating the bushes of Chaucer's text to spring whatever might be found in the way of puns, particularly sexual puns, but some *loci*, where consensus of opinion would certainly recognize the possibility of a pun, warrant a note, and in many instances no such note is forthcoming. This is the case with sexual puns at I, 214: "Unto his order he was a noble post" ("C'était un noble représentant de son ordre"—where the concrete vividness of Chaucer's expression is sacrificed along with the possibility of a phallic pun); I, 3278: "For deerne love of thee, lemman, I spille" ("De mon secret amour pour toi, chérie, je mourrai"); and one crucial, non-sexual pun at VII, 3266: "I kan noon harm of no womman divyne" ("Je ne puis déclarer aucun mal d'aucune femme"), where the alternative reading, "Je ne connais aucun mal d'aucune déesse" protects the Nun's Priest's veiled anti-feminism.

On one occasion at least (I, 3164–66) failure to register a pun disrupts the sense of a more extended passage:

> An housbonde shal nat been inquisityf
> Of Goddes pryvetee, nor of his wyf.
> So he may fynde Goddes foyson there,
> Of the remenant nedeth nat enquere.
>
> (Un mari ne doit pas être trop curieux
> Des secrets de Dieu ni de ceux de sa femme.
> Tant qu'il trouve Dieu en suffisance,
> Du reste il n'a pas besoin de s'enquérir.)

If no pun is perceived on *pryvetee* in the second line, the *there* of line three becomes meaningless, and is silently dropped from the translation, whereby an outrageously liberal defence of feminine promiscuity within marriage, exactly parallel to that urged by the Wife of Bath (III, 329–36), becomes a piously bland acknowledgement of divine bounty.

Between the technical difficulties of achieving a satisfactory literal translation which respects Middle English grammar, idiom, and word play, and the imposed dimension of meaning, here deliberately ignored, which depends upon the individual author's poetic encoding, the translator must further consider the treacherous territory of cultural encoding, that imprecise penumbra of potential connotative significance attaching to any word or phrase which the linguistic context may crystallize into actuality. One could find countless examples of this sort of difficulty if one wished to cavil about ever finer shades of meaning. Let me cite just one instance. The description of the Wife of Bath's pilgrimages (I, 463–66) ends with the statement, "Elle était ferrée en matière de voyages"—a simple and essentially tautological reaffirmation of what precedes. It is a strikingly inadequate rendering of "She koude muchel of wandrynge by the weye," which both reaffirms what has gone before and also reverses its significance with the suggestion that the Wife of Bath's pilgrimages, perverted by her worldliness, merely provide further evidence of the extent to which she has gone spiritually astray. In such instances a translation which appears to offer an adequate, unambiguous equivalent of Chaucer's English text, in that it might discourage any checking of the dictionary range of meanings for the verb *to wander*, for example, might be more of an impediment than an aid in achieving understanding. What is needed to deal with problems of this sort is a more extensive critical apparatus of explanatory notes, without which

Chaucer's characteristic and pervasive ironies may be lost on non-Anglophone readers. Words such as *wandrynge* and *wey* are heavily charged words in the tradition of religious writings in English. Without some indication that *wander* here may mean *errare* ("This is the Wandering Wood, this Error's den": *FQ*, I, i, 13), and that *way* may echo "I am the way, the truth, and the life" (*John,* xiv, 6), or anticipate the Parson's promise (X, 49–51) to show his fellow Canterbury pilgrims "the wey, in this viage, / Of thilke parfit glorious pilgrymage / That highte Jerusalem celestial," non-English speakers will still be left very much in the dark about the full meaning of Chaucer's text.

The notes Professor Caluwé-Dor provides are certainly pertinent and informative. I would hope that in projected future volumes she might consider expanding them to embrace some of the issues raised above, and, perhaps, that her publisher might be persuaded to move them from the back of the book to the foot of the page, where their value for a reader struggling to understand details of Chaucer's text without losing his sense of its linear coherence would be immeasurably increased. Such an expansion of the critical apparatus would make for a considerably more ambitious undertaking than that attempted in this first volume, and it is perhaps unwarranted partisanship to expect that as much might be done in the way of carefully annotated translation to make Chaucer accessible in French as has been done, for example, to make Dante accessible in English. The present translation certainly constitutes a step in the right direction. Let us hope that one of its effects will be to create a demand for more endeavors of this kind, and a consciousness of what, ideally, might still further be achieved.

ROY J. PEARCY
University of Oklahoma

NORMAN DAVIS, Douglas Gray, Patricia Ingham, and Anne Wallace-Hadrill, comps., *A Chaucer Glossary.* Oxford: Clarendon Press, 1979. Pp. xx, 185. Paper $8.95. Cloth $19.95.

For its size and scope, Oxford's new *Chaucer Glossary* is nearly perfect. Having the easy feel of a short paperback novel, it is clearly more convenient than the multivolumed *OED*, the *MED*, or Samuel Singer's three-volume *Sprichwörter des Mittelalters* (1944–47). It is also much easier to use than Francis Henry Stratmann's *Middle English Dictionary* (rev. Henry Bradley, 1891), which covers authors other than Chaucer and, besides being fairly inaccessible, has formidable Old English-looking forms and spellings for the main entries. Remarkably, the coverage in *A Chaucer Glossary* seems almost as full as that in Skeat's excellent but hard-to-come-by glossary (1894), and the crisp format is also similar to Skeat's, consisting of ME term, part of speech, definition, specific representative references to Chaucer's text with shades of meaning carefully delineated, and etymology. The large number of main entries and textual references are the book's best feature, and Chaucer students—undergraduate, graduate, and post-doctoral as well—will find the glossary extremely useful for many years to come.

Given the limited size of the book, it is hard to imagine a more useful glossary. However, the glossaries in the leading classroom texts will still be needed. The student will find some entries in the glossary in Robinson's text that the Oxford glossary does not have (*rendren, wele* 'happiness,' *wyerdes*), and Robinson has more cross-references to variant forms—a very important feature for anyone but a senior Chaucer scholar. In the Oxford glossary, the student will have difficulty finding *wonden, wissh, welk, or bontee*, whereas Robinson has cross-references to *wynden, washen, walken,* and *bountee*. In the Oxford glossary, no main entry will tell him that *wollen* is a form of *wile*, that *wiltow* is a contraction of *wilt thou*, or that *borugh* is a variant of *borwe* 'surety.' The glossary in Baugh's text has a surprising number of specific line references and is a useful complement to Robinson if the Oxford glossary is not at hand. (The Oxford glossary, though, often has two or three times more references than Baugh.) Baugh's glossary is also excellent in giving spelling and morphological variants under main entries, but many variants (like *wonden, wissh, welk,* and *bountee*) are not listed as main entries and therefore are hard to find.

Unlike Robinson and Baugh, the Oxford Glossary gives etymologies—usually one etymological form for each main entry. The principal parts are also given for OE strong verbs, and often the third-person singular present forms are included as well. OE words with short vowels that lengthen in LOE have an accent mark over the vowels, and compounds or derivatives recorded first in ME are marked with the sign +.

This is a great deal of information to have in handbook-glossary and is essentially enough for the beginning student. Much fuller information could be given, of course (e.g., where does the *e* come from in the plural form *thise* 'these'?). Fuller etymologies can be found in the glossary in the back of Oliver F. Emerson's *Middle English Reader* (1905), which has in addition many spelling variants in the several ME dialects and has many EME forms. Another good glossary with etymologies is in Stratmann's dictionary, which also lists variant forms, EME forms, and cognates.

One of the weaknesses in most of the available glossaries is that long and short vowels are too often not clearly marked, much less the open and close *e*'s and *o*'s. This is unfortunate, since the student needs this information in order to know how to pronounce Chaucer's language. The Oxford glossary shares this weakness with the other well-known glossaries. Sometimes long *a, e,* and *o* are doubled in this glossary, using ME spelling practice as the guide (as the Introduction tells us), but since ME spelling practice is inconsistent, the student winds up confused. The Oxford glossary's system of doubling letters to indicate vowel length works very well for words like *de(e)d, ho(l)ly,* and *pa(a)s,* but not for words like *so, speke(n)* and *dame,* which also have long vowels, or for those with long *i* or *u,* like *ride(n)* and *hous.* It is true that the student has the etymological evidence available and that if he knows that OE long vowels stay long in ME he can deduce whether some ME vowels are long or not. But he must also know on his own that OE $æ/ēa$ > ME $ē$, OE $ȳ$ > ME $ī/ȳ$, OE $ēo$ > ME $ē$, and OE $ā$ > ME $ō$.

Even when it is possible to determine from the glossary whether *e*'s and *o*'s are long are short, it is quite impossible to tell whether long *e*'s and *o*'s are open or close. This information, too, is quite important for the student to have in order to know how to pronounce ME. Perhaps another edition can include in the main entries macrons over the long vowels, and dots and hooks where appropriate beneath long close and long open *e*'s and *o*'s. In Robinson one can tell when *e*'s and *o*'s are long and open, since Robinson puts hooks under such vowels, but if no hooks are present it is impossible to tell—without a sound knowledge of OE and ME—whether the *e*'s and *o*'s are short or whether they are long and close. For this information one can go, again, to Emerson, where both the OE and the ME long vowels are marked. Unfortunately, Baugh doesn't make long-short or open-close distinctions. It is hard to tell about these matters even in Skeat; and in Stratmann, although the short-long distinctions are clear, the open-close distinctions are not. There is an obvious need for this information to be readily available to the student of Chaucer, and the *Chaucer Glossary* would be the obvious place for it. (Will the forthcoming edition of Robinson have dots under the long close *o*'s and *e*'s?).

The editors have based their main entry list on the Tatlock-Kennedy *Concordance* and have relied heavily on the *OED*, the *MED* (as far as L), and Skeat's glossary. They have also, as they tell us in the Preface, referred to the glossaries of other editions through 1974 and have consulted scholarly articles pertaining to particular ME words. Editors Gray, Ingham, and Wallace-Hadrill divided up the alphabet for the initial work of compilation, and Norman Davis edited the whole and compiled the prefatory matter and the "Select List of Proper Names" (7 pp.).

In general, the prefatory matter is clearly presented and tells the student as succinctly as possible what he needs to know in order to use the glossary. (However, it is difficult to know what the abbreviation OA means under the rubric "Languages and Dialects," and the explanation "as A" doesn't help.) The "Notes on Inflections" section—broken down by parts of speech—has a great deal of information which the student will find extremely helpful. One cannot imagine more information being presented any more compactly. However, the extreme compactness of the section leads the editor to state rather cryptically that the forms *thise* and *these* are monosyllabic—without any explanation or possibility of exception for these dissyllabic-looking words. Perhaps in the next edition or printing of the book more information on ME spelling, spelling variants, and pronunciation could be included in what is now a great deal of blank space on the pages in the prefatory matter. What we have is so good that it inevitably makes us wish for more, but finally we must allow the editors their own goals and judge them accordingly. What they have set out to do they have done very well indeed.

W. BRUCE FINNIE
University of Delaware

D. H. GREEN. *Irony in the Medieval Romance.* New York: Cambridge University Press, 1979. Pp. x, 431. £27.50; $62.50.

This magisterial study of the role of irony in the medieval romance will justly find its place in the major libraries of the world. Any criticisms that are made of it will have to be addressed to shortcomings in the definition of irony its author offers and to the theory which has grown up around it, rather than to the nuances of interpretation of the various appearances of irony as defined by the author. As to the question with which the book opens, "Does irony exist in the romances of the Middle Ages?" as demonstrated in the works of Chrétien de Troyes, Hartmann von Aue, Gottfried von Strassburg, Wolfram von Eschenbach, (with some attention to *Sir Gawain and the Green Knight,* and to Chaucer's *Troilus and Criseyde*), it should be said in advance that this book demonstrates beyond any shadow of doubt that irony is a pervasive presence in these writers; and from this readers will conclude that irony exists in even purer manifestations throughout virtually the entire corpus of medieval literature.

In brief, Professor Green establishes at the outset a definition of irony which serves him throughout the book:

> Irony is a statement or presentation of an action or situation in which the real or intended meaning conveyed to the initiated intentionally diverges from, and is incongruous with, the apparent or pretended meaning presented to the initiated.

Green admits that the phenomenon is a complex one, then addresses himself to M. S. Batts' objections to the discovery of irony in medieval literature,[1] which he examines with scrupulous care before concluding that irony was known to medieval writers, that it can be demonstrated with some security, and that the poets have in fact given explicit signals of such irony in their works.

---

[1] "Hartmann's humanitas: a new look at Iwein," in F. A. Raven, W. K. Legner, and J. C. King (eds.), *Germanic Studies in honor of Edward Heury Sehrt,* Coral Gables, Fla.: U of Miami P, 1968, pp. 37 ff.

From this point, Green proceeds to lay out the applications of his theory of irony to chivalry, to love, to narrative technique, to verbal manipulations of it, to irony of the narrator and of values, to dramatic irony, and finally to structural irony. These substantives are in fact the chapter headings; each chapter is broken down into smaller sections dealing with a particular author or theme. And finally the book culminates in a series of generalizations accounting for the presence of irony in medieval romance: the poet's status in society, the language of courtesy, the select audience for which poetry is written, written composition, patronage and rhetoric, secularism, the critical spirit, etc. I cite these only to indicate that Green has not neglected the social and aesthetic considerations of his study. So complete is its coverage, within the thesis offered in his introduction and first chapter, that one must conclude that irony as an aspect of medieval composition, both oral and written, and as a legitimate subject for critical evaluation, has come to fruition. His thesis is built up so carefully on every available resource in the scholarly reservoir and is pursued so patiently to its literary locale that as an exercise in comparative literature it stands as a model of scrupulosity and sensitive judgment.

The modern question, one that plagues the theory of irony and its application to literature written prior to the sophisticated theory, namely whether modern literary terminology can be applied to the texts that long preceded it, is correctly dismissed on the grounds of modern intellectual needs and with the clear recognition that criticism must constantly invent a terminology, asking questions of texts "which were for the most part not even realized as possible questions at the time when these texts were composed." And in the process of engaging the texts of his time, any critic explores his text more efficiently when simultaneously he makes advances in the vocabulary to be employed.

The study of irony as a theory, in a welter of books and articles, has been largely the province of the late Norman Knox (*The Word Irony and its Context, 1500–1755,* Durham, N. C.: Duke UP, 1961, and the article "Irony" in the *Dictionary of the History of Ideas*); D. C. Muecke (*The Compass of Irony,* London: Methuen & Co., 1969); and Northrup Frye (*Anatomy of Criticism: four essays,* Princeton: Princeton UP, 1957) curiously absent from Green's wide-ranging bibliography. Knox, Muecke, and Frye, who together have managed to combine virtually everything that can be said about theory of irony into a coherent critical vision, have in recent years made the greatest contribution to our understanding of the complex phenomena of irony, clarifying the field and dispelling many misconceptions in terminology.

This is not to say that from Thirlwall's fine essay of 1833 on the Irony of Sophocles there have not been literally hundreds of essays and several dozen books on the subject. Indeed, so great has been the flood and so drenched have we become in its language that no teacher of literature in any language can discuss the works of a major writer without an underlying assumption of irony at some level of the creative act, whether that level be the act of distancing in writing itself or something more deliberately contrived.

Knox, who more than any other laid down the principles of a theory of irony (too often unheeded), has the virtue of having stated them succinctly; I summarize them here only so that we may have a point of comparison with what in Green is only an underlying system. The four variables of irony are defined as 1) the degree of conflict between appearance and reality; 2) the field of observation (i.e., whether the irony is verbal or dramatic-situational, the latter sometimes called the irony of fate/God/events, etc.; 3) the specifically definable set of relationships between author, audience, and victim; and 4) the degree to which the author and audience sympathize with the victim and his fate: thus, in satiric irony, the victim is viewed unsympathetically; in comic irony, the victim seen sympathetically rises from defeat to triumph; in tragic irony, sympathy for the victim again dominates our other responses; in nihilistic irony, though we share the plight of the victim, and so sympathize with him, our sympathy is counterbalanced by detachment from his plight; and finally, in paradoxical irony, we remain in a vacillation between two poles of response, in an unresolvable non-fusion of identification and detachment.

It would be ridiculous to complain that Green's book does not fit into Knox's system, or into any system for that matter. The difficulty of fitting theory to actual literary practise is nowhere so difficult as in the still emerging theory of irony; Green has found his own system, combining his thematic interests in the subject matter (love, chivalry, courtly values) with certain of the techniques (narrator, verbal signals, dramatic irony) in what is generally a satisfactory series of demonstrations. But much of the refinement which Knox (and Muecke and Frye) provide has not been utilized. And the need still remains for a way of approaching the literature of the past based upon a fuller, accurate survey of the meanings of irony which might enable the reader to recognize that a particular passage combines a variety of techniques of irony, or is, as Muecke suggests, on the borderline between one technique or form and another, or combines ironical with non-ironical elements (p. 41). Green's book manifests the problem inherent in applying any theoretical system to a literary text: the theory undergoes modification; the demonstrations, we find, taken out of context, whether structural or syntactical, sometimes fail to yield a convincingly ironical meaning or, worse, the meaning continues to remain elusive; and occasionally the same passage is utilized to manifest more than one aspect of irony. These minor defects only demonstrate the difficulty of the enterprise.

There are some familiar topics absent here (familiar to us from the work of Frye, for example) that raise the question, not only of the limits of Green's scope, but of possible future work in the field of medieval irony generally, and more specifically, of the way in which even conventionally defined romance is modified from within by the techniques and substantive interests of irony as a way of looking at the world.

There is relatively little said directly, for example, about the range of the hero's power of action, one of the touchstones by which to test the genre, romance. There is much said about the self-deprecating author, but the distinction between naive and sophisticated irony, that is, whether the norms of morality are expressed or merely implied, is largely lost for want of emphasis. A study should be made, perhaps, of the role of arbitrariness or randomness which infects—if that is not a biased 20th century point of view—the narrative line of medieval English romance. And there should be too an examination of the varieties of such a character as the fool whose fate is determined by his impractical innocence and whose life is out of kilter with the practical demands of mundane experience (Troilus, for example, or Sir Gawain, or Parzifal). More needs to be done with the character of the self-deprecating author whose utterances elicit from us emotions for which there is no name, but in which there lurks a strange mixture of self-pity, fawning, and occasionally something like contempt for his audience. Perhaps more should be said about the role of play and parody in the transformation of romance out of liturgy and ritual, in which the role of the victim is inevitably ironical. One might wish, too, for a means of evaluating the way in which romance generally is modified by varying degrees of irony, since some romances, only lightly touched by it, retain full claim to the generic name, while others, more corrosively touched by it, exhibit a different kind of seriousness. Various tales of *The Canterbury Tales* come to mind.

But these are only the smallest considerations. Green has made a judicious presentation. Far from overstating the case for irony (in my view he has understated it), he has seen irony as a positive rather than a negative force, capable of dealing in a balanced way with the courtly ideals of the time. And mercifully, in his quest he has known when to stop, even when the number of examples he might have adduced could have been endlessly expanded.

There can be no question hereafter as to whether medieval irony is merely a fashion of a modern sensibility capable of defining the past in its newly created vocabulary; and no question of whether irony is merely an occasional ornament of the structures that the Middle Ages have bequeathed to us. Irony is fully demonstrated as the inevitable response drawn from the writer by the social and cultural circumstances in which he lived.

PAUL G. RUGGIERS
University of Oklahoma

DOUGLAS KELLY, *Medieval Imagination: Rhetoric and the Poetry of Courtly Love*. Madison: University of Wisconsin Press, 1978. Pp. xvi, 330. Cloth $28.00.

In *Medieval Imagination* Douglas Kelly shuns systematic explanation of his major terms and subjects: Imagination [his capital], rhetoric, courtly love, allegory. One must study his book attentively to discover the underlying system of thought, and even so he may ultimately conclude that there is more than one system. Take Imagination, his title subject. "Imagination is a mental faculty. It governs the invention, retention, and expression of Images in the mind; it also designates the artist's Image, projected as it were onto matter" (p. xii). "Imagination is the visual correlative to the elucidation (*descriptio*) of ideas" (p. 39). "The imposition of meaning onto matter is known as Imagination" (p. 42). These interesting scattered characterizations may or may not be consistent among themselves. Determination of this is left largely to the reader's ingenuity. Kelly does not discuss how Imagination differs from Shakespeare's imagination or that of the Neoclassicists or Romanticists. And while he does give us a rich chapter reviewing the adaptation to poetry of medieval thought about *imaginatio*, no unified conception emerges from it, nor does it supply bases for identifying a separable category, "literature of the Imagination."

This is not to say that Kelly's concept(s) of Imagination is not useful for talking about love poetry of the Middle Ages; it indeed may provide the best way to approach the works he concentrates on. It is to say that Kelly does not make his ideas readily accessible, and one suspects that he himself does not always have a firm grasp on the propositions he throws out. Take, for instance, an intriguing statement in his chapter on Imagination. Having cited the passage in the *Queste* when Galahad is awestruck at the sight of the Grail, Kelly comments: "Such *laetus horror*, the celebration of mystery and truth, dominates the literature of the Imagination in the Middle Ages, and accounts for its fascination. Meaning blends with mystery, order and simplicity emerge from ambagious diversity. Combat and quest, the rose and Ovidian *fabulae* are some sources that amply sustained it. But so long as a moral principle remains absolute, its workings rather than those of the individual soul are paramount. Its fascination lies not in originality, specificity, or uniqueness, but in excellence that transcends even abstract expression, unites all qualities in integrity, and generates Images in the reader's mind" (pp. 38–39). A splendid peroration, it seems, alive with connotation; still, one may have difficulty nailing down its exact meaning.

With most consistency Kelly indicates that the medieval poet uses Imagination to impart corporeal form to abstractions. In literature not based on Imagination, I take it, the process is reversed; the abstract significance arises from the images. The distinction perhaps is expressed in the difference Kelly sees between the chivalric romance and the fourteenth-century *dit*. In the romance, he says (p. 100), a *surplus de sens* is grafted onto a *matière*, while in the *dit* the *sens* "discursively set forth" has a *matière* worked into it. Such distinction strikes me as of great potential value for appreciating the works that are the main concern of Kelly's study, the love poems of Machaut and of those before and after

143

him "from Guillaume de Lorris and Huon de Mery through Froissart to Oton de Grandson, Chartier, and Charles d'Orléans, as well as Chaucer and Gower" (p. xii). It is not entirely original to postulate that in some types of imaginative literature theme is prior to fictional construct, but I think no one has proposed the idea for this whole body of undervalued and misunderstood literature, nor has anyone explored the process as creatively as Kelly does in the course of the book. Unfortunately, he often lets distorted notions of courtly love and of historical evolution of the love poetry lead him into unfruitful discussion. His more enlightening treatments of literary works involve analysis of compositional process rather than of the subject matter.

Kelly illustrates composition by Imagination in several effective analyses. He well chooses Raoul de Houdenc's *Roman des eles* as a simple illustrative example. In this work a bird's flight and the feathers of its wings are allegorized and made into a corporeal embodiment of the notion of Prowess. The same essential process, much complicated, underlies the *Roman de la Rose* of Guillaume de Lorris. Guillaume makes particular use of rhetorical *frequentatio*, involving incremental repetition, to describe the images outside the garden of Deduit; he thereby produces a visual picture of that which is antithetical to love. In the same manner he purveys the concept of delightful love through describing the figures at the carole inside the garden. With Guillaume's fourteenth-century successors, Kelly notes, *frequentatio* continued to be an important device for amplification, but the use of personification receded in importance to be replaced by other tropes, in particular Ovidian mythography.

In his discussion of fourteenth-century poets, Kelly is most clearly effective in analyzing Froissart's *Prison amoureuse* and *Espinette amoureuse*, in both of which Froissart borrows stories directly from Ovid and also invents his own Ovidian narratives. *Prison amoureuse*, Kelly shows, provides a happy example of "Multiple Exposition," whereby various images, including an Ovidian story, and discursive explanations provide means of "converging on the ineffable" (p. 163). His characterizations of these works constitute gratifying recognition of their complexity. He aptly describes *Espinette* as a "poem of varying modes and levels, which includes the sequence of Images and figures, the comparisons more or less amplified, that Froissart uses to elucidate his narrative . . . It includes as well the rhetorical, abstract developments of thought and emotion contained in the fixed forms [i.e., inserted lyrics]. And finally, it underscores a suite of eighteen adventures alternating, as in the *Roman de la Rose*, with solitary reflections, lamentations, expressions of joy and hope" (p. 172). Kelly does well, moreover, in justifying this description. If he did as well for other works and poets he takes up, his book would rank with Daniel Poirion's *Le Prince et le poète* in establishing proper appreciation of the Machaut tradition of court poetry. Unfortunately, he is lured away from such accomplishment by the sirens of courtly love.

In order to understand Kelly's notion of courtly love, one really needs to refer to his 1968 article in *Traditio* on Andreas Capellanus. In the article he claims that Andreas applies the concept of "gradualism" to the various types of love, setting up a hierarchy in which *caritas*, friendship, and marital love rank above courtly love, and mere passion and venal love rank below it. He states that Andreas esteems courtly love in its place as edifying and even obligatory for the courtier. There are numerous problems with his understanding of Andreas as expressed in the article and embedded in the book. The primary one is his failure to understand that Andreas in *De amore* is not writing a philosophical treatise on love any more than Ovid was in *Ars amatoria*. Andreas sets up a variety of fictional situations in which master addresses novice, lover addresses lady and she responds, noblewoman sits in judgment of questions of love, and the God of Love prescribes rules for a knightly lover. He is showing how people may act or think in love situations, not justifying or earnestly teaching methods of adultery to courtiers. Substantial comedy and irony are implicit in his demonstration; and lest his work be taken as serious instruction, Andreas provides Book III, a good moralistic medieval counterpart to Ovid's *Remedia amoris*.

Understood as a presentation of typical behavior, *De amore* has a strong affiliation with the *Roman de la Rose*, both parts, in which the interest also resides in characteristically ironic portrayal of how people act in affairs of love, rather than in any prescription of what they should do. It will not do, despite Kelly's efforts, to make the works of Andreas and Guillaume de Lorris into manuals of courtly love which provided an erotic-philosophic frame of reference for Machaut and his successors. Certainly, the *Roman de la Rose* supplied the fourteenth century with a model for poetic form and with labels useful for love narratives: Danger, Sweet Thought, etc. And it is true that both Guillaume de Lorris and Andreas are interested in the behavior of courtiers, people of social refinement, rather than in the less elegant activities of the lower classes.

Notwithstanding, neither is a docent in a school of courtly love. They are as facetious as Ovid in providing rules and examples. Machaut, though he is far from being all seriousness, has much more of the earnest professor about him. In his works there is an element of art of love and art of poetry which is intended as straightforward instruction. But Machaut also is no instructor in seduction. He changes the subject of his predecessors. He could with propriety teach court people about love only by virtually effacing all reference to coition and its preliminaries. The single instance in his extensive love poetry which presents lovers going to bed—or even talking about it—is a serio-comic scene in the *Voir Dit* involving the aged poet and his youthful lady. And in this case Venus conceals the proceedings, if there are any, by covering the pair with a cloud.

Kelly's exposition of Imagination frequently becomes confused by and lost in his fabrication of a history of courtly love poetry. He sees this poetry as reaching its spiritual height with Guillaume de Lorris, Machaut, and Froissart, and declining thereafter in the work of Granson and the fifteenth-century poets. Numerous works become twisted in this imaginary history. Machaut's *Remede de Fortune* is one. Throughout his book Kelly shows good instinct for the important poem, and he does so in focussing extensive discussion on the *Remede*. Unfortunately, he misinterprets it. His view of the work as Machaut's solution of the courtly lover's quandary ignores most of what happens in the narrative. Kelly finds that the poem presents the lover's successful sublimation of desire to hope. In actuality it shows a typical desperate lover, acting under the encouragement of hope, petitioning his lady for mercy, and shows her in turn accepting him into her service. The lover's desire for acceptance is thus satisfied, not sublimated. Furthermore, the concluding events of the story suggest that Amant may be in a worse predicament than before. After she has accepted him, he comes into a company where she is present; to his anguish, she ignores him, concentrating her attention on others. When he reproaches her she responds that she acts in the interest of "bien celer," and that he must do likewise. Perforce, he accepts her explanation since the lover "ought always to believe his lady;" at the same time, the reader—and perhaps the lover too—can see that another insuperable barrier has been set up between him and his beloved. Certainly, he remains far from consummation, an act which never seems in question. From her acceptance, then, he derives joy for the time being;

at the same time, there is fine irony in his continued willing entanglement in a process that from an objective standpoint is quite circular and involves the most tenuous rewards. This irony is a crucial aspect of the Machaut tradition; take it away and the poetry loses much of its vitality.

Though Kelly covers a substantial number of fourteenth-century poets besides Machaut, and makes sweeping statements about their voluminous works, his generalizations are vitiated by his faulty notion of literary historical progression as well as by incomplete reading. Kelly sees Oton de Granson as a forerunner of the decline of the courtly ideal; however, Granson is much better viewed as a continuator and explorer of Machaut's modes. So is Chaucer in the frame of the discussion, but Kelly sees him too as a poet of the waning ideal, "impressed by the frailty of love, the deleterious effect on the mind of continual sorrow, the world's hostility toward happy love" (p. 199). More rewarding than the schematic observations about Granson, Chaucer, Gower, Christine de Pisan, and Alain Chartier are the treatments of works of Charles d' Orléans and René d'Anjou, since they involve interesting and creative analyses of neglected texts, notably of René's *Livre dou cuer d'amours espris* and Charles' balades and rondeaux.

Kelly becomes involved in a number of large, difficult subjects. In addition to treating the nature of rhetoric and the role of medieval imagination in medieval poetry, and to presenting a history of love literature of the time, he also deals at length with the nature of allegory and the relation between poetry and music. His knowledge and range of reference are broad and impressive. Nevertheless, because of a lack of method in his approach to the various topics, and because of their difficulty and complexity, one generally feels that he does not have sufficient mastery of the subject matter to support his ambitious assertions. The main value I find in the book lies in the new understanding it suggests of the processes of composition that created late medieval love poetry. Kelly properly assumes that the works have both complexity and profundity, and that they merited the esteem they enjoyed in their own time; he discovers in medieval rhetoric and poetic a rationale for the compositional methods he postulates for them; and he illustrates these methods with a number of explications that often constitute pioneering appreciations of misunderstood and neglected works. If the book thereby helps to stimulate a broader appreciation of what the poets were doing, then its difficulty and failures will be largely counterbalanced.

JAMES I. WIMSATT
University of Texas

GREGORY KRATZMANN, *Anglo-Scottish Literary Relations* 1430–1550. Cambridge and New York: Cambridge University Press, 1980. Pp. xii, 252. $29.50.

This is a traditional study of literary influences which builds on the insights of previous critics and refines some generalizations of earlier readers of Middle and later Scots literature. We usually think of Anglo-Scottish literary relations as a one-way process—the influence of English literature on Scots. Kratzmann discusses this phenomenon in five chapters devoted to "The Kingis Quair," Henryson, Douglas, Dunbar, and Lindsay. But he also points to a cross-fertilization in a chapter and a half devoted to discussions of the influence of Scots poetry on the poetry of Skelton, Surrey, and Wyatt.

Kratzmann's initial chapter, "Influences and perspectives," explores the general nature of these influences and sets up a traditional opposition between Chaucer's influence on the Scottish makars and Lydgate's on contemporary English poets. Following Pearsall, Kratzmann asserts that Lydgate's much larger influence is "one of the major reasons for the great differences between contemporary English and Scots poetry" (p. 24). Distinguishing himself from earlier critics, Kratzmann stresses an active relationship between the Scots and English poets and their influences. He asserts that the later poets made informed and deliberate choices based on their poetic needs. Unlike Florence Ridley, Kratzmann accepts the controversial label "Scottish Chaucerians." He feels that although it is inadequate as an account of what is most distinctive about each poet's work, "as a way of denoting the general standard of much Scots poetry . . . the term is not misleading, and its use need not imply any dependence on Chaucer" (p. 23). He explains the Scottish preference for Chaucer as not just a matter of Lydgate's inferiority, but as a response to kindred needs.

Kratzmann stresses the Scots' attempt "to achieve in their form of 'Inglis' what Chaucer had been the first to achieve in 'sudron': an assimilation of continental poetic forms and techniques into new poetry which would dignify the vernacular" (p. 24). He sees the makars as less interested in imitation of Chaucer than in Chaucer's relationship to tradition. Here they could get much less help from Lydgate.

Most crucial for Kratzmann is the similarity of social situation and relationship of poet and audience for Chaucer and the Scots. He emphasizes the sense of the poet's presence and its effect on Chaucer's style as Chaucer's main legacy. He shows how this responded to the needs of the Scots who wrote and performed in a similar court situation, pressed by the same demands to produce court poetry that would be read both silently and aloud. He distinguishes this from Lydgate's writing "to be 'published' " to a wider, more socially diverse audience, and asserts that "the changed circumstances of presentation contributed to the stylistic difference between Chaucer's poetry and Lydgate's" (p. 27). Moreover, he faults Lydgate's longer works for their lack of any sense of the poet's presence.

Far from seeing the makars' response to Chaucer as derivative, Kratzmann stresses their "creative assimilation" of Chaucer as a process which differs markedly from one poet to the next. In his preface he forsees the danger of minimizing the individual merits of the writers discussed. He avoids this by emphasizing the individuality of each makar's work and poetic response in separate chapters. Readers who go to those chapters will find close readings of the texts along with careful presentations of critical agreements and departures. What seems most useful to outline here are some general patterns that emerge about the ways the makars depart from their influences.

In Chapters 2, 3, and 4 Kratzmann presents James I, Henryson, and Douglas in the tradition of readers of Chaucer, arguing that they rework Chaucerian motifs "in such a way that the new poems may be read as critical commentary on their sources" (p. 20). Thus, in the "Kingis Quaire," "Testament of Cresseid," and "Palis of Honour" the continuation of Chaucerian intimacy between poet and audience implies affirmation of Chaucerian attitudes and techniques. The substitution of a pose of experience implies criticism of the Chaucerian pose of detachment; and substitution of an unequivocal commitment to a moral view becomes a comment on the Chaucerian preference for irony, ambiguity, and equivocation. Characteristically, Kratzmann feels "there are no signs that Lydgate's poetry elicited this quality of imaginative response" (p. 20).

Kratzmann consistently places Chaucerian influence as one important influence among many. Thus, Chaucerian readings of the "Testament" and "Palis" are balanced by discussions which emphasize broader European influences on the "Moral Fabillis" and "Eneados." In Chapter 5, not surprisingly, Kratzmann finds the term "Scottish Chaucerian" least helpful to describe Dunbar. Because of crucial differences in tone and effect, he does not feel that "The Tretis of the Tua Mariit Wemen" or "Sir Thomas Norny" should be read as comments on Chaucer. Ultimately, he asserts that the greatest non-Scottish affinity with Dunbar is Skelton. Although he is careful to note that similarities in poems of both "need not necessarily imply indebtedness" (p. 149), he emphasizes their similar unChaucerian use of dream-visions, their comparatively rare shared comic talent, and their sense of personal indignation. Finally, he asserts that the techniques of "The Flyting of Dunbar and Kennedie" influenced Skelton's "Poems Against Garnesche," and that the first part of "Colkelbie Sow" influenced "Elynour Rummyng" (p. 158), and suggests that it may have a broader influence on the "Skeltonic" mode (p. 160).

Chapter 6 develops Kratzmann's thesis about the importance of Douglas' translation of the *Aeneid* to Surrey's, following, in large part, Florence Ridley's edition of Surrey. He then presents much briefer, less convincing, and more tenuous evidence of the influence of Henryson's "The Taill of the Uponlandis Mous" on Wyatt's "extensively philosophical handling" of "My mothers maydes" (p. 193). Kratzmann acknowledges, however, that "Wyatt's probable indebtedness to Scots poetry is a less significant matter than the indebtedness of Scots lyric poets to the work of both Wyatt and Surrey" (p. 193).

Chapter 7, Kratzmann's thesis about the influence of Skelton's *Magnyfycence* on Lindsay's *Ane Satyre of the Thrie Estaitis* is possibly of least immediate interest to readers of this review. This is a pity, because Kratzmann is at his best in his confident and persuasive presentation of the important parallels between the two plays, his illuminating discussion of the structure of Lindsay's play, and his interesting suggestion that with the possible exception of the anonymous Catholic morality *Respublica,* it did not influence English secular drama.

In his final chapter, "The two traditions," Kratzmann answers those critics who would accuse him of presenting a distorted picture of the period he covers. He reminds readers that the borrowings he notes "are so interesting because they are so rare" (p. 228), and demonstrates the more characteristic continuities of Scottish and English literature by reiterating those features which he has identified with the respective influences of Chaucer and Lydgate. As he does so and justifies his focus, however, Kratzmann underscores his obvious bias against Lydgatian poetry, and for the achievements of the Scots. Few would quarrel with these assessments, and they are balanced in part by assertions that the Lydgatians were answering to different needs. But this is not a book to seek out for an appreciation of Lydgatian poetry.

The way Kratzmann's focus can distort can be seen in his strained argument for the influence of Scots poetry on its own tradition. His citation of verbal parallels with "The Kingis Quair" to demonstrate that the Scots may have received Chaucer, at least in part, through their own tradition is weak. Like his attribution of the motif of the self-perpetuation of poetry in other Scots poetry to the local influence of "The Kingis Quair," it overlooks much broader literary traditions. A similar near-sightedness occurs in Kratzmann's peculiar insistence on the "flyting" as an exclusively Scottish form. This results in the assertion that the same Chaucer who orchestrated such vicious "quitting" as that of the Pardoner and the Host would have found the "distinctively Scots . . . verbal and vituperative appeal" of the "flyting" "difficult to comprehend" (p. 134). It also denies the "flytings" multiple written and oral traditions. In fact, in view of Kratzmann's insistence on the importance of performance, it seems strange that he does not emphasize the oral tradition at all.

But these are minor quibbles. For the most part, Kratzmann is very careful to locate the influence he sees as one of several, and does not get carried away by his desire to appreciate the Scots. In fact, one of the strengths of his writing is the great care with which he qualifies his assertions. For this reason, his justifications of focus seem poorly placed. If they represent a continuation of the topos of a plea for the Scots, I think they belong to an earlier age. As they stand, they leave a final impression which detracts from the good and careful work that the book represents.

BARRIE RUTH STRAUS
University of Florida

JOHN P. MCCALL. *Chaucer among the Gods: The Poetics of Classical Myth.* University Park and London: The Pennsylvania State University Press, 1979. Pp. 189. $10.95.

One of the most abiding obstacles to a reviewer producing a useful piece of work for his author and his audience, is the temptation to assess a book in terms of a hypothetical one he might have written on the subject himself instead of in terms of the real book in hand. While reviewers must take full responsibility for the degree to which they withstand or succumb to this temptation, authors sometimes contribute to its seductiveness by opting for titles that look attractive rather than accurately describe the contents they cover. I am afraid the initial impression made by Professor McCall's striking title sustains some qualification through the pages of his book down to the first and last sentences of its concluding paragraph: "In the final analysis, Chaucer was far more interested in people than in gods, in this world than in an airy mythology of antiquity (p. 157).... In truth, when Geoffrey Chaucer strolled among the gods he walked with both feet on the ground" (p. 158). As for the subtitle, somewhat weightier than "airy mythology," nowhere but in the first five pages of the first chapter is there any discussion that could be taken seriously as an account of "the poetics of classical myth." Construed even as Chaucer's poetics of classical myth, the subtitle implies a kind of theoretical discussion we have become conditioned to expect these days despite instances of individual resistance to its currency. Its title notwithstanding, this is really quite an old-fashioned book in which the author in truth walks with both feet on the ground—a fact that is apt to win the approbation of at least some of his readers.

Divided into five chapters and a brief conclusion entitled "Conjectures and Afterthoughts," *Chaucer among the Gods* attempts to explain the conventional status of classical myth in the poet's time and to demonstrate the originality and effectiveness with which he adapted and manipulated it to suit his own ends. Chapter 1, "The Backgrounds," consists primarily of a fourteen-page survey of classical myth from antiquity to the fourteenth century which emphasizes the points that "classical myth of antiquity encompassed a broad variegated tradition [which] included naturalistic, scientific interpretations and an astrologized mythology which survived—to greater and lesser degrees—in the Middle Ages and after. . . . a hodgepodge of traditions" (pp. 5–6), and that during the early Middle Ages pagan myth was not significantly Christianized. To set the scene in the poet's period, McCall, after a disturbingly sketchy discussion of the changes that occurred in the career of classical myth during the twelfth century, states that four "different and not necessarily related things happened to classical myth simultaneously during the later Middle Ages" (p. 12). First, there was an uneasy assumption that a pagan writer could glimpse divine truth and express it through myth. Second, antiquity's standard etymological, natural, and ethical interpretations became the equivalents of literal renderings, e.g., by the fourteenth century Venus is merely a cliché for love. Third, Christian writers were able to transfer classical material into a Christian context, as in a Dantean reference to God as "high Jove." Finally, Christian interpretations were deliberately imposed upon classical myth for ethical or doctrinal purposes.

In Chapter 2, "Brief Allusions: Character, Action, and Theme," McCall analyzes Chaucer's use of classical and mythical allusions in *The Book of the Duchess,* in which they "have moral significance in the sense that they elaborate a distressed condition of mind, heart, and soul" (p. 22); and in *Troilus and Criseyde,* in which they contribute to characterization by establishing simple and typical elements within a more complex whole and to the conflicts and drama in the poem by helping to establish its tragic, non-mythological patterns.

Chapter 3, "Myth and Allegory," the longest in the book, is based on a definition of allegory and allegorized myth as "a discourse more ample and extended than the classical allusions discussed in the previous chapter . . . , one that develops through the course of narrative, drama, or description in such a way that a reader gradually recognizes the dominance of intellectual patterns" (pp. 42–43). Then follows the observation that Chaucer, uninterested in "imposed theological allegorization of myth [and] the sort of moral allegorizing of myth that he had seen in the *Roman de la Rose,* [was] particularly interested in the kinds of moral and philosophical allegorizing of myth that he encountered in Dante and Boccaccio, and these he would adopt with some flippancy, and at times some grandeur, in the *House of Fame,* the *Parliament of Fowls,* and the *Knight's Tale"* (pp. 43–44). By far the most rewarding part of this chapter's treatment of the ways these three poems represent Chaucer's ability to handle received allegorical forms, is the sustained analysis of how allegorized myth approaches having a major effect on the structure, characterization, and language of *The Knight's Tale*.

Chapter 4, "The Classical Scene: Ancient Place and Natural Time," possibly the most intriguing one in the book, begins with the proposition that "setting was for Chaucer largely a matter of metaphor and symbol. In this he resembled those classical poets who conceived of 'place' as a literary *topos*, a motif to suit what happens: to emphasize a moral condition or to amplify an idea" (pp. 87–88). Again, McCall writes effectively on *The Knight's Tale*, indicating the direct relationship between its ancient setting and the moral allegory sustained by the poem's mythological components. He is also stimulating on the *Troilus*, exploring the suitability of the Trojan tragedy as background for the tragedy of Troilus. The treatment of the classical settings of *The Legend of Good Women* and some of *The Canterbury Tales* is notably less compelling, and as the chapter winds down, its compatability with the volume's title and subtitle becomes a minor, nagging question.

Chapter 5, "Classical Myth and Comic Radiance," focusses exclusively on some of *The Canterbury Tales,* including those of the Wife of Bath, the Merchant, the Franklin, and the Manciple. After his discussion of the Pluto and Proserpina episode in *The Merchant's Tale*, McCall makes the following clear and interesting statement:

> The interweaving of classical myth, medieval fabliau, and Canterbury drama constitutes the whole performance of the Merchant. It may also serve as a brief model for what Chaucer does in his most mature work, and in what seems to be his final use of ancient lore. (p. 148)

That use, which serves as the controlling idea of this chapter, is to represent "a curious but understandable perversity" (p. 124) that keeps being revealed in the balanced world of Chaucer's creation.

Professor McCall is a sensitive and perceptive critic, and, as has been already suggested, does his best work in some of the detailed analyses of Chaucer's poems, especially the *Troilus* and *The Knight's Tale*. But there are several moments of self-indulgence and failed discernment in these discussions; for example, when lines are quoted from *The Knight's Tale* to support exclusively a point about the characterization of Troilus (p. 27), when the author ignores the relationship between the *Troilus* and the

Filostrato to speculate (to what end?) that Chaucer could have built the story of Troilus and Criseyde on the mythic structure of the Mars and Venus story (p. 36), and when the optimism of the first three books of the *Troilus* is discussed without the recognition of at least the possibility of the presence of dramatic irony (p. 96). Arguing the significance of the three deities' temples in *The Knight's Tale*, McCall makes a painstaking and absorbing, if not utterly convincing, case for the pervasive effect upon the entire narrative of the embodiment of Aristotle's four moral virtues in Theseus' theater, where "in each oratory an instinctive tendency receives its proper place, its due and complete honor; it then finds itself balanced by other equally valued instincts, and is finally bound in or controlled by 'a just circle' which makes the whole construction a noble work. The theater, in other words, reflects the moral virtue of justice" (p. 72). No matter how attractive or seemingly unassailable, this is interpretation by implication, and I finally prefer, despite McCall's insistence that it has been "overread" (p. 173, n. 27), the "faire cheyne of love" speech—because it is there—as the expression of the poem's chief philosophical perspective. Because great stock is placed in the interpretation of Theseus' growth into an example of Aristotelian moral justice, the character undergoes a series of graduated predications, including the statement, "Theseus is androgynous" (p. 66). Is it possible that the classical myth of androgyny and its foremost Roman poet were completely out of sight and mind when it was made?

Larger issues could be made of what Professor McCall treats lightly. The influence of the literature of the Latin Middle Ages, starting with Boethius, whose importance is minimized, is just not sufficiently reckoned with, nor are some of the vernacular poets from whom Chaucer learned, directly or indirectly, something about handling myth. And courtly love is trivialized—as early as p. 12 Venus is stripped of any possible allegorical or metaphorical value—rather than explored as one of the major forces through which classical myth was conveyed and transformed in medieval culture.

The raising of such issues, of course, brings to mind the observation with which this review began. Nevertheless, I cannot help but wonder how a more thorough accounting of them would have affected the book, or what the results would have been if the author had not resisted, as he apparently did, making profitable use of some pertinent scholarship: John Fleming's *Roman de la Rose: A Study in Allegory and Iconography*

155

(Princeton, 1969); John Block Friedman's *Orpheus in the Middle Ages* (Harvard, 1970); Brian Stock's *Myth and Science in the Twelfth Century* (Princeton, 1972); Winthrop Wetherbee's *Platonism and Poetry in the Twelfth Century* (Princeton, 1972); Emerson Brown's article on Priapus in *The Parliament of Fowls, SP,* 72 (1975), 258 ff., or Susan Schibanoff's on Argus and Argyve in *Speculum,* 51 (1976), 647 ff. (these last two appearing too late, perhaps)—to mention a few published in this country. Still, I'd much rather have *Chaucer among the Gods* as it is than not at all.

GEORGE D. ECONOMOU
Long Island University
The Brooklyn Center

THOMAS E. MARESCA, *Three English Epics: Studies in Chaucer, Spenser, and Milton.* Lincoln and London: University of Nebraska Press. 1980. Pp. xiii, 222. $15.95.

To the unending debate on the genre of *Troilus and Criseyde*, whether it is drama, courtly romance, psychological novel or indefinable anomaly, Thomas E. Maresca adds another suggestion, epic. In *Three English Epics: Studies in Chaucer, Spenser, and Milton*, Maresca argues that the *Troilus* is both in the line of Virgil and Dante and an ancestor of Dryden and Pope, but not until after he has applied his principal definition of the epic, that its central motif is the *descensus ad inferos*, to *The Faerie Queene* and *Paradise Lost*.

Maresca establishes his definition of the epic by studying the commentators on the *Aeneid*, in particular Fulgentius and Bernardus Silvestris, and to a lesser extent, Landino. He sees them as transforming Virgil's epic, the first self-consciously artistic one, into a pattern for later writers. His particular interest is in Bernardus' reading of the poem as the pilgrimage of Everyman through a corrupt world, gaining knowledge, and finally achieving wisdom. Maresca believes the central pattern of epic, therefore, is one of descent, illumination, and ascent which parallels the Neo-Platonic idea of emanation-conversion-return. The epic hero moves from unity or rest to a world of phenomena, of multiplicity, where he must gain knowledge before returning to the peace of the whole. Maresca then proceeds to measure both the heroes and the structures of his three English epics against this three-part paradigm.

Spenser, whom he considers first, fits the argument most readily. There are many descents into the underworld to choose from, most notably Guyon's, which he views as an object lesson in the limits of the material. Maresca sees in Red Crosse's encounter with Error a type of the soul's confusion when it enters the corporal world which leads later to understanding in the Castle of Alma and to triumph over the dragon. Maresca goes on to analyze numerous parallel examples, demonstrating Spenser's concern with making one myth into a multitude of images.

Where his argument becomes most interesting, yet remains finally unsatisfying, is in the discussion of the structure of *The Faerie Queene*. He acknowledges that the poem is "a torso of epic," (p. 2) but then posits a structure for it which given his scheme of descent, illumination, and return would make it a complete epic. For Maresca, Books 1 and 2 represent the descent. He accepts the idea that taken together they form a definition of the mixture of spirit and body which comprises the fundamental nature of earthly experience. Books 3 and 4 represent life in the world and the process of learning about it. Books 5 and 6, then, according to his model, represent the stage of ascent or return. In 5 civic concord is achieved; while in 6 Calidore's vision of Acidale is "an apprehension of perfectibility under the triple modes of poetry, *decensus,* and *The Faerie Queene*" (p. 57). He recognizes that this is only a momentary experience, an intimation of the return to rest, and does acknowledge that the Blatant Beast has not been stilled forever, just as Una and Red Crosse are only betrothed in Book 1, but he never quite answers the question he implies. Did Spenser decide his epic was complete? His consideration of Spenser is balanced and syncretic; nevertheless, it foreshadows the difficulties the rest of the book presents. The pattern is the main concern, and the works are cut to fit it.

When Maresca turns to *Paradise Lost,* he faces a much more complicated task in defining the heroes and in analyzing the structure. Here the poem begins with a literal descent to Hell, but Satan, by definition, cannot ever again make a true ascent, so Maresca sees him as a parody of the Neo-Platonic paradigm. Adam falls, begins his descent, in the course of the epic, but at the end he is only starting his pilgrimage, and never goes beyond the second stage of the model. This makes God and Christ the true epic heroes and the central four books the key to the poem. Maresca also considers Milton himself as one of the epic heroes. Each of the four invocations is a *descensus* in which Divine inspiration comes to Milton and "is transformed in him and returns to God and to man, justifying the ways of God to man and incorporating human creativity into God" (p. 141). In the course of this discussion, which comes at the end of the essay, the poet becomes the most likely candidate for epic heroism.

In his argument for Christ as the hero, Maresca does recognize some difficulties. If Milton were following the *descensus* model accurately, Raphael's narrative ought to mark the conversion stage, yet it concerns the expulsion of the demons and the creation, not the incarnation. He explains this by pointing out that Christ's "incarnation, death, and resurrection are merely logical extensions in time and space of what he has already performed in eternity and spirit" (p. 109). Both the expulsion and the creation are forms of descent, but after the creation, Christ returns to God, having set in motion the three-part drama to be played out by humanity.

Maresca's analysis of the structure is too complicated to summarize, as he applies the three-part structure relentlessly to every aspect of *Paradise Lost*. He does, however, see Milton both as a traditionalist and an innovator who rearranges the usual pattern of the *descensus* by making the central four books the "linchpin" (p. 137).

> Rather than a central unit which in miniature encapsulizes and reflects the sections before and after it, *Paradise Lost* builds itself around a nuclear four books describing the works of the Son (inclusion and exclusion, complication and explication: transformation) which are, as I argued earlier, constitutive of the Son in the poem, and the two wings which surround this nuclear unit reflect it rather than it them (p. 136).

Yet later Maresca contends that Milton's techniques are an outgrowth of Dante who had made the *descensus* his literal and allegorical structure. "Milton has overgone him to the extent that he has completely externalized all of the internals of epic: *Paradise Lost* either contains no allegory or is all allegory" (p. 139).

Throughout each of his three studies, Maresca alludes in passing to other epics and other writers. The book, however, does not consistently make comparisons so that the effect of it is to present three discrete essays. He intends the first two as preparation for the more daring discussion of Chaucer. At the beginning of that essay he rather briefly reminds us that *The Faerie Queene* and *Paradise Lost* end with "both purged vision and restored language, sight and speech returned as it were to grace" (p. 145). Indeed, so does the *Divine Comedy*. Maresca must then show how Chaucer's epic practise differs, as the *Troilus* certainly does not fit the model as he has defined it thus far.

Maresca's argument for the *Troilus* as epic is based partly on what he sees as a variation on the Dido and Aeneas episode and mainly on Chaucer's allusions to Statius' *Thebiad* which imitates Virgil, makes much of Tisiphone and the Furies, and has a coda which resembles "Go, litel book" (V, 1786). This last point is crucial to his argument:

> It identifies the genre of the poem and establishes its pedigree, an epic poem by Chaucer out of "Virgile, Ovide, Omer, Lucan, and Stace" (V, 1792), the greatest narrative poets of antiquity, two of them, Ovid and Lucan, offering models of the kind of apotheosis and illumination Troilus will very shortly undergo, and the other three the great patrons and exemplars of epic. There can be no doubt that Chaucer saw his poem as epic: the real question is what he meant by that (p. 144).

Maresca has no difficulty in establishing Troy as an inferno; what he does have trouble with is seeing Troilus as an epic hero. He considers the choice of a Classical rather than a Christian setting an important departure from Dante which removes the *Troilus* from the tradition of fourfold allegory and enables Chaucer to focus on emotion and psychology. Troilus ought to be learning to reject the fleshly and embrace the spiritual, yet Maresca acknowledges that the stage of ascent is presented only briefly. He finds Troilus a passive, effeminate young man who, in a sense, plays Dido to Criseyde's Aeneas. Certainly he remains in the first stage of the tripartite structure throughout the poem.

The techniques of comedy and satire account for much of Troilus' ambiguity and unsuitability. In fact, in many respects, "he prefigures the heroes of mock epic" (p. 164). Maresca finds in the poem much that resembles later satire: parody in the use of the religion of love, a metaphysical wit, and a comic narrator who is a pander to his audience. Maresca seems to be understanding Chaucer by way of Swift. He implies that as satire makes its points indirectly, inviting the audience to form its own judgments, so does the *Troilus*.

Finding no satisfactory epic figure in the work, Maresca concludes:

> "It is the reader, constantly reminded of Lollius and the artifice of the book and the interpenetration of life and literature, the reader alert to the sympathies and naïveté of narrator and protagonists, who is called upon to make the true epic *descensus*, to send his mind and imagination into the *inferos* of Troy and corporeality, to evaluate what he finds there, and to return to the light instructed and illuminated." (p. 193).

Rather than presenting a hero who stands for Everyman, Chaucer has made Everyman a hero. Maresca tries to see Chaucer as part of the Virgilian-Neo-Platonic epic tradition, but his paradigm has broken down. He appears most interested in making Chaucer a precursor of Pope.

As Maresca candidly admits, his approach is that of a generalist and his purpose is to speculate and suggest. His primary field is the eighteenth century, and he became interested in earlier epic while he was studying the relationship of mock epic to Fielding's *Tom Jones*. Perhaps his true interest in the *Troilus* is most clearly stated in the epilogue: "Chaucer's insistent counterpointing of the frustrations of epic expectations against a grid of epic reference-points forms a coherent pattern that critics ought to recognize: it describes the basic pattern of mock epic" (p. 197). He goes on to reflect on the history of epic, to trace the themes of knowledge and the tension between the life of the body and the life of the spirit until he returns to an earlier point about Milton. *Paradise Lost* put an end to epic by leaving nothing more for poets to do. Only mock epic is possible. Finally, Maresca's book, while it provides some interesting observations along the way, presents some rather conventional views of Spenser, and imposes an ever-increasingly strained paradigm on Milton and Chaucer.

GWENN DAVIS
University of Oklahoma

PRISCILLA MARTIN, *Piers Plowman: The Field and the Tower.* New York: Barnes and Noble; London: Macmillan, 1979. Pp. ix, 172. $22.50.

Piers Plowman enjoyed a particularly rich decade of criticism in the 1970's, with the publication of a number of thoughtful and original essays and monographs concerned with the formal as well as intellectual problems of this most difficult of Middle English poems. This happy period was stimulated in part by the publication in 1969 of a volume of critical essays edited by S. S. Hussey, which contained a fine contribution by Priscilla Martin (Jenkins). That essay, on Conscience and the limitations of allegory, forms the germ and kernel of her present book.

Martin is concerned with allegory, though her emphasis is upon its limitations as a form both for thought and literary expression. The book begins with a chapter on "The Endings", which comments upon the Pardon scene and on Passus XIX and XX of the B Text as examples of how, in *Piers,* forms which propose understanding produce inconsequence or paradox. Thus the Pardon, promised to solve the problems of the *Visio,* in fact only introduces more complications because it is itself ambiguous; the ending of the poem leads to no conclusion, only to more uncertainty and doubt. The book next discusses irony as a pervasive structural device, including a brief analysis of the poem's many "false starts" and its use of dream-vision conventions. The third chapter deals with Will's conversation with Imaginatyf as an attempt by the poet to express his doubts concerning the nature and value of poetry. Entitled "The Christian Poet and the Christian Satirist," it explores in part the problems of language, and Langland's fear of misusing it, embodied in his frequent return to the theme of "good" and "bad" minstrels. Martin comments that satire is a difficult genre for a Christian to use, since it seems to go against the commandment to love one's neighbor. She concludes:

> It is only on the question of satire that Langland can formulate the problem latent in the entire poem: that one might say the right thing in the wrong way . . . It is the clearest—if crudest—example of the paradoxical use of language . . . which is so characterisitc and mysterious in *Piers Plowman"* (p. 70).

The last half of the book is concerned with certain traits of allegory which Martin believes that Langland tests and (in the main) discards in *Piers*: "prejudice", or the tendency in allegory to view the world "as a pattern of intended analogies" (p. 104) which, all too often, seem trite and platitudinous; "idealism", or the tendency to lose the concrete world of experience in order to present "a world of clear-cut moral distinctions" (p. 112); and "spiritualism", or the tendency of "allegorical interpretation . . . to gloss over uncomfortable literal meanings" (p. 141). Martin insists that Langland exposes and rejects in his poetry these tendencies in allegory:

> Allegory is a mode of thought which Langland is investigating and defining through the juxtaposition of allegorical and literal. This reading suggests that the allegorical habit of thought is indispensable in formulating moral concepts, but that, since these concepts are modified by actual situations, allegorisation comes under increasing suspicion. By the end of the poem the mode has been so strained that 'perfect' characters behave inconsistently. Yet the desire for the idealism and intellectual coherence of allegory cannot be abandoned. The final image of the pilgrim reinstates the allegorical, not as a statement of a scheme, but in terms of a quest for the unknown (p. 129).

There is much truth in this statement, but there is also much imprecision and begging of the formal problems presented by the poem, which other critics, like Elizabeth Kirk, Ruth Ames, and David Aers, have analysed with more acumen and critical skill. For example, why "cannot" the desire for coherence be abandoned? What about an allegorical habit of mind is "indispensable" to the formation of moral concepts? Is "allegorisation" a monolithic process, as this analysis assumes? And does *allegory* "come under suspicion" (of what?), or does the "mode of thought" evolve and change in the poem? These are problems which recent studies of *Piers* have dealt with extensively, in the process evolving a vocabulary in which to analyse with some sophistication and accuracy the poem's structure, but their efforts and successes are not evident in Martin's analysis.

One formulation that traps Martin's discussion is her acceptance of a definition of allegory taken straight from Goethe and Coleridge. This admittedly inadequate definition enmires her in a simple opposition of "abstract" and "concrete" which compounds her problems in dealing with *Piers*. "Abstract" and "concrete" are identified with "spiritual" and "material", and thence with "soul" and "body" in a series of correspondences that are ultimately confusing and, I believe, self-defeating. Thus, she speaks of Langland linking "an abstract and a concrete word together in such a combination as 'Mesure is medicine' (I, 35). This terse equation suggests, in form as well as in content, the power of the spirit over the body" (p. 82). But by what standard can *mesure* as a word be considered more abstract than *medicine*? Are not all words by their nature typical, and therefore "abstract"? Do they not depend upon an "abstraction", communication, for their very function and existence? It seems particularly confusing to associate abstraction with spirit and soul, in rigid contradistinction to matter and body, in a poem containing figures like *Anima*, one without tongue or teeth who nonetheless speaks and inhabits a body, or an allegory like that of the Tree of Charity wherein space, time, and apples undergo such rapid material changes in an entirely associative, spiritual logic.

Unfortunately, Martin's theoretical naivety is fundamental in her discussion; she is largely innocent of work on *Piers* published after about 1971, and indeed I had the strong impression that this manuscript was essentially completed about eight years ago. Thus she comments in the text that the function of the diversity of types of characters in the Prologue "has not been much discussed" (p. 111); instead critics have been preoccupied with reading the allegory of the poem and ignoring any analysis of its form (her chief quarrel is with the method of Robertson and Huppé's 1951 study). A footnote on this remark pays graceful tribute to "sensitive discussion" of the diversity of figures in Kirk's study and in mine, but such passing allusion in a book published in 1979 to work published in 1972 and 1973 is simply insufficient. Martin never alludes to Ames on "fulfillment" as a structural principle in *Piers* or to Aers' analysis of its allegorical form, to the work of Alford and Spearing on the influence of sermon structure in the poem, or to Adams' analysis of the ending of the B Text. Kirk is mentioned only in the note I just referred to, even though Martin discusses at several points the relationship of the A and B *Vita*. This practice contrasts completely with her use of earlier critics, to whom she frequently gives full, even lavish, credit, especially to Donaldson, Burrow, and Muscatine; oddly, however, she does not discuss Salter's 1960 study of allegorical form in the poem. She does make use of work by Anne Middleton (1972) and by me, but the effect merely compounds one's impression of her non-acquaintance with most of the work on *Piers* of the last decade.

Martin's method is that of the old "new criticism", a reading devoted entirely to formal problems, the irony and paradox they produce, and rigorously focused upon the text (mostly B). There are several good discussions of particular scenes and passages, such as the role of Conscience, the "plante of pees" metaphor in Lady Holy Church's speech, and the figure of Pees. There is also an interesting discussion of the importance Langland accords to the performance of miracles as a stage in spiritual growth (for example in the accounts of the life of Jesus in B, Passus XVI and XIX). Miracles provide "a resolution of one of Langland's favorite dichotomies, works and words" (p. 138), because they are symbolic works, exempla as well as literal manifestations of the divine in the world. I was, however, frequently bothered by Martin's tendency to duck the harder, but often more interesting, critical questions, and to assert truths about the poem without arguing them through. For instance, after discussing the "plante of pees" metaphor at some length and with sensitivity, she concludes "it would be perverse—or impossible—to chart the abstract and concrete associations of the imagery" because it achieves "a brilliant synthesis of the material and the spiritual" (p. 85). Perversity indeed; but not emanating from the poet or poem.

The text used is the Kane–Donaldson B Text, though I had the impression that this choice did not seriously affect any of Martin's readings. For some reason the publisher elected not to reproduce Kane-Donaldson's editorial marks, only their regular punctuation, an odd policy to apply to a scholarly book, though perhaps justified in a book intended, as this one seems to be, for a general student audience. She uses Kane's A Text (also without marks) and Skeat's Early English Text Society C Text, as Pearsall's C Text was apparently not available to her (though she makes no allusion to its imminent appearance). In sum, this is a modest and agreeable book, which makes a good, general, readerly introduction to the experience of *Piers Plowman*, but it does seem an anachronistic beginning to published studies of the poem for the nineteen-eighties.

I caught two evident errors: on p. 113, "and" makes nonsense of the sentence, and must surely be a mistake for "the"; on p. 121, the quotation of B, XIII, 203 should read "shalt" instead of "halt". In general, however, the manuscript and quotations have been carefully checked.

MARY CARRUTHERS
University of Illinois
at Chicago Circle

JOHN NORTON-SMITH, introd., *Bodleian Library MS. Fairfax 16.* London: Scolar Press, 1979. Pp. xxix, 682. £95.

Scolar Press has done an excellent job in the production of this attractive, carefully written, and extremely important manuscript. As all Chaucerians know, Fairfax 16 is of vital importance as a witness to the texts of Chaucer's vision poems, in particular, of course, for *The House of Fame,* and for several minor poems as well.

The facsimile is of fine quality; the virgules seem to be easily visible, shades of ink determinable, and the membrane of the vellum distinct. The binding is scarcely beautiful, but it is a very serviceable brown buckram designed for tough use, and even though the book is quite heavy, I suspect that the binding will stand up for some time. Scolar by now must be a very experienced press in the printing of such facsimiles, for they are responsible not only for this one and the Auchinleck, which are under their own name, but also for the printing of the two Derek Brewer, Ltd., facsimiles, Corpus Christi Cambridge MS. 61 (*Troilus*) and the first volume (of three projected) of Cambridge MS. Gg. 4. 27.

The most profitable use of this facsimile of Fairfax 16 will probably not, in the near future, be made by students of Chaucer's texts; the ms has been readily available in the Bodleian and freely consulted by editors of Chaucer. Its great use will be as an example, for graduate students, of medieval book-making. The intricate discussions by Chaucer bibliographers and textual critics make real sense only when one is able to follow their arguments with the book, or a close approximation of it, in hand. And each of the major Chaucerian manuscripts seems to be a somewhat different kind of book. The Corpus Christi Cambridge MS. 61 is a book which was intended for commission sale and designed to be finished and illustrated on a lavish scale; it was never completed, and was left frozen, as it were. The exact natures of the great Hengwrt and Ellesmere MSS. are still in dispute in spite of Parkes's and Doyle's learned commentary, and Cambridge Gg. 4. 27 has always been a vast puzzle (we hope to see much light shed on this ms by the forthcoming introductions by Parkes and Richard Beadle). Fairfax 16 seems to be an example of an ordinary commercial operation, compiled in booklets at the order of a customer, all the booklets done in the same hand, but clearly from exemplars of widely varying closeness to what we might think of as the originals. It is generally dated in the middle of the fifteenth century, and Norton-Smith agrees with this in his introduction.

The introduction in general is solid, emphasizing the construction of the book and the possible circumstances of its compilation. Norton-Smith's main contribution to textual studies comes in his support for Brusendorff's suggestion that, although Chaucer apparently took no special trouble over collecting his minor poems into a single authoritative edition, he had originally "published" or "multiplied" them in a set of six basic booklets: 1) *The Legend of Good Women,* 2) *The House of Fame,* 3) the *Complaints of Mars* and *Venus,* 4) *The Parliament of Fowls,* 5) *Anelida and Arcite,* and 6) the minor poems contained in Booklet Two of Fairfax 16 (the *Complaint unto Pity, An ABC, Fortune, Envoy to Scogan, Complaint to His Purse, Lenvoy de Chaucer a Bukton, Lack of Steadfastness, Against Women Unconstant*). Booklet One of Fairfax 16 contains the vision poems, the *Complaints of Mars* and *Venus,* and the *Anelida.* Norton-Smith speculates (p. ix) that the possible reason why no manuscript of the minor poems which antedates Fairfax 16 has survived is that the small booklets proved too fragile (he excludes Cambridge Gg. 4. 27 as not being a collection of the minor poems).

Norton-Smith's notes on the texts of the individual poems are quite useful, citing in each case the place of the Fairfax 16 text in the editorial tradition of the poem. His comments are careful, and his remarks upon the classification of the manuscript copies of *Lack of Steadfastness* make a contribution, suggesting a new way of grouping the manuscripts on the basis of a convincing authorial variant.

One reads the introduction with admiration and instruction, but finally comes away, or this reader comes away, wondering whether in our reaction to the unjustified assumption of a much earlier age of scholars that Chaucer had edited and seen after his poetic children as carefully as a modern poet would have, we have not gone to the opposite extreme in assuming an almost total lack of concern by Chaucer (in spite of the poem to Adam) about the text and the preservation of his poems. This lack of concern we are likely to associate with a vague notion current now of what was "medieval," just as an earlier age attempted to extrapolate from the nineteenth- and twentieth-century poets' preoccupation with their texts and apply it to medieval poets. It is surely obvious that Gower was concerned with his texts, and so was, bless him, John Lydgate, and, we have reason to believe, so were Dante, Petrarch, and Boccaccio. Why Chaucer should be assumed to have been the lone standard-bearer of the now current "medievalism" among critics and scholars is something that should puzzle us all.

I must add that, though I have justly praised Norton-Smith's accurate scholarship and close attention to his masters in his introduction, I find a certain note in his writings, here and elsewhere, a bit annoying. It amounts to an impertinent condescension to, or dismissal of, other scholars which has a harsh and self-congratulatory tone even when criticism is justified. This condescension leads Norton-Smith occasionally even into error and downright misrepresentation. For example (p. ix), he remarks that ". . . Dr. Doyle and Mr. Parkes have argued persuasively that the Ellesmere Manuscript of the *Canterbury Tales* is an editorial, didactic rearrangement, as far as one can get from Chaucer's own original intention. So much for the editorial complacency of Rickert, Manly and Robinson." This is a statement stunning in its arrogance and ignorance to one who has studied with care these far from complacent scholars. And to be able to speak of getting ". . . as far as one can get from Chaucer's own original intention. . . ." suggests a breath-taking assumption, that one, anyone, now knows Chaucer's own, original intention. Parkes and Doyle do not, nor do they claim to. Robinson, Manly, and Rickert did not, nor did they claim to. Does Mr. Norton-Smith? Norton-Smith further twists the line of the Parkes and Doyle argument. Learnedly and persuasively, Parkes and Doyle merely argue much more carefully and with more corroborative detail, what most textual scholars would for many years have argued, but to less effect: that *The Canterbury Tales* manuscripts were in the hands of scribes and editors who made the best sense they could of what they had and found, and, as a result, no organization or relationship can be with confidence described as "authorial" in origin. These are also the assumptions of Rickert, Manly, and Robinson, three scholars of at least as great learning (not the specific learning of Parkes and Doyle) as any in the field today. Robinson, for example, clearly states (pp. 888–89) that he knows that the Ellesmere is not authorial, but seems to be the best that can be had, both for text and pleasing and reasonably consistent order. Manly and Rickert constantly remind us that, however exacting and ingenious their redaction of Chaucer's text, they have no hope of getting beyond O^1 to Chaucer himself, that they regard all manuscripts as non-authorial. There are many errors in the Manly-Rickert edition, and, owing to the circumstances of its production and hasty publication long after the death of Edith Rickert and shortly after the death of Manly, there are several inconsistencies of method which undercut its still enormous usefulness. But complacency is the last quality which one would, I hope, ordinarily assume in the work of these scholars. Without Manly and Rickert, our knowledge of the text of *The Canterbury Tales*, and even Mr. Norton-Smith's knowledge of the Chaucerian texts, would be far poorer than it is. It is sad to see a fine piece of scholarship marred by such unnecessary, pointless, and ultimately foolish thrusts.

Scolar Press has earned our gratitude not only by the highly satisfactory general lay-out and quality of the book, but also by the splendid full-scale, full-color reproductions of the illustration to *The Complaint of Mars,* and of the opening page of the same poem. Norton-Smith's brief discussion of the iconography of the illustration (pp. xii-xiii) is illuminating in its pointing to the religious model for the picture's composition and its drawing analogues to other artists' treatments; he has used Alexander's work well and made his own observations.

It is to be hoped that economic recession and rising costs will not prevent, on both sides of the Atlantic, what appears to be in the making—a whole library of the most important Chaucerian and other medieval manuscripts, accessible to all serious students in a great variety of institutions, a *studium paleographicum* for everyman which was unthought of (or even desired *if* thought of) in the early days of the Roxburghe Club and in the case of the printers of the Manchester Ellesmere facsimile, the latter now an extremely rare and extraordinarily expensive book. Perhaps even the Ellesmere might one day be made available again, though, of course, a judicious facsimile would inevitably be much more expensive than the one under review.

DONALD C. BAKER
University of Colorado

MAUREEN QUILLIGAN, *The Language of Allegory: Defining the Genre*. Ithaca and London: Cornell University Press, 1979. Pp. 305. $15.

Professor Quilligan has constructed a conceptually energetic argument for allegory as a distinct literary genre with its own rules and expectations.

She rejects the traditional understanding that allegory "says one thing and means another" as a creation of critics rather than readers of allegory. *Readers* of allegory know that is draws fully on the polysemous possibilities of language to reveal itself horizontally as a simultaneous discovery of meanings both literal and figurative, rather than vertically as a hierarchy of different "levels" of meaning.

So crucial in her view is the polysemy of words to the operation of allegory that she regards this quality of language as the essential precondition of allegory, whether in the fourteenth, sixteenth, or twentieth century. She argues that all allegorists regard language as having a potent existence of its own in the world, independent of the mundane world of things. Carried to its limit, this is the "suprarealist" attitude toward language, "in which abstract nouns not only name universals that are real, but in which the abstract names themselves are perceived to be as real and powerful as the things named" (p. 156). This attitude toward language pervades works as various as *Piers Plowman*, the *Faerie Queene*, *Pilgrim's Progress*, *The Confidence Man*, and *Gravity's Rainbow*.

At times, the ambitious scope of this study leads to statements from which the reader may well quail, such as the assertion that allegories by Alain de Lille, Jean de Meun, Spenser, and Thomas Pynchon all "work in exactly the same way" (p. 46). Fortunately, Professor Quilligan usually balances such sweeping claims with more particular and perceptive observations about the working of allegory in each of the works under discussion. She maintains that each of these works shares an implicit relation to what she calls a "pretext" (a punning reference both to its antecedence and to its role as an occasion for the allegory), which is usually the Bible itself. Yet she observes insightfully that the role of the Bible as pretext differs in each case: it is present typologically in the *Commedia*, as a sacred book in its own right in *The Faerie Queene*, in a reified and authoritative form in *Pilgrim's Progress*, and in a series of equivocal and possibly parodic allusions in *Gravity's Rainbow*. She maintains that all these works use language to create a reading process which forces the reader into a "self-reflexive" role which involves redefinition, reconsideration, and final, self-defining choice. Yet she describes with skill the differing terms of the choice which each work thrusts on its reader.

Professor Quilligan's argument that all these works share certain self-reflexive verbal techniques (and demand certain self-reflexive reader responses) is quite persuasive. Less persuasive is her central contention that allegory is a distinct genre to which all these works belong while other works which have traditionally been regarded as allegories do not. For example, her contention that *Gravity's Rainbow* is an allegory because of its attitude toward the sacramental possibilities of language but that *House of Fame* falls short of being truly allegorical because it lacks a "self-conscious textual presentation" (pp. 246–47) is compelling only in the particular terms of her study, and conviction melts as I set her book aside. Finally, this study would be more tenable and no less useful if she had abandoned the debatable contention that allegory is a distinct genre and treated it instead as a mode or device which authors of different periods and traditions employ in varying ways.

Other medievalists may also share my concern that Professor Quilligan's approach, while quite sensitive to differing tonalities and objectives among the works discussed, nevertheless treats allegory in an essentially a-historical way. She does acknowledge some temporal developments in her boldly-conceived description of the changing attitudes toward language and the shifting status of the Bible as sacred pretext through some 600 years. Yet she does not avail herself of an historically-grounded sense of the development of allegorical theory. She is quick to upbraid theorists as eminent as Quintilian and Dante if their advice seems inapplicable to her sense of the reader's experience of an allegorical text, but she does not take advantage of those points in the development of allegorical theory which support her own interpretations. I am thinking, for example, of the Victorines, and their twelfth-century anticipation of her argument that the literal surface of the text must be encountered and valued in its own right, rather than simply decoded and thrown away.

Such qualifications aside, this remains a work of considerable theoretical energy, keen textual sympathy, and admirable lucidity in the face of frequently perplexing subject matter. Although it does not address the concerns of literary historians, it will be of special interest to those reader-theorists who have enjoyed the works of Honig and Frye and—more recently—Fish, Foucault, and Derrida.

PAUL STROHM
Indiana University

MARY SALU, ed., *Essays on Troilus and Criseyde*. Chaucer Studies, III. Cambridge: D. S. Brewer, Ltd., 1979; Totowa, New Jersey: Rowman & Littlefield, 1980. Pp. 143. £10.00; $23.75.

In recent years, *Troilus and Criseyde* has finally come back into its own. For three hundred years after Chaucer's death, *Troilus* was by far his most popular work and the principal reason he was considered, in Usk's phrase, "the noble philosophical poete in Englissh." During the eighteenth and nineteenth centuries, however, readers generally preferred the human comedy of *The Canterbury Tales* and frequently judged the *Troilus* to be "tedious" and much too long.

Now that most Chaucerians can face both sexual love and medieval thought squarely, the *Troilus* is once again highly regarded. In recent years several books on this one poem alone have appeared, and now D. S. Brewer's admirable press offers a volume of seven original essays by British and American scholars. *Essays on Troilus and Criseyde* contains no single theme or approach (the editor, Mary Salu, notes that "the range in this book is wide"), and there is no sense here of radically new readings or fresh ground broken. Nevertheless, none of the essays is without merit, and together, while not representing an accurate cross-section, they may suggest some general tendencies in contemporary *Troilus* studies. For example, we may note the great respect in which the poem is held even when passages are found awkward and confused, they are said to have been deliberately constructed so. Additionally, many old topics no longer seem of interest: although love is frequently discussed, the "system" of courtly love is not once mentioned, nor do the roles of Pandarus and the narrator attract much attention. Paradoxically, the best essays here, at least in the opinion of this reader, are the one that is most technical (by Windeatt) and the two that are most free-ranging and subjective (by David and Lambert).

In "The Text of the *Troilus*," Barry Windeatt makes a strong case against R. K. Root's widely accepted view that the first version of *Troilus* was carefully revised by the poet so as to form three distinct texts (α, β, and γ), most obviously through the addition of three long passages—Troilus' song in Book III (1744–71), his soliloquy on predestination in Book IV (953–1085), and his ascent to the spheres in Book V (1807–27)—as well as in numerous passages marked by differences in language and line sequence. Windeatt notes that "the same evidence for authorial addition may turn out to be evidence of scribal omission." He demonstrates that even in those mss where the three passages are missing or added later, the context shows that they were always part of the poet's original conception. Since the *Troilus* is "a patchwork and embroidery" of passages added to its main source, Boccaccio's *Filostrato*, Windeatt suggests that the composition of the poet's copy may have involved "a series of layers—perhaps physical layers—of writing." Thus what appear to be distinct versions of the poem in the mss need not indicate authorial revision but might just as plausibly reveal "scribal misunderstandings *after the event* of the layers of composition present in a confusing exemplar, of which loose sheets may always have been lost." As for those smaller changes (usually of a word or phrase), which Root took as further evidence of distinct versions of the *Troilus*, Windeatt argues in detail that many such variants are merely scribal and that even those that may represent genuine authorial reworking are too sporadic and minor to be considered evidence of the kind of systematic revision found in Gower and Langland. Windeatt's essay is useful not only for its argument that the *Troilus* was never seriously revised, but also for its conception of the work as a "layered poem," the implications of which may eventually be as interesting to the literary critic as to the textual scholar.

Two essays, by James Wimsatt and John McKinnell, that attempt to identify new literary sources of the *Troilus* suggest that most of the corn in this field of study may already have been reaped by previous scholars so that today we are left to glean subtler (and thus harder to prove) influences. In "Realism in *Troilus and Criseyde* and the *Roman de la Rose*," Wimsatt argues that the realism (a difficult term that is never adequately defined) of *Troilus* makes it "a new kind of literature." Two neglected *genres* are said to have contributed to this realism: the Arts of Love tradition from Ovid to *Pamphilus* and Platonic cosmic fables from *Timaeus* to Alain of Lille. The former *genre*, whose primary influence in the *Troilus* is on the character of Pandarus, helps both the French and English poems "maintain a close connection with the world of fact and of practical action"; the latter, which despite its abstract qualities is realistic because "concerned with typical affairs of human life, the sphere of realism," adds profundity to both poems. Although the influence of Platonic cosmic fables on the *Roman* and Chaucer's *Parliament* is undeniable, Wimsatt's claims for its use in the *Troilus* is more doubtful and rests primarily on the perception that the love between Troilus and Criseyde, for all its faults, is archetypal and partakes of the universal order.

Like Wimsatt, McKinnell in his "Letters as a Type of the Formal Level in *Troilus and Criseyde*," considers *Troilus* in terms of contemporary literary expectations. He argues that if the letters between Troilus and Criseyde, which are greatly changed from Boccaccio, are read with a knowledge of the rules of the *artes dictandi* tradition—especially the five-part model offered by pseudo-Alberich—they are able "to provide a sensitive listener with a critical commentary on the narrated characters who are supposed to write them." McKinnell's essay contains much useful information (e.g., his observation that in the Middle Ages "real life letters were regarded chiefly as a storing of the spoken word") and some good close analyses of individual letters, but his central claim that Chaucer is consciously using and departing from the *artes dictandi* tradition is finally not proven.

One critical question that will not disappear concerns the fundamental tone and meaning of *Troilus and Criseyde*, and specifically the attitude the reader should have toward the love affair. Although all the essays in this collection wisely avoid the excesses of absolute condemnation or approval, two (by Gaylord and Frankis) view the lovers critically and two others (by David and Lambert) more sympathetically.

In a good, if not especially original, essay, "The Lesson of the *Troilus*: Chastisement and Correction," Alan Gaylord first argues against two modern, overly complex interpretations of the *Troilus*, which view the love story benignly, before suggesting that the author's call for courtly correction masks serious Christian instruction. Chaucer teaches this lesson by inviting the reader first to identify with the story and then "to disengage from it—not by moralistic condemnation, but through a process of perfected understanding based upon self-examination." Like Ida Gordon and others, Gaylord shows the ways in which the characters deceive themselves while refusing to take responsibility for their actions; Criseyde wrongly assumes that she is helpless, and Troilus' soliloquy on predestination is analyzed as a declaration of "intellectual bankruptcy." The real tragedy of the lovers is their despair, according to Gaylord, and he argues that the poet's final appeal for correction to his friends "moral" Gower and "philosophical" Strode "is conclusive evidence that Chaucer means us to take more meaning than sad mutability from the conclusion of his poem." The reader learns that Troilus and Criseyde need not have acted as they did, and he is forced to correct his own vision "for it is *choice* which is at the heart of Chaucer's lesson."

John Frankis, in "Paganism and Pagan Love in *Troilus and Criseyde*," like Gaylord, finds the characters wanting and sees their story as a negative *exemplum* to the audience. Although he raises some interesting questions about the role of paganism in the poem, Frankis' answers are somewhat limited and questionable. He argues that even though Troilus sees further than his fellow pagans, he can never reach the truth of Christianity. Specifically, his love of Criseyde is unable to succeed because Troy lacks the Sacrament of Marriage which would unite divine and earthly love. This argument leads to some doubtful readings (e.g., that IV, 555 means Troilus thought of asking for Criseyde's hand in marriage) and odd interpretations (that the pagan worlds of *The Franklin's* and *Knight's Tales* are more favorable to proto-Christian marriages than the world of Troy), and the argument finally depends on the assumption that Chaucer viewed marriage positively, though one might easily argue that we never see a happy, functioning marriage in any of his works.

Perhaps the most stimulating essays in this collection are those by Alfred David and Mark Lambert, both of which, while accepting the fitness of Chaucer's moral ending, concentrate on the first half of the poem. Without denying the tragedy of Troilus, these critics are more interested in the comedy of Criseyde.

In "*Troilus*, Books I–III: A Criseydan Reading," Lambert argues that the "markedly timid heroine," who has no taste for extremes and must be persuaded that "love isn't going to hurt one bit," is at first closer to the reader than is Troilus: "To experience the first half of the *Troilus* is to be charmed by the unheroic." The Troy we find in the poem "is not truly of the great world," but is a city of kindliness, friendship, and childhood. Even the extraordinary Helen of Troy has become "altogether domesticated" and "seems to have put on a few pounds." In such a setting Troilus' stiff, humorless heroism initially appears quite silly. Although Lambert may underestimate some of the darker, more serious aspects of *Troilus* present even in its early books, his exploration of the "deep Criseydan counter-current" is welcome. Lambert acknowledges that Troilus' heroic qualities are appropriate to the second part of the story and make him "the most dignified of the major characters," but he also believes that Criseyde remains closer to the poet's own sensibility and may even be autobiographical: Chaucer is a "poet of the unheroic who knows (or suspects) the heroes are finally correct."

Even more than Lambert, Alfred David in "Chaucerian Comedy and Criseyde" emphasizes Criseyde's humor and love of "game"; both she and Pandarus, unlike Troilus, are given to what David calls "bodily laughter," which, though it laughs at the body, "does so out of sympathy in order to affirm, not to deny, the body's values." David, like Lambert, sees that "Criseyde's whole nature is opposed to death and tragedy," and he suggest that she is neither conquered by nor rises above Fortune but constantly goes around in circles on Fortune's wheel, unable to imagine the future but pluckily dealing with whatever comes: she is a survivor. David is especially good at not taking Criseyde too seriously, especially in his analyses of her more emotional scenes, which he regards as genuine if somewhat facile and necessary "to satisfy the demands of Criseyde's romantic conception of herself." Although only some will go as far as David and believe that Criseyde's story remains comedy until the end and that she herself is sister to the Wife of Bath, many will agree that she is "a comic creation of such vitality that it challenges the idea of tragedy and the authority of the advice that bids us to repair 'hom fro worldly vanyte'." Challenges but does not overturn. Undoubtedly both Lambert and David represent the kind of modern correction of Chaucer about which Gaylord complains, and yet surely they describe a genuine response to the poem and one of the reasons for its renewed popularity six hundred years after its composition.

C. DAVID BENSON
University of Colorado

TSUTOMU SATOW, *Sentence and Solaas: Thematic Development and Narrative Technique in* The Canterbury Tales. Tokyo: Kobundo Publishing Company, 1979. Pp. 400. 8000 yen.

That Chaucer studies should flourish in Japan should not surprise us: English is a second language for many Japanese, and in school and university curricula literary study has traditionally accompanied linguistic training. An analogous situation exists in Germany where, for generations, students have learned not only phonetics and grammar but Old and Middle English literatures as well. In addition, German scholars have of course given the world some of its most significant Middle English scholarship—in the past, much of it philological, but today critical in most senses of that word.

Japanese Chaucer studies have followed the German pattern: there have been philological works such as the study of the structure of the rhyme-words by Michio Masui (Tokyo: 1964). Professor Satow's book is a critical study of a sort familiar to us all. As he says in his Introduction (pp. 6–7): "We will engage in literary research in Chaucer's greatest work the *Canterbury Tales* by 'new criticism' and sometimes by 'historicism.'"

There is not much of the latter: Satow speculates, for instance, that the *geaunt* that opposes Thopas may in some oblique way refer to John of Gaunt. Most of the book is concerned with structural matters—parallels and contrasts among the tales, for example—viewed from a point of view that I suppose we may, with the author, label "new critical."

Satow has profound, and readily acknowledged, debts to English and American critics, notably Bowden, Corsa, Kittredge, Lumiansky, Ruggiers, and Whittock. The insights are therefore for the most part familiar. Satow shows that *The Knight's Tale* establishes a triangular pattern that is reflected in its successor, *The Miller's Tale;* and that this same arrangement of incidents and characters may be found in *The Shipman's Tale* and *The Merchant's Tale* as well.

There is a more sophisticated critical perception in Satow's treatment of *The Physician's* and *Pardoner's Tales,* both of which deal with the "gift" of death. And the author provides a vigorous appreciation of the Wife of Bath—somewhat flawed, perhaps, by his apparent unawareness of details such as the Wife's (or Chaucer's) alteration of incidents in Ovid's Midas-story.

Thus, though the critical perceptions are familiar, they make up a full-length study of *The Canterbury Tales* that should be of value to the advanced Japanese student of English literature. It might be suggested, on the other hand, that such students would have welcomed more observations drawn from the writer's own culture. In the immensely rich Japanese history and literature, there must be parallels and contrasts that a scholar like Professor Satow might have called upon—but he takes advantage of this possibility only three or four times in his book. For instance, he points out that the pilgrimage is a Japanese tradition, as it was in fourteenth-century England (p. 17): "Take the Japanese for example. They go on a pilgrimage for the purpose of great enjoyment." But the motives are different: for the European (p. 19), "each shrine is likened to the recovery of paradise. This is quite different from the Japanese pilgrimage." In the same passage, Satow suggests some tentative parallels with the Japanese poet Basho. He also draws upon his own traditions when dealing with *The Physician's Tale* (pp. 220–21): "The dialogue and persuasion between Virginius and his daughter is very interesting and *kabuki*-like. Since the knight could never accept the shame as the Japanese samurai could never do, he withdrew his sword and cut off his daughter's head." He also observes (p. 320): "Such questions and answers between the Host and the Canon's Yeoman continued in a way that intrigued and puzzled, just as in *kakeai* in Japanese *Rakugo*," traditions of which I confess I have no knowledge.

Most of the book reflects European and American views almost exclusively. Until recent times, Japan had a feudal system perhaps analogous in some ways to that of Europe, a circumstance that would seem to have provided Professor Satow with unique opportunities for comparison with Chaucer's life and works. The institution of literary patronage springs to mind.

The non-native speaker of English encounters titanic difficulties when dealing with the language of 600 years ago. I can imagine the problems that I might confront if I chose to write in Japanese about the poet Basho. I hope it will not be considered ungenerous of me, therefore, if I point out a few of the book's shortcomings. There are countless misprints. On one page of the bibliography (p. 382) we find "Geoffffrey . . . J. J. Rarry [Parry] . . . Edingburgh . . . Walfgang Clemen . . . Perspecticves . . . Michigan (Oklahoma). . . Germain Dempster . . . Eliason, *The Language of Chaucer's Poetry,* 1927 [1972]."

More important are some undeniable—and some probable—errors of fact: Emelye is described as Theseus' daughter (p. 28); Absolon borrows from Gerveys "a red-hot poker"(p. 56); the secular clergy are distinguished from the "religious" (p. 93—i.e., the regular); *The Merchant's Tale* includes a reference to the marriage of "Paris and Esther" (p. 185); *The Pardoner's Tale* has "a strong . . . antisexual bias" (p. 228); Thopas' seemly nose "may have an obscene double meaning, as reference to the nose sometimes does in Shakespeare" (p. 259); "because we can easily imagine that most of 'a court audience' consist of court ladies" (p. 303).

English, Middle as well as Modern, is a maddening tongue: those who learn it as a second language have understandable problems with tense sequence, presence and absence of the article, and the use of the elusive apostrophe. Modern English idioms are also difficult, and for the record some of the infelicities in this book should perhaps be recorded: "he dear reveal Arcite's identity"; "medieval ages"; "we can accept the argument of P. G. Ruggiers as available"; the Host "tries to shunk him [the Miller] up"; "Walter, emblematic of God and the subtle serpent that is wicked in the Book of Job, in the trails of Griselda's patience, selects her mysteriously and unexpectedly"; "the fruit-bearing deity, Priapus"; "January is drowned in kindled erotic reveries"; "women are always foible"; "Harry Bailly is a practical critic with powerful emotions of his own contemporary articulation"; Virginius bursts out into "the frenzy of topical illusion"; Thopas runs home "to fetch his amour"; the Prioress wears a "plated wimple."

These are flaws that a more thorough-going revision might have corrected. Despite them, Professor Satow's book is welcome evidence of Japanese university interest in Chaucer's work.

THOMAS W. ROSS
Colorado Springs, Colorado.

NATHANIEL B. SMITH and JOSEPH T. SNOW, eds., *The Expansion and Transformations Of Courtly Literature*. Athens: University of Georgia Press, 1980. Pp. xii, 235. $15.00.

"The Expansion and Transformations of Courtly Literature" was the general topic of the Second Triennial Congress of the International Courtly Literature Society held at the University of Georgia in 1977, and it serves as the title for the volume under review; the book consists of a selection of twelve papers from among those delivered at the congress, together with an introductory essay by the editors, Nathaniel Smith and Joseph Snow.

The essays cover a broad range of literature. In the first paper, the late Eugène Vinaver (to whose memory the volume is dedicated) restates some of his earlier conclusions on Arthurian romance; next, William Calin reviews the by now familiar shortcomings of D. W. Robertson's analysis of medieval love; Friederike Wiesmann-Wiedemann examines the character of King Mark in various versions of the Tristan story (he is basically good in Eilhart, basically villainous in the other accounts); Terence Scully interprets Chrétien's *Erec* in terms of the poem's final episode; and Matilda Tomaryn Bruckner isolates a "hospitality" convention in several twelfth-century French romances. Of these five essays, the first three are grouped under the rubric "Courtly Literature and the International Legends," whereas the last two come under the heading of "Twelfth-Century Changes." The next six papers deal with later works, and are all grouped under "Expansion and Transformations." Lowanne E. Jones studies four narrative forms somehow inspired by the troubadour lyrics, namely the *novas* (short story in couplets), the allegorical narrative, the prose life of individual troubadours, and the prose explanation of individual poems. Sara Sturm-Maddox examines the love lyrics of

Dante and Petrarch, and also Dante's prose explanations in the *Vita nuova*, while John M. Bowers writes of love in Chaucer's *Troilus*, and Donald Maddox discusses a drama, *L'estoire de Griseldis*, written in 1395. We move to the turn of the sixteenth century in Florence Ridley's paper, which analyzes and classifies the poetry of William Dunbar, and to the end of the sixteenth century in Winifred Gleeson Keaney's discussion of Book VI of Spenser's *Faerie Queene*. The last paper, by William Melczer, is a call for scholars in different disciplines to study in concert the various aspects of specific "courts," that is, political and cultural centers.

The editors have felt called upon not only to perform the usual introductory task of finding unity in a disparate collection of papers, but also to define the nature and purposes of the International Courtly Literature Society by arriving at a working definition of courtly literature, which in turn contains a definition of courtly love. In a way, these two purposes are contradictory, for on the one hand the editors stress the need for coherency of meaning (hence their new definition), and on the other hand they defend the lack of such coherency in the papers they are recommending to our attention. After admitting "for the moment" that there are "many courtly loves," they say that each of the essayists in the volume who uses the term courtly love "knows what he and others mean by it." Unfortunately, this is not the case. Vinaver, for instance, in a rather obscure statement cited with approval by the editors, says that "courtly love" is the best way that has been found to characterize the peculiar kind of argumentation about love manifested in the works of Chrétien de Troyes. In so speaking, Vinaver has actually come up with a new definition of courtly love while at the same time maintaining that it faithfully reflects what everyone else has meant by the term.

The book has other examples of authors who know what they mean by courtly love and who assume that all others agree. Keaney, for instance, takes it for granted that courtly love is coterminous with "pure love" (as explained by Andrew the Chaplain and Alexander Denomy), and seems to think that various scholars whom she mentions (including two Kellys mistakenly given the same first name) differ only in deciding "when and how often" courtly love gave way to "mixed love."

Sometimes there is no indication of what an author means by courtly love; an example occurs when Bruckner in a note refers to "the role of love—courtly or otherwise—as a motivation of wild-man transformations." There is a double danger in such a casual usage of an ambiguous term. One runs the risk, on the one hand, of being thought ignorant of scholarly debate by those who are aware of such debate, and, on the other hand, of being misunderstood by those whose favorite meaning of the term differs from the author's. The author may be thinking primarily of adulterous love, for instance, while a reader is thinking first and foremost of knightly service or sophisticated behavior.

The same cautions apply to "courtly literature," or anything else that is said to be courtly. Smith and Snow argue for the virtues of "fluctuating meaning," but surely individual writers should say exactly what they mean by the word, or they should set forth a range of possible meanings, as Ridley does in her essay on Dunbar. There she brings out something that the editors do not explicitly acknowledge, that "courtly literature" is not simply or always a short-hand expression for "courtly-love literature," but can have other meanings unconnected with love and can even deal with courts.

In order to get an insight into the variety and contradictoriness of present-day usages, it may be of help to look at the meanings of the term *courtois* as it was originally applied to love and literature. Most scholars assume that Gaston Paris, in the often-cited but seldom-read article in the 1883 volume of *Romania,* used the term *amour courtois* to characterize the love conventions of the troubadours, but in fact he introduced the term to distinguish a new kind of love which combined troubadour conventions with the chivalry of the Arthurian court, and which was first given literary expression in Chrétien's *Lancelot. Courtois* in this context means "courteous and chivalric." But it was also common, though not for Gaston Paris, to speak of *poésie courtoise,* with reference primarily to troubadour poetry and the literature that was influenced by it. Alfred Jeanroy in *Les origines de la poésie en France au moyen âge* (1889) found the term to be suitable, because Provençal poetry was produced for the amusement of the courts, rather than for the people at large. When Gaston Paris reviewed Jeanroy's book (*Journal des savants,* 1891–92), he accepted, at first hesitantly but then matter-of-factly, this use of *courtois* to mean "artistic and aristocratic" as opposed to "popular."

It is clear that there was a promise of confusion from the very beginning in these disparate usages of the same word. The promise has been abundantly fulfilled in the twentieth century and is illustrated in the present volume. For instance, Wiesmann-Wiedemann finds Thomas and Gottfried to be courtly because their characters are more subtle than

181

those of the "uncourtly" Eilhart and the author of the *Prose Tristan,* even though Eilhart is admittedly more interested in court society than the courtly poets. Thomas' lovers belong to "courtly culture" or "the courtly world," which affirms the rights of love over legal rights, whereas in Gottfried "the concept of courtliness" has the negative connotation of selfishness, which gives way to a higher religious element (though it is not clear how Gottfried's lovers are either religious or unselfish). For Vinaver, on the other hand, "courtly romance" is simply distinguished from "epic," and it is not clear that "courtly" is meant to add anything to "romance."

One essayist, John Bowers, avoids the word "courtly" altogether in his discussion of "How Criseyde Falls in Love." The reason seems to be, if we may judge from his harshly moralistic interpretation of the *Troilus,* that he subscribes to the views of D. W. Robertson; but it would have been better if he had clarified the matter himself. The moral, then, is that one must explain one's nonuse as well as one's use of "courtly"; Bowers' paper demonstrates that there is still a need for the kind of rebuttal that Calin offers. I should point out that in defending the existence of various kinds of *fin' amors* (which he identifies with courtly love and romantic love) in the Middle Ages, Calin admits the basic similarity of such love throughout the ages. Such is the pit that scholars have dug for themselves, that this basic truth, which was common knowledge at the turn of our century, must be painfully reclaimed. Calin attributes chiefly to Peter Dronke the insight that "romantic love was not the invention of the twelfth century," and to Denis de Rougemont the insight that romantic love outlived the Middle Ages and lasted into the Renaissance, while he himself can testify to "the extraordinary resurgence of romantic love since the First World War."

There is not space for me to summarize the virtues and vices of all of the essays, and I will limit myself to a remark about Vinaver's "Landmark's in Arthurian Romance." As in the past, Vinaver tends to overestimate the achievement of Malory's "last work," by comparing it to the French Arthurian prose cycle as a whole. But Malory's *Tale of the Death of King Arthur* should be compared only to the independently authored *Mort Artu,* which contains most of the virtues supposedly first found in Malory, and which in many ways surpasses Malory in artistry, particularly in psychological realism and tragic intensity.

As a whole, the volume offers little that is both new and striking, but much that is solid and interesting, especially when the authors are not formulating or drawing upon suspect generalizations but are giving concrete analyses of specific literary works. Melczer's statement of the need for interdisciplinary piecework is particularly important, and Ridley's study of Dunbar in the context of the court of James IV shows that one does not have to wait for congresses or collaborators to take advantage of the methods and results of other fields of scholarship.

H. A. KELLY
University of California,
Los Angeles

SIEGFRIED WENZEL, *Verses in Sermons:* Fasciculus Morum *and its Middle English Poems.* Cambridge, Mass.: The Mediaeval Academy of America, 1978. Pp. 234. $20.00.

This latest contribution by Siegfried Wenzel to our understanding of the rhetoric of preaching and its possible impact on imaginative literature will appeal not simply to those who are interested in didactic literature per se, but also to the broader audience concerned with lyric forms and meditative poetry in general.

Wenzel begins his introduction with the bold statement that "Middle English lyrics owe a profound and multiform debt to contemporary religious beliefs and institutions," and he then proceeds to develop this thesis throughout his work. First of all, he describes the "Little Bundle of Morality," a Latin treatise which was meant to teach friars the art of effective oratorical delivery (an outline is provided at the end). He then proceeds to put the *Fasciculus* in an historical and aesthetic perspective, and finally he offers a complete critical edition of the 61 English poems that are scattered through some of the manuscripts of the treatise (their number being exceedingly variable, as is shown in a table on pages 106–07).

Wenzel's work is, as a whole, the most complete commentary on the text to date, and his edition of the poetry surpasses those of his predecessors because of its completeness and accuracy; indeed, the entire book, with its many difficulties in a variety of languages, is remarkably free from errors in any.

The book is divided into three main chapters. In the first, Wenzel places the *Fasciculus* in the Franciscan tradition, where it stands as an important English contribution to the literature of the Seven Deadly Sins. Wenzel then describes the twenty-eight manuscripts of the treatise, including R, which serves as the base for his own edition of the poems. He shows that the work, in several forms, was widely read throughout England in Chaucer's day, functioning as a clergyman's guide. Wenzel next wrestles with the problem of dating, settling on the latter years of the reign of Edward I as the most likely time for its composition. The author then reveals himself as an excellent detective as he sifts through the evidence offering four different candidates for authorship. He decides, in a way that is perfectly reasonable, that the greatest claim belongs to Robert Selk.

The first chapter ends with a very interesting discussion of the fortune of the *Fasciculus* through references to it by other people, and concludes with some generalizations on the art of popular preaching. Wenzel notes that many allusions in these works are drawn from natural science, but, rather surprisingly at first glance, few from the world of the clergy; the greatest number of allusions is related to the world of the common man, and this makes sense when one considers the audience. The world of the Plowman provides the backdrop for the world of the Parson, precisely as Chaucer portrayed the characters in his *Prologue,* side by side. When one considers Chaucer's own great predicators—such as the Pardoner or Chauntecleer—one sees that the milieux of the barnyard and the tavern are never very far removed from the ecclesiastical forum. This blending of the lowly with the sublime, which formed the center for Auerbach's great essay on *Sermo humilis,* and which reached its optimum of expression in Dante's *Comedy,* can be seen rather more humbly in this English work.

Chapter II explores that phenomenon of blending the poetic with the prosaic that is shown in the *Fasciculus.* Wenzel documents the widespread practice of writing treatises with mixed styles, and decides that the poems were inserted in sermons because "they were mnemonic, rhetorical, or meditative, or simply an outlet for wit and verbal skill" (p. 66). Clearly, when one reads the poems, one sees that they crystallize certain beliefs or dramatic situations in ways that could impress unlettered folk and allow them to take these ideas home for further thought. Later, Wenzel rightfully backs away from claiming that the *Fasciculus* reaches the intense meditative profundity of a Donne, yet at the same time these simple poems are capable of possessing a trenchant power that can approach the epigram. Let us remember Ball at Blackheath in 1381. Wenzel notes, after an historical rundown, that the tradition slackens during the later fifteenth century, but does not offer any hypotheses for the decline. Perhaps no one can.

Chapter III offers the poems themselves, preceded by a defense of their originality and diveristy, with the general disclaimer that they are "at best third- or fourth-class citizens in the kingdom of lyrics" (p. 121). It is true that when these poems are excised from their original context, with the prose introductions, they do appear rather truncated and naked. Yet that can be said of many short lyrics. To make the poems stand forth in whatever glory they originally possessed, one needs the entire treatise. Wenzel himself compares the works to "punch-lines," and punch-lines can only be effective with the proper lead-ins. The reader who wants the whole story will be pleased to learn that Wenzel himself is contemplating a fuller edition that includes the Latin text, along with a translation even of the Middle English, which, despite the editor's excellent glosses, is often hard. Students who demand from literature more than superficial delight will look forward to its arrival.

JAMES J. WILHELM
Rutgers University

CHARLES R. YOUNG, *The Royal Forests of Medieval England*. Philadelphia: University of Pennsylvania Press, 1979. Pp. ix, 220; 3 maps. $14.00.

Hitherto, non-specialists inquiring about this subject have usually first consulted J. C. Cox, *The Royal Forests of England* (1905), and despite its anecdotal and antiquarian character Cox's book is in many respects not fully outdated; but as a political and administrative history it is quite superseded by C. R. Young's excellent new monograph. In narrative histories of the Middle Ages the forests are usually given minor treatment or considered an antiquarian curiosity. But, as Young reminds us, at their height of importance they may have comprised as much as a quarter of the arable land in England; they were in themselves subject not to the common law but to the king and his officials; in the twelfth and thirteenth centuries they were an immensely important source of royal income—in cash, kind, fees, etc. (see esp. pp. 130–34)—and from the late twelfth to the early fourteenth century their limits and the king's privileges in them were the subject of intense controversy between the king and his barons.

This study, amply documented from original sources and modern studies, is chiefly concerned with the period of controversy, from Henry II to the first years of Edward III, but some attention is given to the later fourteenth century. It is to a great extent a work of synthesis, with few major novelties, but it is nevertheless welcome and even necessary. The maps are enlightening, and although the technical terminology (eyre, swanimote, purpesture, agist, etc.) is unfamiliar and unexplained, Cox and the *OED* explain it. After reading Cox and Young, the interested reader can pursue the subject further by means of Young's exemplary and wide-ranging bibliography, the only major omission from which, from a literary standpoint, is E. F. Shannon, Jr., "A Medieval Law in Gamelyn" (*Speculum,* 26 [1951], 458–64). Marcelle Thiebaux, *The Stag of Love: The Chase in Medieval LIterature* (1974) probably appeared too late for inclusion.

Young devotes most of his attention to the causes and the effects of two periods of crisis involving royal-baronial conflict about the forests: in 1217 and following and in 1297 and following. According to him, a statute of 1 Edward III (1327) "may be taken as a turning point leading to the decline of the royal forest in the later fourteenth and fifteenth centuries" (p. 147). Thereafter, significant disafforestation occurred, and the administration of the forests decayed and was neglected. Young suggests that the diminished importance was due to declining revenues from the forests, to "the development of a system of public finances based upon taxes that could be levied on the growing commercial wealth of the nation" (p. 158), and to the necessity for taxation to conduct foreign wars under Edward I and later under Edward III and Richard II. Thereafter, "the attenuated royal forests were neglected and, having become insignificant for the economy, they declined into the hunting preserves from which they had begun" (p. 158). Writers before and after Shakespeare often imply that the great and familiar historical personages in and of themselves determined the issues and events of the reigns of Edward III and Richard II. It is salutary to be reminded that the decline of the forests and the consequent, necessary, and hateful introduction of such taxes— especially the poll taxes of 1377–80—were among the determining economic factors.

Young glances occasionally at literature. His discussion of the Robin Hood ballads and of other related matters confirms the popular impression, derived from those ballads, and their derivatives, of the harshness of forest law towards the common man (a harshness often tempered by practical inefficiency, however) and of the frequent corruption of forest officials. Even after the early fourteenth century, when the forests were no longer a political issue and the severity of punishment for infractions of the forest law had been reduced, a statute of 13 Richard II (1389–90) restricted hunting to the gentry. "Gamelyn" and Robin Hood provide the briefest of glimpses of the lower classes' dislike of and oppression by the aristocracy. In *Piers Plowman* (A VII; B VI; C IX), hunting is defended as an aristocratic privilege, whereby the commonalty's land is kept free of pests. Apparently, less humble folk than Piers himself often saw the matter differently.

Otherwise, none of the principal literary works of the age of Chaucer is relevant to Young, and this is a pity because his book is of the sort that can and should be used by non-specialists. Neither does he discuss the Petherton Forestership, held both by Geoffrey Chaucer and, after an interval, by Thomas Chaucer. (See Crow and Olson, *Chaucer Life-Records*, Ch. 24) But Young's demonstration that by this time such posts were often sinecures, and (though the case is not quite parallel) often hereditary, should be noted, however. Some years ago, in his *Chaucerian Problems, Especially the Petherton Forestership and the Question of Thomas Chaucer* (1932), Russell Krauss contended, as part of his argument that Thomas Chaucer was really John of Gaunt's son, that Geoffrey Chaucer's appointment to the post was due to Sir Peter de Courtenay and not to the Mortimers, who were closely allied to Richard II. J. M. Manly, however, demolished this contention (*RES*, 10 [1934], 257–73). Some literary historians apparently consider the matter still open; but—although this is to end this review on something of a tangent—one need not adopt the tone of an A. L. Rowse to assert that in historical matters even some literary historians may profit from the thorough acquaintance with primary sources shown by Manly and, in the study under consideration, by C. R. Young.

SUMNER FERRIS
California State College
California, Pennsylvania

An Annotated Chaucer Bibliography
1979

Compiled by John H. Fisher
University of Tennessee

With the assistance of:

Virginia E. Leland, *Bowling Green State University*; Robert ap Roberts, *California State University, Northridge;* Sumner Ferris, *California State College, Pennsylvania;* Thomas W. Ross, *Colorado College*; Edmund Reiss, Christopher B. Kennedy, David G. Allen, *Duke University*; Beverly Taylor, *University of North Carolina, Chapel Hill*; Daniel G. Ransom, Nancy Zorn, J. Lane Goodall, Nan Arbuckle, *University of Oklahoma*; N. F. Blake, *University of Sheffield*; Stanley Hauer, *University of Southern Mississippi*; Claire Clements, Penelope Minick, Timothy Shonk, Ute Stargardt, Michael Tierce, *University of Tennessee, Knoxville*; James Wimsatt, *University of Texas Austin*; Shinsuke Ando, *Tokyo University*; Werner Bies, *University of Trier*; Robert L. Kindrick, *Western Illinois University*; Constance Hieatt. D. F. Chapin, *University of Western Ontario*; Karl P. Wentersdorf, *Xavier University, Cincinnati*; Beryl Rowland, *York University*; Lorrayne Y. Baird, Janet Britton, Anne Davis, William Flynn, Elton Greer, Cynthia Logan, Mary Sue Michael, Virginia Monseau, Betty Romanello, Arlene Troyer, Kathleen Tuskan, Mary Lynn Varley, Ruth Vukovich, *Youngstown State University*.

This bibliography continues those since 1975 published in previous volumes of *Studies in the Age of Chaucer*. Bibliographical information up to 1975 may be found in Eleanor P. Hammond, *Chaucer: A Bibliographical Manual* (1908; rpt. New York: Peter Smith, 1933); D. D. Griffith, *Bibliography of Chaucer 1908–1953*, Seattle: Univ. of Washington Press, 1955; W. R. Crawford, *Bibliography of Chaucer 1954–1963*, Seattle: Univ. of Washington Press, 1967; Lorrayne Y. Baird, *Bibliography of Chaucer 1964–1973*, Boston: G. K. Hall, 1977; and J. H. Fisher, Bibliography for 1963–1974 in *The Complete Poetry and Prose of Geoffrey Chaucer*, New York: Holt, Rinehart and Winston, 1977.

The annotations are based upon listings in the 1979 *MLA International Bibliography*, with additions. Additions and corrections should be sent to John H. Fisher, Department of English, University of Tennessee, Knoxville, Tenn. 37916. Authors' own annotations (75 words for articles; 150 words for books) are invited. Preferably they should be sent on 5 x 8 index cards, and comply with the form of *SAC*'s published entries; for a list of abbreviations for Chaucer's works, see page 261. We will search the major journals for reviews published in any given year. However, authors are urged to send us citations to reviews which might otherwise be overlooked.

Classifications

General Treatments   1–3
Bibliographies and Dictionaries   4–12
Biography and Background   13–20
Scribes and Printers   21–22
Language and Prosody   23–35
Continental and Latin Influences   36–39
Chaucer's Influence   40–56
Narrative Technique, Characterization   57–64
Imagery, Symbolism   65–70
Canterbury Tales—Translations   71–72
CT—Manuscripts   73–75
CT—Design   76–77
CT—Genres   78–80
CT—Criticism   81–85
CT—Marriage Argument   86–88
CT—General Prologue   89
CT—The Knight and His Tale   90–91
CT—The Miller and His Tale   92–93
CT—The Reeve and His Tale   94–95
CT—The Cook and His Tale   95
CT—The Man of Law and His Tale   96–103
CT—The Wife of Bath and Her Tale   104–11
CT—The Friar and His Tale   112–13
CT—The Summoner and His Tale   114
CT—The Clerk and His Tale   115
CT—The Merchant and His Tale   116–21
CT—The Squire and His Tale   122
CT—The Franklin and His Tale   123–25
CT—The Physician and His Tale   126–27
CT—The Pardoner and His Tale   128–29
CT—The Shipman and His Tale   130–31
CT—The Prioress and Her Tale   132–35
CT—*The Tale of Sir Thopas*   136–37
CT—*The Tale of Melibee*   138

CT—The Monk and His Tale   139
CT—The Nun's Priest and His Tale   140–47
CT—The Second Nun and Her Tale   148
CT—The Canon's Yeoman and His Tale   148
CT—The Manciple and His Tale   149–50
CT—The Parson's Tale   79, 138
CT—The Retraction   151
Troilus and Criseyde—General   152–54
TC—Text   155
TC—Literary Relations   156–64
TC—The Theme of Love   165–69
TC—Narrative Technique   170–74
TC—Characterization   175–80
TC—Verbal Texture and Imagery   181–86
Book of the Duchess   187–92
Parliament of Fowls   193–200
House of Fame   201–05
Legend of Good Women   206–09
Short Poems   210–18
Boece   219–20
Book Reviews   221–32

Journal Abbreviations

AI	American Imago
AN&Q	American Notes and Queries
AnM	Annuale Mediaevale
CR	The Critical Review
ChauR	Chaucer Review
DAI	Dissertation Abstracts International
DQR	Dutch Quarterly Review of Anglo-American Letters
E&S	Essays and Studies
EAS	Essays in Arts and Sciences
ECS	Eighteenth-Century Studies
ELN	English Language Notes
ES	English Studies
JMRS	Journal of Medieval and Renaissance Studies
JWSL	Journal of Women Studies in Literature
KPAB	Kentucky Philological Association Bulletin
Lang&S	Language and Style
LangQ	Language Quarterly
LeedsSE	Leeds Studies in English
LHY	Literary Half-Yearly
MÆ	Medium Aevum
M&H	Medievalia et Humanistica
MP	Modern Philology
MSE	Massachusetts Studies in English
N&Q	Notes and Queries
Neophil	Neophilologus
NLH	New Literary History
NM	Neuphilologische Mitteilungen
PBSA	Papers of the Bibliographical Society of America
PLL	Papers on Language and Literature
PMLA	Publications of the Modern Language Association
PQ	Philological Quarterly
RES	Review of English Studies
SAC	Studies in the Age of Chaucer
SIcon	Studies in Iconography

SMC	Studies in Medieval Culture
SN	Studia Neophilologica
SP	Studies in Philology
StHum	Studies in the Humanities
TSLL	Texas Studies in Language and Literature
UTQ	University of Toronto Quarterly
YES	Yearbook of English Studies
WGCR	West Georgia College Review
YWES	Year's Work in English Studies

Bibliographical Citations and Annotations

General Treatments

1. Aers, David. *Chaucer, Langland and the Creative Imagination.* London: Routledge & Kegan Paul, 1979.

Aers explores the conflict between traditional Christian ideology and social and individual realities in *Piers Plowman*, and Langland's criticism of abuse of power in all ranks of the clerical hierarchy. Langland calls for reformation within traditional ideology, resolving the tensions apocalyptically in his poetry, but at the end rejecting a millenarian renewal, and sees conscience pursuing grace alone. Chaucer's "reflexivity" is seen in the Wife of Bath's mockery of ecclesiastical traditions, and in the Pardoner's exposures. *TC* reveals Chaucer's concern with the manipulative pressures that subordinate human relationships to patriarchal militaristic glory. The "marriage group" except for *FranT* in *CT* show how both sexes were engulfed in an orthodoxy which maintained women as subservient and marriage as a commodity exchange. *KnT* shows the realities of and human attitudes involved in militarism.

2. Mehl, Dieter. "Chaucer, Geoffrey," In *Enzyklopädie des Märchens.* Ed. Kurt Ranke. Vol. 2, Berlin: de Gruyter, 1979. Cols. 1256–67.

Emphasis on Chaucer's sources and narrative patterns in the light of fairy tales and the oral tradition.

3. Rowland, Beryl, ed. *Companion to Chaucer Studies*, revised ed. New York: Oxford UP, 1979.

The essays are listed under their separate authors.

Bibliographies and Dictionaries

4. Bazaire, Joyce and David Mills. "Middle English: Chaucer." *YWES* 57(1976):89–100.

5. Davis, Norman, and Douglas Gray, Patricia Ingham, and Anne Wallace-Hadrill. *A Chaucer Glossary*. Oxford: Clarendon, 1979.

A glossary based largely on the Tatlock and Kennedy *Concordance*. It does not go beyond A of *Rom*, nor does it cover the *Equatorie*. Different meanings are cited by line references; etymologies are provided; there is a useful introductory note on inflections.

6. Fisher, John H., et al. "An Annotated Chaucer Bibliography, 1975–76," *SAC* 1(1979): 201–55.

7. Kirby, Thomas A. "Chaucer Research in Progress: 1978–79." *NM* 80(1979): 280–86.

8. ———."Chaucer Research, 1978: Report No. 39." *ChauR* 14(1979):74–95.

9. Oizumi, Akio. "Chaucer Scholarship in America and the New Chaucer Society." *Eigo Seinen* 125(1979): 30–31. Kenkyusha Publishing Co. Ltd.

A survey of Chaucer scholarship in America.

10. Ridley, Florence. "The State of Chaucer Studies: A Brief Survey." *SAC* 1(1979):3–16.

Two major trends of the past two or three decades have been the attempt to define the Chaucerian aesthetic and to focus sharply on the poetry itself. Recently, there is a great increase in those critics who read medieval poetry in terms of modern, clinical psychology.

11. Shikii, Kumiko. "A Survey of Chaucerian scholarship." *SELLA* (1979): 61–77. Shirayuri English Language and Literature Association.

Some typical references are introduced to classify the characteristics of each period of Chaucerian scholarship from the fourteenth century to the present time. The paper also shows the necessity of trying a religious approach especially to *CT* to appreciate Chaucer's mind.

12. Tsuchiya, Tadayuki. *A Concordance and Glossary to the General Prologue of the Canterbury Tales*. Privately published, 1975.

A complete concordance to *GP* based on Robinson's second edition. All the words in *GP* are glossed on the basis of *OED* and *MMED*.

Biography and Background

13. Ackerman, Robert W. "Chaucer, the Church, and Religion." In *Companion to Chaucer Studies* [Item 3], pp. 21–41. Added in the second edition, replacing Olson's "Chaucer and Fourteenth-Century Society."

References to popular Christianity pervade Chaucer's work, especially *CT* and the shorter poems, but these usually concern the lower clergy and routine matters. His canon does not include ponderous didactic allegory or theological treatises.

14. Baugh, Albert C. "Chaucer the Man." In *Companion to Chaucer Studies* [Item 3], pp. 1–20. Repr. from the first (1968) edition, with updated bibliography.

Despite several still unresolved problems, Chaucer's life is well documented in the nearly 500 citations of the Crow and Olsen *Chaucer Life Records*, based on the previous researches of Manly, Rickert, and Redstone.

15. Hieatt, Constance B. " 'to boille the chiknes with the marybones': Hodge's Kitchen Revisited." In *Chaucerian Problems and Perspectives: Essays*

Presented to Paul E. Beichner, C.S.C. Ed. Edward Vasta and Zacharias P. Thundy. Notre Dame, Ind.: U of Notre Dame P, 1979, pp. 139–63.

Food and eating provide central images and activities in Chaucer's poetry. Misunderstanding the foods mentioned, Chaucer's readers may miss points essential to their comprehension of his poetry. The revolution in tastes and eating habits may be more a matter of emphasis than of basic techniques and ingredients.

16. Hira, Toshinori. "Chaucer's laughter." *Bulletin of the Faculty of Liberal Arts, Nagasaki University*, 20(1979): 27–42.

Chaucer as a court poet adapts himself to the pattern of sentiments of the court audience. He views the bourgeois pragmatism from the aristocratic standpoint. However, in his fabliaux he could deliberately make fun of the attitude of the aristocrats.

17. Mehl, Dieter. "Chaucer's Audience." *LeedsSE* 10(1978):58–74.

Chaucer obviously expects his audience to be familiar with his person, his previous writings, and his reputation as an author. He also expects his audience to reflect about the moral function of poetry. He draws his audience into his poetry by using his text to emphasize the importance of the reader's intelligent and imaginative responses. The greatness of his text allows him to evoke the desired responses.

18. Wentersdorf, Karl P. "The Clandestine Marriages of the Fair Maid of Kent." *Journal of Medieval History* 5(1979):202–31.

The obscure circumstances surrounding the three marriages of Joan of Kent are clarified by reference to the original documents. In 1340, at age 12, she secretly married Sir Thomas Holland. In 1341, while Holland was crusading in Prussia, she was compelled to marry William Montague, son of the Earl of Salisbury. In 1349, after protracted litigation, Holland secured a curial verdict annulling the marriage of Joan and Montague. When Holland died in 1360, Joan secretly married Edward, Prince of Wales, to the annoyance of his father who was trying to arrange a dynastic wedding.

19. Wood, Chauncey. *"Chaucer and Astrology."* In *Companion to Chaucer Studies* [Item 3], pp. 202–20. Repr. from the first (1968) edition, with updated bibliography.

Chaucer's many references to astrology have often been discussed, but only recently (as in Wood's *Chaucer and the Country of the Stars*) have there been any book-length studies of the subject and of its function in his poetry.

20. Woolf, Rosemary. "Moral Chaucer and Kindly Gower." In *J. R. R. Tolkien: Essays in Memoriam*. Ed. Mary Salu and Robert T. Farrell. Ithaca: Cornell UP, 1979. Pp. 221–45.

The epithets "moral" and "kindly" have for centuries been applied, respectively, to Gower and Chaucer, with a deleterious effect upon critical evaluation of the two poets. The epithets can revealingly be reversed. Gower is seen as kindly in his treatment of sexual matters (notably rape and incest in tales from the *Confessio Amantis*, for instance; while Chaucer's morality, though never obtrusive, is to be found even in such "immoral" tales as *MerT*, *FranT*, and *WBP*.

See also: 119   123   136   162   187

Scribes and Printers

21. Blodgett, James E. "Some Printer's Copy for William Thynne's 1532 Edition of Chaucer." *Library* 6th ser. 1(1979):97–113.

Identifies through examination of printer's marks the printer's copy for Thynne's text of *Rom, Bo, The Assembly of Ladies*, and the final six stanzas of *La Belle Dame sans Merci*.

22. Windeatt, Barry A. "The Scribes as Chaucer's Early Critics." *SAC* 1(1979):119–142.

Scribal transcriptions of Chaucer's work offer line-by-line "active readings" through numerous intentional variations in word choice and syntax. Comparisons of the mss yield inverse criticism which reflects the scribes' tendency for poetic cliché and emphasizes Chaucer's originality.

See also: 213   220.

Language and Prosody

23. Burrow, J. A. " 'Young Saint, Old Devil': Reflections on a Medieval Proverb." *RES* 30(1979):385–96.

Implicit in the proverb are two distinct views of the order of human development: the order is either a "high norm to be achieved" or a "low norm to be transcended." Although Chaucer never directly cites the proverb, evidence found in *KnT* and *PrT*, combined with the contrasts between the Knight and Squire and their respective tales, suggests he ascribed to the less orthodox view—the "nature ideal."

24. Cosmos, Spencer. "Toward a Visual Stylistics: Assent and Denial in Chaucer." *Visible Language* 12(1978):406–27.

Variations in spelling of words for 'yes' and 'no' are systemic in the literate language of Chaucer in that they distinguish the meanings of *no* and *nay*, *yis* and *yea*. As such, they are manifestations of visible language. Variant spellings of similar words exist in free variation in records of oral verse and are manifestations of audible language. Hence writing is not merely a mode of expressing speech, but a language in its own right.

25. Crépin, André. "From 'swutol sang scopes' to 'rum, ram, ruf,' or the Problems of Alliteration." *Actes du 2e Colloque de langue et de littérature écossaises (moyen âge et renaissance)*. Ed. Jean-Jacques Blanchot and Claude Graf. Université de Strasbourg, 1978, pp. 113–24.

In discussing the standard alliterative line in medieval English poetry, notes Chaucer's attitude toward alliteration in *ParsP* and, focussing on *TC*, shows the diminishing role of alliteration in Chaucer. Alliterative patterns and phrases provide ornaments for, not the structure of, his poetry.

26. Hoya, Katusuzo. Latin and French loan words in the 'General Prologue' to the *Canterbury Tales*." *Memoirs* 30(1979):39–51. Faculty of Liberal Arts and Education, Yamanashi University.

A complete list of the Latin and French loan words in *GP*, including proper nouns. Chaucer is indebted to earlier borrowings, especially to those in the *Ancrene Riwle*. The number of Chaucer's own borrowings is indicated. A high ratio of the borrowed verbs, next to the nouns and adjectives, proves the profundity of borrowing.

27. Ito, Eiko. "Reflexive verbs in Chaucer." *Studies in English Literature, English number* (March, 1978): 65–89. The English Literary Society of Japan.

An analysis of reflexive verbs in Chaucer within the case grammar framework. It shows the possibility of the semantic motivation of the reflexive pronoun and of a finer distinction of reflexivity in terms of the semantic relationship among the verb, reflexive pronoun, and other elements of the sentence.

28. Kuhn, Sherman M. "The Language of Some Fifteenth-Century Chaucerians: A Study of Manuscript Variants in the *Canterbury Tales*." *SMC* 4(1974): 472–82.

The four volumes of manuscript variants added to the Manly-Rickert edition of *CT* have been neglected too long.

29. Mustanoja, Tauno F. "Chaucer's Prosody." In *Companion to Chaucer Studies* [Item 3], pp. 65–94. Repr. from the first (1968) edition, with updated bibliography.

Chaucer's meters are of mixed Romance and native origin, but the details of scansion—whether the verse is accentual or syllabic and the pronunciation of final *e*—are still in dispute.

30. Nakao, Yoshiyuki. "Chaucer's use of proverbs—an aspect of Chaucer's convention and invention." *Phoenix* 15(1979):3–20. Graduate School of English Philology and Literature, Faculty of Letters, Hiroshima University.

Connotations of proverbs depend on their contexts—addresser, addressee, situation, purpose, etc. Chaucer's maturity in art is particularly discernible in his 'misapplication' of them. This deviant use provides him with ample linguistic resources to show his irony and humor.

31. Ogura, Mieko. "Metrix of Chaucer: an analysis based on the Kiparsky theory." *Lexicon* 8(1979):1–15. Iwasaki Linguistic Circle.

In view of Kiparsky's new theory (1977), we can show the differences of the metrical rules in the specific types of mismatches allowed in each of Chaucer's works. We can say that the constraints on mismatches became severer in an orderly way from Chaucer's early poetry to his late poetry.

32. Payne, Robert O. "Chaucer and the Art of Rhetoric." In *Companion to Chaucer Studies* [Item 3], pp. 42-64. Repr. from the first (1968) edition, with updated bibliography.

Scholars of the early twentieth century such as Naunin and Manly denied any significant influence of medieval rhetoric upon Chaucer. In more recent days, however, this attitude has been reversed, so that Payne (*The Key of Remembrance*) could claim that Chaucer's critical attitude quite closely resembles that of the rhetoricians.

33. Scheps, Walter. "Chaucer's Use of Nonce Words, Primarily in the *Canterbury Tales*." *NM* 80(1979):69–77.

Nonce words in *CT* illustrate a correlation between conventionality in subject matter and conventionality in diction. Because nonce words increase as Chaucer's career progresses, their frequency can be used for relative dating. Following this process, one would conclude that *Anel* is part of Chaucer's *juvenilia* and that the F version of the *Prologue* to *LGW* comes after either the G version or the legends themselves.

34. Shimogasa, Tokuji. " '–less' words in Chaucer." In *A Collection of Essays in Honour of Professor Hiroshige Yoshida*. Shinozaki Shorin Press, 1980, pp. 30–43.

Chaucer's '-less' words deserve our special consideration. Some ninety percent of all the '-less' words occur in verse. Though the total frequency is not so high, they may be said to fulfill an important function seen from a syntactical, stylistical, rhythmical, metrical and rhetorical viewpoint in Chaucer's poetry-making.

35. Shoaf, R. A. "Notes Toward Chaucer's Poetics of Translation." *SAC* 1(1979):55–66.

Fluent in English, French, Latin, and Italian, Chaucer realized the burden of responsibility in translating another poet's work. Also highly aware of the mutability of language, he sought to re-create new meaning in translations which he hoped would endure into the future.

See also: 46 54 68 92 94 98 131 134 137 149 178 182 183 186 210 219

Continental and Latin Influences

36. Braddy, Haldeen. "The French Influence on Chaucer." In *Companion to Chaucer Studies* [Item 3], pp. 143–59. Repr. from the first (1968) edition, with updated bibliography.

The French strain in Chaucer's poetry (though obviously strongest in his earlier career) pervades his *ouvre*. So far as is known, however, Chaucer himself never wrote an original line in that tongue.

37. Fyler, John M. *Chaucer and Ovid*. New Haven: Yale UP, 1979.

Unlike Ovid and Dante, who speak for fate and the universal order, Chaucer and Ovid speak for "the comic pathos of human frailty and human pretensions." The central concern of Chaucer's *HF, BD, PF, LGW, TC, KnT*, and *NPT* is with the attempt, and failure, of the narrator or his surrogate to remain detached and to control the flow of events. This Ovidian paradigm provides a fresh reading of the poems.

38. Hoffman, Richard L. "The Influence of the Classics on Chaucer." In *Companion to Chaucer Studies* [Item 3], pp. 185–201. Repr. from the first (1968) edition, with updated bibliography.

Chaucer's favorite Latin author was Ovid, followed by Virgil and Statius, as well as several prose writers. The central problem in evaluating the Latin influence on Chaucer is to determine what sorts of manuscripts he used—not just texts, but glosses, commentaries, and the entire apparatus of his contemporary medieval scholarship.

39. Ruggiers, Paul G. "The Italian Influence on Chaucer." In *Companion to Chaucer Studies* [Item 3], pp. 160–84. Repr. from the first (1968) edition, with updated bibliography.

Chaucer made at least two authenticated journeys to Italy whereby he gained a knowledge of the works of Dante, Petrarch, and Boccaccio. Curiously, though he borrowed extensive narrative material from Boccaccio, Chaucer never mentions him by name as he does the other two. Chaucer's use of Petrarch is slight, and the influence of Dante (aside from the tragedy of Ugolino) is mostly confined to images.

See also: 110   120   125   158   160   192   196   200   209   218

Chaucer's Influence

40. Benson, C. David. "Troilus and Cresseid in Henryson's Testament." *ChauR* 13(1979):263–71.

In Henryson's poem, contrary to traditional interpretation, Troilus is the more limited character and Cresseid the more noble.

41. Berry, Reginald. "Chaucer Transformed 1700–1721." *DAI* 40(1979) 231A.

The poets' adaptations of Chaucer's work in this era reflect the nature and principles of Chaucerian transformation for the eighteenth century. In his *Fables*

Dryden emphasized the moral nature of the original poems and thus established a tradition which Pope and the members of the Scriblerus Club, among others, were to follow. By the time of Urry's 1721 edition, the scholarly and popular traditions of the seventeenth century had coalesced in the common reader.

42. ———. "Chaucer and Absalom and Achitophel." *N&Q* 26(1979): 522–23.

The discovery of Dryden's indebtedness to Chaucer (*TC*, V, 817: "That Paradis stood formed in hire yen") for a line in *Absalom* ("And *Paradise* was open'd in his face") is attributed in the California edition of Dryden's works to an article published in 1943. In fact, the indebtedness was noted much earlier—in 1720 by George Sewell.

43. Clogan, Paul. "Chaucer and Leigh Hunt." *M&H* 9(1979):163–74.

Like most of the early nineteenth-century critics, Leigh Hunt strove to bring about a popular revival of Chaucer. But more important, he was among the first to attempt a technical analysis of Chaucer's poetry and to link his poetry with the idea of music. Hunt added greatly to the Romantic conception of the poet.

44. Flahiff, Frederick T. "*The Great Gatsby:* Scott Fitzgerald's Chaucerian Rag." In *Figures in a Ground: Canadian Essays on Modern Literature Collected in Honor of Sheila Watson*. Saskatoon: Western Producer Prairie, 1978, pp. 87–98.

The movement of *Gatsby* was compared to that of *TC* by Nancy Hoffman in 1971. However, the differences are as significant as the similarities. Fitzgerald's story reflects different preoccupations, a different age. Chaucer created something poised and terrible and elegant. Fitzgerald produced a story of the 20's, something equivalent to his own Age of Confusion.

45. Hunter, Michael. "Alexander Pope and Geoffrey Chaucer." In *The Warden's Meeting: A Tribute to John Sparrow*. Oxford: Oxford Univ. Society of Bibliophiles, 1977, pp. 29–32.

Hunter describes a copy of the 1602 edition of Chaucer in his possession signed "A. Pope." The volume is defective, lacking the first gathering. The signature comes at the beginning of gathering B. There are no marginalia. Presumably this was a duplicate in Pope's library. In the Hurd library at Hartlebury Castle, Worcestershire, there is a copy of the 1598 Chaucer inscribed "Ex libris Alexandri Popei" with marginal annotations. Presumably this was Pope's working copy.

46. Jeffery, C. D. "Anglo-Scots Poetry and the *Kingis Quair*." *Actes du 2e colloque de langue et de littérature écossaises (moyen âge et renaissance)*. Ed. Jean-Jacques Blanchot and Claude Graf. Université de Strasbourg, 1978), pp. 207–21.

By means of vocabulary items, characteristics of Chaucerian English as found in the *Kingis Quair* are noted in passing.

47. Miskimin, Alice. "The Design of Douglas's *Palice of Honour*." *Actes du 2e colloque de langue et de littérature écossaises (moyen âge et renaissance)*, ed. Jean-Jacques Blanchot and Claude Graf (Université de Strasbourg, 1978), pp. 198–206.

Discussion of the literary background of Douglas's poem takes account of Chaucer's references to music, especially in *HF* and *PF*.

48. ———. "The Illustrated Eighteenth–Century Chaucer." *MP* 77(1979):26-55.

Two sets of Chaucer illustrations altered the late eighteenth-century and early Romantic readers' perception of Chaucer: George Vertue's for Urry's edition (1721), and Thomas Stothard's for Bell (1782–83). Stothard's illustrations were later developed into his large "cabinet picture," *The Procession of Chaucer's Pilgrims*, engravings of which had wide sale and popularity far greater than Blake's Chaucer work. Blake rejected the Roman-type editions of Tyrwhitt and Urry and returned to the black-letter of Speght (1687) for quotations in his *Advertisement* for Chaucer engravings (1809–12).

49. Newlyn, Evelyn S. "Of Sin and Courtliness: Henryson's Tale of the Cock and the Fox." *Actes du 2e Colloque de langue et de littérature écossaises (moyen âge et renaissance)*. Ed. Jean-Jacques Blanchot and Claude Graf. Université de Strasbourg, 1978, pp. 268–77.

Whereas Henryson's tale focuses on flattery and pride, and with the relationship of these sins to language, Chaucer's *NPT*—a likely source for Henryson—emphasizes the rhetoric of heroic poetry and the question of women's opinions. These different emphases are reflected in the structures of the two poems.

50. Reisner, M. E. "Effigies of Power: Pitt and Fox as Canterbury Pilgrims." *ECS* 12(1979):481–503.

Blake's portraits of the Pardoner and Summoner in *Chaucer's Canterbury Pilgrims* bear strong resemblances to contemporary satirical portraits of William Pitt the Younger and Charles James Fox, respectively. The descriptions of the two pilgrims in *GP* and in their individual tales closely parallel the physical traits, tastes, abilities, and personalities of the historical figures.

51. Reiss, Edmund. "Dunbar's Self-Revelation and Poetic Tradition." *Actes du 2e colloque de langue et de littérature écossaises (moyen âge et renaissance)*. Ed. Jean-Jacques Blanchot and Claude Graf. Université de Strasbourg, 1978, pp. 326–38.

Dunbar's so-called autobiographical references are comparable to Chaucer's references to himself in his poetry. Also Dunbar's references employ conventions that may be found in Chaucer.

52. Robbins, Rossell Hope. "The Structure of Longer Middle English Court Poems." In *Chaucerian Problems and Perspectives: Essays Presented to Paul E. Beichner, C.S.C.* Ed. Edward Vasta and Zacharias P. Thundy. Notre Dame, Ind.: U of Notre Dame P, 1979, pp. 244–64.

English fifteenth-century court verse, comprising formal lyrics and Chaucerian apocrypha, has been neglected because it is not major, not easily accessible, and lacks appropriate criticism. Bases for a critical rationale include awareness of its purpose: the diversion of a small, elite group; of the two genres of the brief poems—salutations and complaints; of the structure of the longer poems, extensions of the two genres by the use of formal rhetorical devices.

53. Schöwerling, Rainer. "Chaucer's *Troilus and Criseyde* in der Englischen Literatur von Henryson bis Dryden." *Anglia* 97(1979):326–49.

Schöwerling investigates the influence of Chaucer's *TC* on four writers of the fifteenth through seventeenth centuries. Writers and works discussed include: Henryson's *Testament of Cresseid*, Sidnam's paraphrase of *TC*, Shakespeare's *Troilus and Cressida* and Dryden's *Troilus and Cressida, or Truth Found too Late*. Henryson's work is tragic in tone and imparts a moral. Conversely, Sidnam's paraphrase is best described as a tragicomedy. Shakespeare's *Troilus and Cressida* is the most innovative, while Dryden's heroic tragedy includes a major fall for Hector, Troilus, and Criseyde.

54. Stevens, Martin. "The Royal Stanza in Early English Literature." *PMLA* 94(1979):67–76.

The rhyme royal stanza takes its name from the fact that it was used in ballade contests in the fourteenth century to address real or imaginary royalty. Chaucer employed the stanza first for royal address in *PF* and *TC*. In *MLT* he used it to create a high style. "Prose" in *MLT* means formal stanzas of equal length.

55. Straus, Barrie Ruth. "The Role of the Reader in the *Kingis Quair*." *Actes du 2e colloque de langue et de littérature écossaises (moyen âge et renaissance)*. Ed. Jean-Jacques Blanchot and Claude Graf. Université de Strasbourg, 1978, pp. 198–206.

Reading is more important to the meaning of the *Kingis Quair* than it is to the meaning of Chaucer's dream poems. This point is demonstrated by an analysis of *PF*.

56. Swart, Felix, "Chaucer and the English Reformation." *Neophil* 62(1978):616–19.

The Plowman's Tale, first appearing in Chaucer's *Works* in 1542, and the *Pilgrim's Tale*, printed not earlier tha 1536, both clearly based on earlier material, could be clever forgeries or retouched, but substantially genuine, medieval poems. Their intended effect was to make Chaucer posthumously support the English Reformation.

See also: 121 127 161 163

Narrative Technique, Characterization

57. Grossman, Judith. "The Correction of a Descriptive Schema: Some 'Buts' in Barbour and Chaucer." *SAC* 1(1979):41–54.

John Barbour in *The Bruce* (1375) depicts Sir James Douglas as conforming to the knightly ideal in character and manner, but not in physical appearance. In Chaucer's *TC* Criseyde occasionally departs from the pattern of idealized heroine. Through observing the complexity of individuals, Barbour and Chaucer develop a new criterion for criticizing and correcting prescribed description.

58. Jordan, Robert M. "Chaucerian Narrative." In *Companion to Chaucer Studies* [Item 3], pp. 95–116. Repr. from the first (1968) edition, with updated bibliography.

Emphasis has shifted from the study of Chaucer as a realist and proto-novelist to the examination of his mode of presentation and his esthetics: principles of rhetoric, uses of style, and poetic theory.

59. Minnis, A. J. "Medieval Discussions of the Role of the Author: A Preliminary Survey, with Particular Reference to Chaucer and Gower." *DAI* 37(1976–77):1534C.

Theological commentators in the Middle Ages distinguished between the roles of *auctor* and *compilator*. Gower seems to have modeled his main literary stances (as *propheta* in the *Vox Clamantis* and *sapiens* in the *Confessio Amantis*) on the theological descriptions of the authorial role. By contrast, Chaucer gradually became aware of the potential of the *compilatio*, which he fully exploited in *CT*. The literary stances which he adopted in this work resemble the compilers' descriptions of their role.

60. Rowland, Beryl. "What Chaucer Did to the Fabliau." *SN* 51(1979):205–13.

Like his French predecessors, Chaucer employs a commonplace detail and dialogue to impart to his fabliaux a sense of domestic, small town, and rural life. However, while unity in design and treatment characterize the French fabliaux,

Chaucer's are disjunctive and digressive. He juxtaposes discrete materials, thereby interrupting continuous development. Recurring patterns of imagery and irony help to conceal the disjunctive character of the stories.

61. Salter, Elizabeth, and Derek Pearsall. "Chaucer's Realism." In *English Poetry*. Ed. Alan Sinfield. London: Sussex, 1976, pp. 36–51. (Edited oral dialogue.)

It can be difficult to be sure what is "realistic" and what "typical," "idealized," or traditionally "patterned" in Chaucer's work, especially when "realism" of different degrees and types is often woven into a formal structure which is anything but realistic in intent. Irony, comic exaggeration, moral structure, and convention qualify what we can see of character development and realistic content.

62. Sato, Tsutomu. *Sentence and Solaas: Thematic Development and Narrative Technique in the Canterbury Tales*. Tokyo: Kobundo-Publishing Co., 1979.

The author investigates some of the ways in which Chaucer exploited the scheme of *CT* to enlighten us about the nature of the art of narrative, and demonstrates some of the modern senses in which the poet dramatized the medieval pilgrims with reference to both fictional and real characters, and represented to us an eternal human comedy. The author especially pays attention to a full understanding of the pilgrim-tale relationship which affords the fundamental dramatic principle of *CT*. At the same time he fixes his attention on the invention of Chaucer the pilgrim-narrator who tells the whole Canterbury event as persona of Chaucer, the poet, who has created the total poetic structure, the various elements of narration, and the narrative technique.

63. Stolz, Anne Crehan. "The Artifice of Temporality: A Study of Unfinishedness in Chaucer." *DAI* 39 (1979):5498A.

The signs of unfinishedness which appear most prominently in Chaucer's unfinished pieces are also present in the more finished pieces, where they make a major contribution to Chaucer's meaning. Chaucer's unfinishedness is due in part to the uses he found for incomplete or non-definitive statement and due in part to the aesthetic tradition he inherited. The richness of vision and the multiplicity of meaning which characterize his work are due in large part to the philosophical unfinishedness of his art.

64. Strohm, Paul. "Form and Social Statement in *Confessio Amantis* and *The Canterbury Tales.*" *SAC* 1(1979):17–40.

Gower's *Confessio* and Chaucer's *CT* reflect a process of mediation in which problematic social realities are restated or reconceived. The two writers treat two medieval aesthetics, unity-in-diversity and hierarchies, though Chaucer encourages contrary possibilities while Gower seeks to reconcile old forms and new content.

See also: 86 98 102 149 203

Imagery, Symbolism

65. Heffernan, Ann Falve. "Wells and Streams in Three Chaucerian Gardens." *PLL* 15(1979):339–57.

The functioning of wells and streams in Chaucer's employment of the garden *topos* suggests that, where the secular materials are drawn from the courtly love tradition, as in *PF* and very largely in *MerT*, religious echoes expose the illusiveness or inadequacy of romantic love. The primary effect of the merger in *FranT* is that religious and secular materials, classical as well as romantic, support the impression that love on earth can be a 'verray paradise.'

66. Kanno, Masahiko. "Subtlety in Chaucer's expression—a dual view." *Hiroshima Studies in English Language and Literature,* 29(1979):54–68. The English Literary Association of Hiroshima University.

The simile applied to the Friar—"His nekke *whit* was *as the flour-de-lys*"—functions externally and internally. The outward sign of his neck is symbolic of his inner degraded state of mind, which shows physiognomically a mark of licentiousness or depravity.

67. Kleinstück, Johannes. "Chaucer." In *Wörterbuch der Symbolik*. Ed. Manfred Lurker. Stuttgart: Kröner, 1979.

Emphasis on Chaucer's use of symbols.

68. Parr, Roger P. "Chaucer's Art of Portraiture." *SMC* 4(1974): 428–36.

Chaucer's art of characterization is an act of poetic creation rather than the mere use of rhetorical convention. By employing rhetorical devices which vivify emotion and intensify dramatic action, or which infuse suggestion of movement, Chaucer subordinates technique to artistic vision and releases narrative art from static rhetorical conventions.

69. Rowland, Beryl. "Chaucer's Imagery." In *Companion to Chaucer Studies* [Item 3], pp. 117–42. Repr. from the first (1968) edition, with updated bibliography.

Chaucer's figurative language is mostly traditional, but its effect usually transcends the merely visual: it is emotional and intellectual—aiming at more than concrete realism. Often, however, the nature of this imagery eludes us because Chaucer's world is so different from ours.

70. Windeatt, Barry A. "Gesture in Chaucer." *M&H* 9(1978):143–61.

Chaucer frequently gives his characters gestures which are not in his sources in order more fully to reflect the inner lives of the actors. His most frequent gestures center on eyes and faces.

See also: 82   115   135   148   184   185

Canterbury Tales—Translations

71. Caluwé-Dor, Juliette de, tr. *Les Contes de Cantorbéry, Ière partie*. Ktēmata 5. Ghent: Éditions Scientifiques E. Story-Scientia, 1977.

This translation into French of *GP, KnT, MilT,* and *NPT,* representing the first part of a projected complete translation of *CT,* aims to present a text as faithful to Chaucer's English as the French language allows. With a few exceptions it is based on Robinson's edition. The notes at the end serve to explain the text—especially obscure allusions and strange terms—or to justify translations.

72. Donohue, James J., ed. *Chaucer's Canterbury Tales Complete, in Present-Day English.* Dubuque: Loras Coll. P, 1979.

CT—Manuscripts

73. Blake, N. F. "The Relationship between the Hengwrt and the Ellesmere Manuscripts of the 'Canterbury Tales'." *E&S* 32(1979):1–18.

El is based on Hg, the first published text. Hg arranged the thirteen apparently unrelated fragments of the one copytext left by Chaucer not by geographical and chronological features which exercise modern critics but by a sequence of tale-link-tale. The Wife of Bath's role and the spurious *CYT* led El's editor to improve this order by positioning *WBPT, MerT,* and *ClT* as closely as possible and by creating the sequence *SNT, CYT, MancT.*

74. Keiser, George P. "The Collation of the Cardigan Chaucer Manuscript." *PBSA* 73(1979):333–34.

The explanation for the condition of quire 10 in *CT* is that the leaves became disarranged after the scribe had completed the first half. The order that resulted from his error was ii-iii-i-iv-v-vi. After this faulty order was corrected, the order of the second half became vii-viii-ix-xi-xii-x. In order to correct this problem and facilitate binding, another scribe recopied x onto a folio with a stub. This stub now appears between iii and iv.

75. Killough, George. "The Virgule in the Poetry of the *Canterbury Tales.*" *DAI* 39(1979):5496A.

Virgule placement in the Hengwrt and Ellesmere mss. is highly regular. Syntactic and metrical rules can be used to predict 80 percent of the placements. The two mss agree in virgule placement 77 percent of the time. The 23 percent rate of disagreement indicates that the scribes must have placed the virgules

213

according to the same sort of rules rather than from an examplar. The practice of midline poetic punctuation has precedent in Latin grammatical theory.

See also: 28

CT—Design

76. Owen, Charles A., Jr. "The Design of the *Canterbury Tales.*" In *Companion to Chaucer Studies* [Item 3], pp. 221–42. Repr. from the first (1968) edition, with updated bibliography.

Since Kittredge, we have come to see a dramatic structure at the heart of *CT*, with interaction not only among the tellers but also among the tales themselves. Many points, however, are still in dispute: the order of the tales, the question of symbolic interpretations, and the nature of *ParsT* and *Ret*.

77. Thundy, Zacharias P. "Significance of Pilgrimage in Chaucer's *Canterbury Tales.*" *LHY* 20, ii(1979):64–77.

Chaucer is careful to dwell on the pilgrimage to Canterbury as an interior, not merely as an exterior, experience, thus giving it an allegorical significance. This allegory can be seen as twofold: a journey from reason to faith and a movement from human to divine love.

See also: 59 73

CT—Genres

78. Brewer, Derek S. "The Fabliaux." In *Companion to Chaucer Studies* [Item 3], pp. 296–325. Repr. from the first (1968) edition, with updated bibliography.

The advance of the fabliaux in critical estimation is perhaps the major development of twentieth-century Chaucer studies. The fabliau—an *upper*-class genre ridiculing the buffooneries of the *lower* classes and clergy—flourished in thirteenth-century France but was moribund by the time Chaucer resurrected and refined it in England.

79. Ebin, Lois. "Chaucer, Lydgate, and the 'Myrie Tale'." *ChauR* 13(1979):316–36.

In *CT* Chaucer defines and redefines "myrie tale." Ultimately it is neither mere entertainment, nor pure instruction, nor even sentence and solace. A truly "myrie tale" must be "fructuous," i.e., truly edifying. Only *ParsT* fits, for poetry is inherently ambiguous, unreliable, fruitless. Lydgate disagrees. In his "Canterbury Tale," *The Siege of Thebes*, he gives poetry a political dimension and makes the tale a moral speculum that is beneficial practically as well as spiritually.

80. Severs, J. Burke. "The Tales of Romance." In *Companion to Chaucer Studies* [Item 3], pp. 271–95. Repr. from the first (1968) edition, with updated bibliography.

Chaucer's romances include *KnT, SqT, WBT, FranT,* and *Th*; but "Chaucer's realism, humor, and interest in character all tend to transform his romances into something beyond what one usually finds in the genre."

CT—Criticism

81. Dove, Mary. "The Criticism of Medieval Literature: A Sermon and an Exemplum." *CR* 21(1979):36–44.

It is a common misconception that the criticism of medieval literature is different from that of modern literature and thereby less satisfactory. The proper goal of the critic of medieval literature should be to discern (1) how the work was formed by its period, (2) how it informs us about that period, and (3) how it is independent of its period. A brief study of the description of the Yeoman from *CT* shows how complex this process can be.

82. Fleming, John V. "Chaucer's Ascetical Images." *Christianity and Literature* 28,iv(1979):19–26.

Chaucer is the rule for vernacular poets rather than the exception. His appropriation of monastic patterns of thought and ascetic ideas and imagery were a tradition already becoming a classic in his time. In *CT*, the Summoner's portrait, the Pardoner's portrait, and the friar of *SumT* all adhere to and exemplify the exegetical traditions of Christian asceticism. Most significant is the manner in which Chaucer makes traditional exegetical details his own.

83. Miller, Robert P. "Allegory in the *Canterbury Tales*," In *Companion to Chaucer Studies* [Item 3], pp. 326–51. Repr. from the first (1968) edition, with updated bibliography.

The much-disputed allegorical criticism of *CT* is a fairly recent phenomenon. Chaucer's allegories may be either "formal" (e.g., *ClT*) or "informal" (*KnT*)—both styles deriving from "a reservoir of established meanings shared by the poet and his audience."

84. Ramsey, Vance. "Modes of Irony in the *Canterbury Tales*." In *Companion to Chaucer Studies* [Item 3], pp. 352–79. Rep. from the first (1968) edition, with updated bibliography.

Irony—"the Chaucerian pose"—is of five basic types in *CT*: verbal, structural, dramatic, and philosophic irony, as well as irony of manner.

85. Rudat, Wolfgang E. H. "The *Canterbury Tales*: Anxiety Release and Wish Fulfillment." *AI* 35(1978):407–18.

The Canterbury pilgrimage is, among other things, an attempt by some of the pilgrims to sublimate the sex drive. The Merchant indirectly admits his sexual inadequacy (he is January); the Prioress her fear of the opposite sex (the little "clergeon's" murder is a form of castration); the Monk his desire to masturbate (God, after all, made Adam with his "owene fynger"); and the Pardoner his sexual fraudulence (he is a eunuch). Such confessions as these pilgrims make help to release their fears and anxieties.

See also: 33 48 50 62 64

CT—The Marriage Argument

86. Knapp, Janet Schlauch. "A Grammar of Narrative." *DAI* 38(1978):6690A.

The basic narrative unit is limited to nine possible combinations. These combinations can be illustrated by application to the four tales of the Marriage Group in *CT*. These nine relationships can also be applied to characters, to the relationships among speech acts, and to the relationships of the participants in story-telling sessions. All of these interactions serve to illustrate the difference between successful and unsuccessful narratives.

87. Richmond, Velma Bourgeois. " 'Pacience in Adversitee': Chaucer's Presentation of Marriage." *Viator* 10(1979):323–54.

Marriage has important positive values in medieval narrative, including Chaucer's. The "Marriage Group" constitutes not so much a debate over sexual dominance in marriage as a varied demonstration of the need for mutual consideration and forgiveness, and a condemnation of force, selfishness, and illicit sexuality: it is generally a man who has most to learn and/or to gain through forbearance or reconciliation. These views are also clear in *TC, MancT,* and *Mel*.

88. Takimoto, Jiro. "Re-examination of the marriage group in the *Canterbury Tales*." *Baika Review* 12(1979):1–24. English and American Literature Society, Baika Women's College.

Kittredge's dialectical interpretation of the Marriage Group in *CT* is re-examined in terms of the different views presented by W. W. Lawrence, D. R. Howard, J. L. Hodge, and C. C. Olson. The conclusion is that there seems little to be revised in Kittredge's fundamental thesis.

See also: 104

CT—General Prologue

89. Kirby, Thomas A. "The General Prologue." In *Companion to Chaucer Studies* [Item 3], pp. 243–70. Repr. from the first (1968) edition, with updated bibliography.

GP not only is a brilliant poem in itself but also sets the tone for the entire work to follow. It skillfully blends the real with the ideal world—all seen through the device of a narrative persona. Chaucer uses several devices for description, but varies them for dramatic effect; he describes, for example, only one representative for each profession.

See also: 12   26   50   82   148

CT—The Knight and His Tale

90. Boheemen, Christel van. "Chaucer's *Knight's Tale* and the Structure of Myth." *DQR* 9(1979):1–27.

The fundamental distinction in *KnT* is not between Palamon and Arcite, but between them and Theseus. The Dionysian misrule of Thebes is symbolically contrasted to the Apollonian order of Athens. The mythic structure of the narrative prepares a gradual process of overcoming the distance separating Theseus and the knights.

91. Roney, Lois Yvonne. "Scholastic Philosophies in Chaucer's Knight's Tale." *DAI* 39(1979):5498A.

KnT is a scholastic romance whose primary subject is universal human nature conceived in varying combinations of will and intellect, and its overriding concern is man's freedom. From its position as the first Canterbury tale, one might infer that human nature will be the concern of the links and tales that follow. Since Theseus becomes a better man figuring out the significance of events, one might infer that the significance of the tales will also depend on the mind of the reader.

See also: 23   57   80   83   93   122   148

CT—The Miller and His Tale

92. Blake, N. F. " 'Astromye' in 'The Miller's Tale'." *N&Q* 26 (1979):110–11.

Twice the carpenter in *MilT* uses "astromye": is it a malapropism, an acceptable variant, or a scribal error? Since according to Manly-Rickert all mss of *CT* record "astromye," the last of these is not tenable. And since the word thus misused does not take on the form of another word, it cannot be a malapropism, though the evidence we have for these matters come 200 years after Chaucer wrote. It must therefore be considered an allowable variant without any connotation of barbarism or illiteracy.

93. Reiss, Edmund. "Chaucer's *deerne love* and the Medieval View of Secrecy in Love." In *Chaucerian Problems and Perspectives: Essays Presented to Paul E. Beichner, C.S.C.* Ed. Edward Vasta and Zacharias P. Thundy. Notre Dame, Ind.: U of Notre Dame P, 1979, pp. 164–79.

Although giving the impression of belonging to the world of courtesy, *deerne love* is actually more pertinent to the activities detailed in fabliaux. But secrecy, even when it would appear to be taken seriously, causes destruction of love and lovers. While directing Chaucer's narrative in *MilT*, it also suggests comically the true nature of the passion. It also provides a comment on the love described in *KnT*.

See also: 60   95   148   168

CT—The Reeve and His Tale

94. Blake, N. F. "The Northernisms in *The Reeve's Tale*." *Lore and Language* 3,i(1979):1–8.

Despite Tolkien's praise of Chaucer's "accurate observation" of dialects in *RvT*, examination of the mss of *CT* reveals that Chaucer's knowledge of northern dialect was in no way exceptional and that many of the northern speech characteristics of the two students were added by later scribes.

95. Spearing, A. C., and J. E. Spearing, eds. *The Reeve's Prologue & Tale*. Cambridge: Cambridge UP, 1979.

Despite its low reputation, the artistry and comic power of *RvT* supply outstanding examples of Chaucer's mature art. The manner in which it springs from *MilT* is proof of Chaucer's ingenious linking of tales. In the same manner, *CkT* and its *Prologue* are also effectively linked to *RvT* and *CkT* in a single volume allows the reader to examine Chaucer's methods of connecting one tale with another in a more than superficial way.

See also: 60

CT—The Cook and His Tale

See: 95

CT—The Man of Law and His Tale

96. Burch, Beth. "Chaucer's 'Man of Law's Tale' and 'The Handless Maiden'." *LangQ* 17, iii-iv(1979):50–51.

Chaucer's version of *MLT* is more like Trivet's the folktale version identified as "The Handless Maiden." If Chaucer knew this folktale version, his choice of Trivet's more sophisticated version is another tribute to his art.

97. Clasby, Eugene. "Chaucer's Constance: Womanly Virtue and the Heroic Life." *ChauR* 13(1979):221–33.

Constance is not, as Delany (1974) claims, a character who embodies and recommends self-degradation and abject submission to power in all its forms. What is important is that Constance discovers in the course of her experience that Providence, not Fortune, governs and establishes the meaning of her life.

98. Clogan, Paul M. "The Narrative Style of the Man of Law's Tale." *M&H* 8(1977):217–33.

MLT relies less on organic structure than on the "exemplary episodic narrative sequence" of hagiographic tradition. Likewise the rhetorical flourishes of the narrator recall the learned stance expected of the hagiographer.

99. Farrell, Robert T. "Chaucer's Man of Law and His Tale: the Eccentric Design." In *J. R. R. Tolkien: Essays in Memoriam*. Ed. Mary Salu and Robert T. Farrell. Ithaca: Cornell UP, 1979, pp. 159–72.

Previous criticism often finds an unresolved tension between tale and teller in *MLT* and in the tale itself, leading a critic like Edward A. Block to declare the work "poor art." However, the admitted tensions within the tale between a feeling of despair and the slim hope of salvation, ultimately reveal the teller as "an acutely troubled intelligence."

100. Loomis, Dorothy Bethurum. "Constance and the Stars." In *Chaucerian Problems and Perspectives: Essays Presented to Paul E. Beichner, C.S.C.* Ed. Edward Vasta and Zacharias P. Thundy. Notre Dame, Ind.: U of Notre Dame P, 1979, pp. 207–20.

The story of Constance is not especially appropriate to the Man of Law. Chaucer was attracted to it because it is a good piece of fiction and because it gave him the perfect opportunity to set forth and justify his belief in astrology. The story illustrates perfectly how a Christian could believe in astrology and not be a complete determinist.

101. Manning, Stephen. "Chaucer's Constance: Pale and Passive." In *Chaucerian Problems and Perspectives: Essays Presented to Paul E. Beichner, C.S.C.* Ed. Edward Vasta and Zacharias P. Thundy. Notre Dame, Ind.: U of Notre Dame P, 1979, pp. 13–23.

Constance is not the passive ninny she has been accused of being. She possesses a presence which demands and receives forcible response; she moves in her world with self-sufficiency; her virture is heroic; her ability to accept what God sends gives her an imposing strength. Constance's force of soul is such that she can remain detached from what befalls her. She is always aware of the emotional cost of yielding to Providence.

102. Theiner, Paul. "The Man of Law Tells His Tale." *SMC* 5(1975):173–79.

In *MLT* Chaucer does not change the events found in Trivet, but, rather, transforms their telling so as to alter our perceptions of them. His purposeful complicating expresses the Man of Law's narrative technique.

103. Weissman, Hope Phyllis. "Late Gothic Pathos in the *MLT*." *JMRS* 9,i(1979):133–53.

Past opinions are either that Chaucer was profoundly involved with the tale and reflected the period's emotionalism or that he was detached and disenchanted with the narrator. Actually the tale is an exposure of the "publicly sentimentalizing sensibility" of the age. Chaucer aligns his aesthetic with that of late medieval devotional art in its most ornamental and histrionic form. But adherence to such an aesthetic may lead to spiritual complacency, which Chaucer seeks to unsettle by converting the tale into "a profoundly earnest jest," with some outright parody.

CT—The Wife of Bath and Her Tale

104. Berggren, Ruth. "Who *Really* Is the Advocate of Equality in the Marriage Group?" *MSE* 6(1977):25–36.

Contrary to received opinion, the Wife of Bath argues implicitly for equality in marriage; she and the loathly lady in her tale gain dominance only to relinquish it. On the other hand, the Clerk, Merchant, and Franklin present views of women which deny the viability of marital equality.

105. Carruthers, Mary. "The Wife of Bath and the Painting of Lions." *PMLA* 94(1979):209–22.

Alisoun has learned through experience that her marital happiness depends on practical economic control rather than on surrender to the ideal of feminine subservience espoused by authorities. Her tale parodies these authorities in its mock-idealistic reversal of emphasis from masculine to feminine dominance.

106. Hamel, Mary. "The Wife of Bath and a Contemporary Murder." *ChauR* 14(1979):132–39.

Recent proposals that Alisoun and Jankyn may have murdered her fourth husband are analyzed and rejected. Their violent quarrel arises not from mutual guilt but from Jankyn's suspicions about Alisoun, and from his association of murder and female lust. Such an association attacks female sexuality, that which Alisoun values most highly in herself, and compels Alisoun to a lively defense of her nature.

107. Rhodes, Jewell Parker. "Female Stereotypes in Medieval Literature: Androgyny and the Wife of Bath." *JWSL* 1(1979):348–52.

The Wife of Bath has served as an example of a medieval feminist. However, it would be more accurate to describe her as an androgyne—a person possessing both male and female characterisitcs. While it can be argued that she has liberated herself from certain societal constraints because of her dual character, one must consider the morality involved in her selection of experiences. Though androgyny may have served as a practical survival technique in medieval society, the wife succeeds only in becoming "spiritually corrupt" in both sexist role systems.

108. Roth, Elizabeth. "On the Wife of Bath's 'Embarrassing Question'." *AN&Q* 17(1978):54–55.

Fisher's reading "wight" (1977) in *WBT* 117 is preferable to Donaldson's "wrighte." *FranT* 867–72 contains phrasing which is reminiscent of Fisher's proposed meaning of *WBT* 117: "And created by so wise a Being."

109. Sanders, Barry. "Chaucer's Dependence on Sermon Structure in the Wife of Bath's 'Prologue' and 'Tale'." *SMC* 4(1974):437–45.

WBP/WBT are best read as one woman's satire of both preachers and their anti-feminist propaganda. Attacking antifeminism in medieval preaching, she uses the structure of the medieval sermon.

110. Thundy, Zacharias P. "Matheolus, Chaucer, and the Wife of Bath." In *Chaucerian Problems and Perspectives: Essays Presented to Paul E. Beichner, C.S.C.* Ed. Edward Vasta and Zacharias P. Thundy. Notre Dame, Ind.: U of Notre Dame P, 1979, pp. 24–56.

An important immediate source of Chaucer's work is the Latin *Lamentations of Matheolus,* a thirteenth-century French cleric, whose work Jean le Fèvre translated into French and expanded in the fourteenth century. In excess of one hundred parallels between *Lamentations* and *WBP/WBT* are proposed. In French and in Latin the work survives in fourteenth-century mss in the British Library. It is also a source for Deschamps' *Miroir de Mariage*, not published until after 1406, and obviously not a source for Chaucer.

111. West, Philip. "The Perils of Pauline Theology: The Wife of Bath's Prologue and Tale." *EAS* 8(1979): 7–16.

The Wife of Bath is, in B. J. Whiting's phrase, "an oxymoron in the flesh," and modern structuralist criticism helps us to see the mythic implications of her parodies of Paul's dicta concerning marriage, apostolic experience, and beatific vision.

See also: 20   80

CT—The Friar and His Tale

112. Havely, N. R. "Chaucer's Friar and Merchant." *ChauR* 13(1979):337–45.

The Friar's varied activities are recounted in terms that have both commercial and non-materialistic applications. Ambiguous diction points toward deeper questions about the use of wealth and, together with the sexual innuendoes and the enumeration of activities commonly shared by mendicants and merchants in antifraternal writing, establishes the Friar as a harbinger of the Merchant.

113. Nicholson, Peter. "Analogues of Chaucer's *Friar's Tale*." *ELN* 17, ii(1979–80):93–98.

Archer Taylor's account, in *Sources and Analogues*, of the analogues to *FrT* is incomplete and misleading. Exempla from two fourteenth-century English manuscript collections show that it is possible to be much more precise about Chaucer's indebtedness.

CT—The Summoner and His Tale

114. Pratt, Robert A. "Albertus Magnus and the Problem of Sound and Odor in the Summoner's Tale." *PQ* 57(1978): 267–68.

Jankyn's theories of the dissemination of sound and odor coincide precisely with those of medieval science as presented by Albertus Magnus in his *Liber de sensu et sensato*. Chaucer draws upon these widely disseminated medieval views rather than upon the opinions of classical writers such as Euclid, Ptolemy, Vitruvius, or Boethius.

See also: 82

CT—The Clerk and His Tale

115. Gilmartin, Kristine. "Array in the *Clerk's Tale*." *ChauR* 13(1979): 234–46.

Griselda's several robings and disrobings are used to suggest the difficulty of knowing the constant reality behind shifting appearances. The behavior of Griselda and Walter becomes more coherent through the different meanings they see in clothing: Griselda sees it as a symbol of her constancy; Walter sees it as a potentially deceptive status-symbol. Array, since it conceals and reveals, expresses the theme of knowledge in the tale.

See also: 83 88 104

CT—The Merchant and His Tale

116. Adams, John F. "The Janus Symbolism in 'The Merchant's Tale'." *SMC* 4(1974): 446–51.

MerT is both fabliau and romance, both realistic and allegorical. Janus was god of gates and of marriage beds. January falls under Aquarius, associated with old age; May, under Gemini, was associated with youth. The name of the sacred Roman gate was Iannus Geminus.

117. Andrew, Malcolm. "January's Knife: Sexual Morality and Proverbial Wisdom in the *Merchant's Tale*." *ELN* 16(1978–79):273–77.

The point of the proverb that a man may not sin with his own wife or cut himself with his own knife is reversed in *MerT*. Chaucer intends the effect of surprise to create a sense of the nature and significance of January's wrong headedness.

118. Benson, Donald R. "The Marriage 'Encomium' in the *Merchant's Tale*: A Chaucerian Crux." *ChauR* 14(1979):48–60.

Rhetorically nearer to exhortation than to encomium, the didactic structure of this passage rises in a series of contradictions that confuse doctrines and undercut ironic perceptions. None of the proposed assignments of the passage resolves the problematical aspects of this anomaly, which may point toward an incomplete stage of revision.

119. Brown, Emerson, Jr. "Chaucer, the Merchant, and Their Tale: Getting Beyond Old Controversies: Part II." *ChauR* 13(1979):247–62.

In the Merchant and *MerT* Chaucer objectifies his own cultural bias against women and his own interest in financial profit. The Merchant is like January (Janus was the god of merchants), and Chaucer (born into a family of merchants) is like the Merchant. However, through the portrayal of this cynical character Chaucer reaches a certain self-understanding, and expresses with it a keen awareness that antifeminism and crass mercantilism vitiate human love.

120. Donovan, Mortimer J. "Chaucer's January and May: Counterparts in Claudian." In *Chaucerian Problems and Perspectives: Essays Presented to Paul E. Beichner, C.S.C.* Ed. Edward Vasta and Zacharias P. Thundy, Notre Dame, Ind.: U of Notre Dame P, 1979, pp. 59–69.

Glosses in Class Alpha mss of Claudian's *De Raptu Proserpinae*, which Chaucer could have used at school, explain his description of Pluto and Proserpina as Fairies, his "many a lady" following Proserpina, the terrifying tone of Pluto's "grisely carte," the trickery practised by the gods, the offense January gave to Nature, and the January/May, Pluto/Proserpina contrasts.

121. Hoy, James F. "A Twentieth-Century Analogue to Chaucer's *Merchant's Tale*." ChauR 14(1979):155–57.

A previously uncollected analogue emerges in the form of a joke in Kansas. Structural parallels include the motivating action, the consummation in a tree, and the refusal of the husband to believe the evidence of his own eyes.

See also: 20   65   85   104   112   192

CT—The Squire and His Tale

122. Hatton, Thomas J. "Thematic Relationships between Chaucer's Squire's Portrait and Tale and the Knight's Portrait and Tale." SMC 4(1974): 452–58.

The Squire's concupiscence and selfishness contrast with the Knight's love of chivalric virtues. Through the Squire and his tale Chaucer may be suggesting that the knights of Richard II's court return to the values represented by his own perfect knight.

See also: 80

CT—The Franklin and His Tale

123. Luecke, Janemarie. "Dorigen: Marriage Model or Male Fantasy." *JWSL* 1(1979):107–21.

FranT, although a declared romance, has been judged almost universally by real–life standards of conduct in marriage. Two real-life women of Chaucer's period, Margaret Paston and Christine de Pizan, provide a standard of conduct in their own writings. In comparison to them, Dorigen is neither an adult person nor one capable of any willed action. And Arveragus is delineated as a suitable husband.

124. Manning, Stephen. "Rhetoric, Game, Morality, and Geoffrey Chaucer." *SAC* 1(1979):105–18.

Richard Lanham's game ("play") theories contribute to an understanding of *FranT* and *PardT*. The study of rhetoric as game emphasizes Chaucer's creative vision rather than a moral vision.

125. Reisner, Thomas A., and Mary Ellen Reisner. "A British Analogue for the Rock-Motif in the *Franklin's Tale*." *SP* 76(1979):1–12.

The eighth-century legend of St. Balred, who moved a rock dangerous to sailors, may have suggested to Chaucer the motif for Aurelius' task.

See also: 20 65 80 104 108 188 210 216

CT—The Physician and His Tale

126. Waller, Martha S. "The Physician's Tale: Geoffrey Chaucer and Fray Juan García de Castrojeriz." *Speculum* 51(1976):292–306.

Certain parallels suggest that Chaucer may have used Castrojeriz' Castilian version of the *De regimine principum of* Aegidius Romanus in writing *PhyT*.

127. White, Robert B., Jr. "Chaucer's Physician: An Uncollected Allusion 1611." *N&Q* 26(1979):102–03.

In his *Physicall and approved Medicines* . . . (London, 1611) Edmund Gardiner cites Galfridus Chaucer as one of his authorities and quotes a version of *GP*, I(A), 443–44: "For Gold in Physicke is a cordiall: / Wherefore he loved Golde in speciall."

CT—The Pardoner and His Tale

128. Bolton, W. F. "Structural Meaning in *The Pardoner's Tale* and *The Nun's Priest's Tale*." *Lang & S* 11(1978):201–11.

The Pardoner, making, through structure, game of his tale's morality and morality of its game, wishes the Pilgrims to play gullible churchgoers and to depose the Host, who rebuffs him. *NPT*'s structure reveals covert anti-feminism manifesting the Confessor's superiority over the Prioress, who like Pertelote listens to lower reason.

129. Rowland, Beryl. "Chaucer's Idea of the Pardoner." *ChauR* 14 (1979):140–54.

If the Pardoner is taken as a hermaphrodite, it is easier to approach the question of how he can explain his false practices and still expect his listeners to be taken in by them. According to late medieval writers, the hermaphrodite's dual nature represented a duplicity, a doubleness of character. The Pardoner's physical ambivalence is both counterpart and cause of his conduct.

See also: 82   85   124

CT—The Shipman and His Tale

130. Coletti, Theresa. "The Meeting at the Gate: Hagiography and Symbol in the Shipman's Tale." *SIcon* 3(1977):47–56.

The image of the merchant's wife waiting for him at the gate at the end of *ShT* (VII, 673–76) may be a reflection of a popular iconographic motif, the meeting of Anne and Joachim, parents of the Virgin Mary, at the Golden Gate of Jerusalem.

131. Pearcy, Roy J. "Punning on 'Cosyn' and 'Cosynage' in Chaucer's *Shipman's Tale*." *AN&Q* 17(1979):70–71.

The likelihood that Chaucer in *ShT* was consciously punning on *cousin/cozen* is increased by the appearance of such a pun in a *ronde* which belongs to a special subgroup of *chansons de mal marié(e)*.

CT—The Prioress and Her Tale

132. Cutts, John P. "Madame Eglentyne's Saint Loy." *StHum* 7, ii(1979):34–38.

Chaucer's characterization of the Prioress mirrors the struggle of "a country bumpkin trying to upgrade herself." The St. Loy of her oath might best be identified with St. Louis IX, King of France. The Bell edition of 1890 cites St. Loy as the spelling for St. Louis in the 1543 edition of the French translation of *Legenda Aurea*. St. Louis was noted for his simple humanity. The Prioress was attempting to refine and embellish her own simple humanity.

133. Davidson, Audrey. "*Alma Redemptoris Mater*: The Little Clergeon's Song." *SMC* 4(1974):459–66.

The text of the *Alma Redemptoris Mater* in *PrT* may have been written by Hermannus Contractus. A reconstruction of its tune must depend on the Use of Sarum. This particular text and this tune are especially appropriate to the themes of the tale.

134. Ferris, Sumner. "A Hissing Stanza in Chaucer's *Prioress's Tale*." *NM* 80(1979):164–68.

Lines 1748–54 (558–64) of *PrT* are a *tour de force* of sustained onomatopoetic alliteration, with thirty-one [*recte*, thirty-two] sibilants, in hissing imitation of "the serpent Sathanas." Chaucer's artistry here is more subtle and varied than in the cruder, "rum ram ruf" alliterating passages in *KnT* and *LGW*.

135. Frank, Hardy Long. "Chaucer's Prioress and the Blessed Virgin." *ChauR* 13(1979):346–62.

Chaucer and his fellow pilgrims saw Madame Eglentyne as the Virgin's handmaiden, reflecting in her foibles and virtues the Queen of Heaven, whose *amor vincit omnia*. Support for the existence of the Marian echoes includes the use of "simple and coy" in a fourteenth-century *serventois* to the Virgin, the fact that eglantine is a common symbol for the Virgin, and the likelihood that St. Eloy would have been especially pleasing to the Virgin.

See also: 23 85

CT—The Tale of Sir Thopas

136. Brewer, Derek. "The Arming of the Warrior in European Literature and in Chaucer." In *Chaucerian Problems and Perspectives: Essays Presented to Paul E. Beichner, C.S.C.* Ed. Edward Vasta and Zacharias P. Thundy. Notre Dame, Ind.: U of Notre Dame P, 1979, pp. 221–43.

Recognition of the arming of the warrior *topos* guides us to many formal arming passages: in the Babylonian epic, the *Iliad*, the Bible, the *Aeneid*, Irish literature, *Beowulf*, the *Chanson de Roland*, *Erec et Enide*, the Arthurian series, fourteenth-century English romances, rhymed and alliterative. Elaborations of the *topos* and the order followed are familiar from the *Iliad* onwards. The *Gawain*-poet finally naturalized the topos, and, in *Th*, Chaucer effectively killed it.

137. Gaylord, Alan T. "Chaucer's Dainty 'Dogerel': The 'Elvyssh' Prosody of *Sir Thopas*." *SAC* 1(1979):83–104.

Most critics agree *Th* parodies Middle English tail-rhyme romances. A regularity of stress, external rhyme, internal alliteration, stanza pattern, and a "bobbing" meter reflect Chaucer's polished craft. While offering an ample measure of *sentence* and *solace*, Chaucer illustrates the tension between ornamentation and sincerity.

See also: 80

CT—The Tale of Melibee

138. Ruggiers, Paul G. "Serious Chaucer: *The Tale of Melibeus* and the Parson's Tale." In *Chaucerian Problems and Perspectives: Essays Presented to Paul E. Beichner, C.S.C.* Ed. Edward Vasta and Zacharias P. Thundy. Notre Dame, Ind.: U of Notre Dame P, 1979, pp. 83–94.

Chaucer gives large emphasis and exaggerated length to the didactic. *Mel* and *ParsT* are so solidly 'there' in the structure of *CT* that we would not understand the dynamics of the poem if we did not take them into account. Chaucer vies with Dante in making materials inimical to poetry the large stepping stones across which we walk more confidently into the poem as a whole.

See also: 87

CT—The Monk and His Tale

139. Waller, Martha S. "*The Monk's Tale:* Nero's Nets and Caesar's Father—An Inquiry into the Transformations of Classical Roman History in Medieval Tradition." *Indiana Social Studies Quarterly* 31(1978):46–55.

Waller examines the transmission of two classical traditions—Nero's fishnets, and Julius Caesar's ancestry, both found in Chaucer's *MkT*. From the second-century historian Suetonius, to the fourteenth-century historians, the "fishnets" have remained unchanged. By contrast, apocryphal stories regarding Caesar's low birth as well as other personal deficiencies were rampant in medieval Europe. The tradition of humble birth, ultimately deriving from a misinterpretation of Suetonius seems to be peculiar to Chaucer and other English writers.

See also: 85

CT—The Nun's Priest and His Tale

140. Bishop, Ian. *"The Nun's Priest's Tale* and the Liberal Arts." *RES*, NS 30(1979):257–67.

A framework for the function of the medieval world of learning in *NPT* can be found in the scheme of the Seven Liberal Arts (grammar, rhetoric, dialectic, astrology, arithmetic, geometry, and music). Although arithmetic and geometry are too abstract to be considered here, the other five merit exploration, with dialectic being the most important for a study of Chaucer's intentions. Under the influence of feminine charm, Chauntecleer gives up the dialectician's ability to make significant distinctions.

141. Bloomfield, Morton W. "The Wisdom of the Nun's Priest's Tale." In *Chaucerian Problems and Perspectives: Essays Presented to Paul E. Beichner, C.S.C.* Ed. Edward Vasta and Zacharias P. Thundy. Notre Dame, Ind.: U of Notre Dame P, 1979, pp. 70–82.

Generically and rhetorically *NPT* is a fable devoted to the teaching of wisdom, undercut by its mock quality, by its characterization, by its scholastic reasoning; but finally leading us back, on a higher level, to its original didactic purpose. *NPT* is about the subversion of wisdom and its reinstatement. *NPT* preaches courage and humanity and sheer delight in mankind's endless ingenuity which even self-deception cannot completely destroy.

142. Brody, Saul Nathaniel. "Truth and Fiction in the *Nun's Priest's Tale." ChauR* 14(1979):33–47.

By constantly breaking the dramatic illusion, the Nun's Priest forces his audience to consider the implications not only of his storytelling but of storytelling itself. The interruptions of his narrative, the comparisons of chickens and people, the stories within the story, and the parodies of literary styles, make it impossible to suspend disbelief. The result is that the Nun's Priest sharpens the perception of his tale.

143. Crider, Richard. "Daniel in the 'Nun's Priests's Tale'." *AN&Q* 18(1979):18–19.

Though Chauntecleer's citation of Daniel is usually taken as an allusion to Daniel vii, Daniel iv contains a more pertinent dream. In Nebuchadnezzar's dream there is a fall from greatness through pride and a reversal of misfortune when he regains his reason. Similarly, Chauntecleer falls prey to the fox, is caught, and finally escapes.

144. Cullen, Dolores L. "Chaucer's *NPT*." *Expl* 38, i(1980):11.

Following the contention that the name "Pertelote" means "one who confuses someone's lot or fate" [R. A. Pratt, "Three Old French Sources of *NPT*," *Speculum*, 47(1972),655], the author suggests that Pertelote tries to effect a change in Chauntecleer's future by the use of a laxative which, from the point of view of augury, would, through improving the condition of the bird's entrails, improve his destiny.

145. Lall, Rama Rani. *Satiric Fable in English: A Critical Study of the Animal Tales of Chaucer, Spenser, Dryden, and Orwell*. New Delhi: New Statesman Publishing Co., 1979.

The satiric fable, with oral origins among the Orientals and Greeks, is usually characterized by economy, light-heartedness, and singleness of impression. The popularity of the genre continued into the Middle Ages and beyond not only because of its beguiling literal surface but also because it was a safe allegorical vehicle for social and political criticism. In Chaucer's *NPT* (Chapter 3), the Nun's Priest serves as a mouthpiece for Chaucer, who can speak equivocally and yet disavow responsibility for his words. Although the cock and hen are convincing both as birds and as representatives of the human race, the tale in its mock heroics overleaps the boundaries between human truth and beast fiction.

146. Rex, Richard. "Chauntecleer's 'Sisters'." *StHum* 7, ii(1979):39–42.

Evidence from several sources indicates that "susters" in *CT*, VII, 4057 may be a triple-entendre: sibling sisters, nuns, and paramours. This heightens the implied parallel between Chauntecleer and the Nun's Priest.

147. Trüter, Wolfgang. "Geoffrey Chaucer, *Die Erzählung des Nonnenpriesters*: Zeilenkommentar." *DAI* 38(1979):4698C.

A line-by-line commentary on *NPT* reveals that the primary difficulties of the poem are not linguistic, but lie rather in the tremendous range of subjects from which Chaucer draws in the work: medicine, theology, astrology, and music, among others.

See also: 37   49   128   188

CT—The Second Nun and Her Tale

See: 148

CT—The Canon's Yeoman and His Tale

148. Taylor, Paul B. "The Canon's Yeoman's Breath: Emanations of a Metaphor." *ES* 60(1979):380–88.

Zephirus' breath in *GP* contrasts to the parody of divine inspiration in *CYT* and *CYT Prol* and to the piety of *SNT*. *CYT* stands in relation to *SNT* as *MilT* stands to *KnT*. Both *CYT* and *SNT* exploit the metaphor of creative breath.

See also: 81

CT—The Manciple and His Tale

149. Dean, James. "The Ending of the *Canterbury Tales*, 1952–1976." *TSLL* 21(1979):17–33.

In *MancT*, Chaucer intentionally thwarts his narrative skills, thus creating an "anti-tale" or a "farewell to his book." Providing "images of linguistic destruction," the tale prepares for the Parson's new direction in language and thought.

150. Davison, Arnold B. "The Logic of Confusion in the *Manciple's Tale.*" *AnM* 19(1979):5–13.

Though aspects of *MancT* seem hopelessly irreconcilable, the tale itself is a coherent whole, its incongruities intentional. While the Manciple cunningly pretends to be a fool, he is, in a different sense, a far greater fool than he pretends to be. By effectively portraying a protagonist who deliberately deceives his immediate audience while remaining self-deceived, Chaucer achieves the subtly ironic Christian comedy that characterizes the best work in *CT*.

See also: 87

CT—The Parson's Tale

See: 79   138

CT—The Retraction

151. Reiss, Edmund. "Chaucer and Medieval Irony." *SAC* 1(1979):67–82.

The inherent irony of *CT* stems from a Neoplatonic or Augustinian world view in which poetic tale-telling is an inadequate reflection of reality. This particularly medieval irony necessitates the inclusion of *Ret*, whereby art leads beyond time and space to Truth.

Troilus and Criseyde—General

152. McCall, John P. "*Troilus and Criseyde.*" In *Companion to Chaucer Studies* [Item 3], pp. 446–63. Repr. from the first (1968) edition, with updated bibliography.

Comprehensive readings of *TC* fall into two basic categories: sympathetic/ dualistic, and ironic. In the first, the essentially admirable courtly love of Troilus and Criseyde is seen to contrast (in varying degrees) with the orthodox Christian world at the end of the poem. In the ironic view, Troilus is a self-pitying sinner who anchors himself only to the fickleness of this world.

153. Maresca, Thomas E. *Three English Epics: Studies of Troilus and Criseyde, The Faerie Queene, and Paradise Lost*. Lincoln: U of Nebraska P, 1979.

Chaucer explicitly identifies *TC* as an epic. Like most epics, it uses the structural and thematic device of the *descensus*. It also contains many reminders of and allusions to other epic masterworks. Chaucer's "classical" subject matter not only establishes a link with other epics, but also frees him from the confines of Christain allegory and allows him to focus on human emotions in a human landscape. However, even though *TC* focuses on human emotions, it still lacks a legitimate, conventional hero. For this reason, the reader serves the function of the hero; Everyman becomes an epic hero. The *imitatio christi* and the *imitatio troili* are the two alternatives confronting Everyman; he can journey to the city of man or to the city of God. *TC* is a roadmap of such a journey. It prepares Everyman for the choice that must be made.

154. Takeshi, Miyata, trans. *Troilus and Criseyde*. The Anglo-Norman Research Centre, 1979.

A fully annotated Japanese translation.

See also: 37 44 53 87 210 216

TC—Text

155. Windeatt, Barry A. "The Text of the *Troilus*." In *Chaucer Studies III: Essays on Troilus and Criseyde*. Ed. Mary Salu. Cambridge: D.S. Brewer; Totowa, New Jersey: Rowman and Littlefield, 1979, pp. 1–23.

Distinctions among extant *TC* mss have been widely accepted as evidence that Chaucer issued two or even three versions of the poem. Supposed instances of *TC* revision bear no relation to Chaucer's extended rewriting of the Prologue to *LGW* or to the types of revision surviving in the mss of Gower or Langland. None of the various groups of *TC* mss has consistent integrity throughout equivalent to a distinct state of the author's text.

TC—Literary Relations

156. Barry, Gregory L. "Chaucer's Mnemonic Verses and the Siege of Thebes in *Troilus and Criseyde*." *ELN* 17(1979–80):90–93.

The short verse argument to the *Thebaid* prefixed to most manuscripts of *TC* had probably been memorized in Chaucer's youth and was used for the later books of *TC*. While the siege of Troy continues, Cassandra completes the story of the siege of Thebes; at the center of both narratives is a man betrayed by a faithless woman.

157. Benson, C. David. " 'O Nyce World': What Chaucer really found in Guido delle Colonne's History of Troy." *ChauR* 13(1979):308–15.

Guido's *Historia Destructionis Troiae* uses an objective historical tone, mixed with outbursts of personal lamentation. From this Chaucer developed his narrator, a philosophical historian who is affected as a man by his own story, to accent in *TC* the beauty of love and the nature of human ignorance.

158. Clayton, Margaret. "A Virgilian Source for Chaucer's 'White Bole'." *N&Q* 26(1979):103–04.

In the astrological setting of *TC* (II, 54–55), Chaucer refers to Taurus as a "white Bole." The epithet probably came from Virgil (*Georgics*, I, 217–18), perhaps through the intermediary of Macrobius' *Commentary on the Dream of Scipio*. It is suggested that it was "to Chaucer an obvious symbol for that in human behavior which is apparently attractive but actually ugly and destructive, specifically, unrestrained indulgence of sexual desire."

159. Donaldson, E. Talbot. "Briseis, Briseida, Criseyde, Cresseid, Cressid." In *Chaucerian Problems and Perspectives: Essays Presented to Paul E. Beichner,*

C.S.C. Ed. Edward Vasta and Zacharias P. Thundy. Notre Dame, Ind.: U of Notre Dame P, 1979, pp. 3–12.

Other enduring attributes of the Criseyde character complicate and perhaps mitigate her infidelity. From the start, as Homer's Briseis, she engages sympathy as a woman unwillingly transferred from one man to another. Dares made Briseida attractive; Benoit realized her sense of insecurity. Later Criseydes, Boccaccio's, Chaucer's, Henryson's, are frankly passionate. Shakespeare emphasized her lack of security and her high sexuality. Only Chaucer and Shakespeare understood that Criseyde, treated like a pawn, could not behave like a queen.

160. Frost, William. "A Chaucer-Virgil Link in 'Aeneid' XI and 'Troilus and Criseyde' V." *N&Q* 26(1979):104–05.

In *TC*, V, 804, Diomede is said to be "of tonge large," a phrase that perhaps owes a debt to the *Aeneid* (XI, 338), where Drances is described as "largus opum et lingua melior." Koch's view in "Chaucers Belesenheit in den römischen Klassikern" that "deutliche Beziehungen zu B. VIII and XI [of the *Aeneid*] sind jedoch nicht vorhanden" perhaps needs to be revised.

161. Gransden, K. W. "*Lente Currite, Noctis Eqvi*: Chaucer, *Troilus and Criseyde* III, 1422–70; Donne, *The Sun Rising*; and Ovid, *Amores* I, 13." In *Creative Imitation and Latin Literature*. Ed. David West and Tony Woodman. Cambridge: Cambridge UP, 1979, pp. 157–71.

The *aubade* of Troilus shows its indebtedness to Ovid's *Amores* (I, 13) in both references and tone, but the effect is transformed by the poet's playing off of medieval complaint and Ovidian satire. Donne makes a similar combination but transforms it into a triumph for lovers by use of a metaphysical conceit.

162. Griffin, Salatha Martha. "*Troilus and Criseyde* from the Perspective of Ralph Strode's *Consequences*." *DAI* 39(1979):6754A.

In *TC* the questions of free will and predestination are analyzed in argumentative patterns which may be related to Strode's *Consequences*. Measured against Strode's rules, these patterns reveal that the most valid logic is used by the character whose reference is faith rather than reason. Chaucer's concern for such topics as the Primary Mover, predestination, and free will may have been reinforced by his contacts with Strode.

163. Patterson, Lee W. "Ambiguity and Interpretation: A Fifteenth-Century Reading of *Troilus and Criseyde.*" *Speculum* 54(1979):297–330.

References to *TC* in a fifteenth-century treatise *Disce Mori* illustrate how the poem may have been read in the Middle Ages, with both a sensitivity to its psychological reality and at the same time moralizing its sentiments.

164. Wimsatt, James I. "Realism in *Troilus and Criseyde* and in the *Roman de la Rose.*" In *Chaucer Studies III: Essays on Troilus and Criseyde.* Ed. Mary Salu. Cambridge: D. S. Brewer; Totowa, New Jersey: Rowman and Littlefield, 1979, pp. 43–57.

The realism repeats, develops from, or combines the genres of previous works: the Arts of Love and the Platonic cosmic fables. The character of Pandarus links *TC* and the Arts of Love genre. Archetypal patterns in the later Platonic fables are also basic.

TC—The Theme of Love

165. Frankis, John. "Paganism and Pagan Love in *Troilus and Criseyde.*" In *Chaucer Studies III: Essays on Troilus and Criseyde.* Ed. Mary Salu. Cambridge: D. S. Brewer; Totowa, New Jersey: Rowman and Littlefield, 1979, pp. 57–73.

Though the primary function of the pagan imagery in *TC* is to provide local color, it has a more serious and constructive function. The supreme happiness of fulfilled love in Book III leads Troilus to a partial perception beyond the limits of this paganism. As the course of the tragedy reveals the duplicity of the pagan gods, the narrator turns to contempt of all the transient things the pagan gods represent.

166. Green, Richard F. "Troilus and the Game of Love." *ChauR* 13(1979):201–20.

Throughout *TC* Chaucer uses the social play of "luf-talkyng" as a vehicle for irony and as a means of establishing man's inability to attain an ideal. Troilus plays the love game too earnestly and so is both truly comic and, in terms of final action, tragic. His attainment of distance for veiwing his failure in the end warns against playing too seriously.

167. Morgan, Gerald. "The Significance of the Aubades in *Troilus and Criseyde*." *YES* 9(1979):221–35.

The ironic treatment of the lovers in Book III may be clarified by examining representations of *charitas* and *cupiditas*. Chaucer juxtaposes them throughout the poem and with special effect in the proem and aubades of Book III. His use and narration of source material allow the poem to create its own irony, underlining the stability of divine love as opposed to the transience of earthly love.

168. Renoir, Alain. "The Inept Lover and the Reluctant Mistress: "Remarks on Sexual Inefficiency in Medieval Literature." In *Chaucerian Problems and Perspectives: Essays Presented to Paul E. Beichner, C.S.C.* Ed. Edward Vasta and Zacharias P. Thundy. Notre Dame, Ind.: U of Notre Dame, 1979, pp. 180–206.

TC reveals on a serious level a sexual pattern similar to that of the ludicrous *MilT*. In spite of disparity of social status, Alisoun and Criseyde offer the same promise to a would-be lover; Absolon and Troilus suffer in similar ways; the same kind of parallel exists between Nicholas and Diomede. Male sexual frustration in *MilT* and *TC* contrasts to the woman's tragedy in the Icelandic *Gunnlaugssaga*.

169. Windeatt, Barry A. " 'Love that oughte ben secree' in Chaucer's *Troilus*." *ChauR* 14(1979):116–31.

Chaucer increases Boccaccio's emphasis on the social situation of the lovers to dramatize the separation between personal and public lives. Pandarus, ever conscious of the social context, trains Troilus as the "literary" lover. The action reflects repetitive romance patterns and shows both the beauty and sincerity, and the strain and inconsistency of a literary love in a normal social scene.

TC—Narrative Technique

170. Gaylord, Alan T. "The Lesson of the *Troilus*: Chastisement and Correction." In *Chaucer Studies III: Essays on Troilus and Criseyde*. Ed. Mary Salu. Cambridge: D. S. Brewer; Totowa, New Jersey: Rowman and Littlefield, 1979, pp. 23–42.

The lesson of the *Troilus* relates to the theme of exemplification. Chaucer's technique invites the reader first to identify with the example and gradually to disengage from it. The sign of the process of disengagement comes in the call for correction at the end of the poem.

171. Lambert, Mark. "*Troilus*, Books I–III: A Criseydan Reading." In *Chaucer Studies III: Essays on Troilus and Criseyde*. Ed. Mary Salu. Cambridge: D. S. Brewer; Totowa, New Jersey: Rowman and Littlefield, 1979, pp. 105–25.

From the opening through the end of Book III the reader's experience is more like Criseyde's than like Troilus'.

172. McKinnell, John. "Letters as a Type of the Formal Level in *Troilus and Criseyde*. In *Chaucer Studies III: Essays on Troilus and Criseyde*. Ed. Mary Salu. Cambridge: D. S. Brewer; Totowa, New Jersey: Rowman and Littlefield, 1979, pp. 73–90.

The letters in *TC* are able, largely by their status as letters, to provide a sensitive listener with a critical commentary on the characters who are supposed to write them; yet they do not endanger the sympathy of the audience or make the Narrator unduly perceptive or didactic. This idea of a letter as witness speaking for or against the writer can also be paralleled in medieval practice.

173. Shigeo, Hisashi. "The 'epilogue' of *Troilus and Criseyde* reconsidered." *The Meiji Gakuin Review* (March, 1979):137–69. Meiji Gakuin University.

The "epilogue" of *TC* apparently reveals Chaucer's denial of worldly love. However, it should be interpreted as the poet's complexity and uncertainty in his attitude towards "love", one of his major themes.

174. Vance, Edward. "Mervelous Signals: Poetics, Sign Theory, and Politics in Chaucer's *Troilus.*" *NLH* 10(1978):293–337.

The Middle Ages had developed a sophisticated semiotic theory. The legend of Troy permitted poets to explore language as the living expression of the social order. The principal sphere of action of *TC* is words, not swordblows or even kisses. Pandarus sees everything as a disguise where everything is disclosed by its contrary. Diomedes, *of tonge large*, "is less a soldier than a cunnilinguist." Troy is a city where people have forgotten to use signs properly: the figural violence within ignores the actuality of the true violence without. The conclusion is itself a linguistic act, confronting the Logos itself in the person of Christ.

TC—Characterization

175. Aers, David. "Criseyde: Woman in Medieval Society." *ChauR* 13(1979): 177–200.

Chaucer sets up Criseyde's behavior, from first love to betrayal, as a reflection on woman's perilous social state. In so doing he questions the judgment passed on her by a male-centered society and religion, even though it is represented in his own palinode.

176. Carton, Evan. "Complicity and Responsibility in Pandarus' Bed and Chaucer's Art." *PMLA* 94(1979): 47–61.

Chaucer illustrates the reciprocity of hearing and speaking by demonstrating how perfectly the characters of *TC* understand each other's indirectly spoken meanings. The reader's complicity in this implicit communication is stressed particularly in the narrator's intimation of incest between Pandarus and Criseyde directly after her first night with Troilus.

177. David, Alfred. "Chaucerian Comedy and Criseyde." In *Chaucer Studies III: Essays on Troilus and Criseyde*. Ed. Mary Salu. Cambridge: D. S. Brewer; Totowa, New Jersey: Rowman and Littlefield, 1979, pp. 90–104.

Crisyede is a comic creation of such vitality that it challenges the idea of tragedy and the authority of the advice that bids us repair "hom fro worldly vanitee." Criseyde's message is rather that our home is here on "This litel spot of erthe."

178. Jimura, Akiyuki. "The Characterization of Troilus and Criseyde through adjectives: 'trewe as stiel' and 'slydynge of corage'." *Phoenix*, 15(1979): 101–22. Department of English, Hiroshima University.

A discussion of the characterizations of Troilus and Criseyde by investigating the meanings of adjectives attached to each noun illustrating their natures. Troilus, who languishes for love, is represented as a strong, faithful, idealistic knight and courtier; Criseyde is a beautiful and charming lady, who shows her subtle and delicate feeling with a suggestion of something fragile to touch.

179. Sakai, Satoshi. "Some women in middle English literature (3): A portrait of Chaucerian women." *Journal of Tokyo Kasei Gajuin College* (May 1980).

Chaucer's strenuous effort to protect Criseyde from harsh criticism against her is an indication that he is a man with interests in humanity in the dawn of the Renaissance rather than a medieval writer.

180. Taylor, Ann M. "Troilus' Rhetorical Failure." *PLL* 15(1979): 357–69.

Chaucer presents Troilus' appeal to Crisyde as ominous in its accuracy, sincere in its passions, yet faulty in its rhetoric. Troilus fails to appear confident, to inspire Criseyde's good will; through faulty emphasis he loses the effect of his plan for a romantic escape. Diomede's argument noticeably lacks the errors made by Troilus. Character, circumstance, destiny all oppose Troilus; his argument is an analogue for his earthly condition.

See also: 40   57   169   171

TC—Verbal Texture and Imagery

181. Brennan, John P. "*Troilus and Criseyde* IV, 209–210." *ELN* 17, ii(1979–80):15–18.

The alliterative phrase "here and houne," usually related to "hare and hound," may derive from an unattested OE formula meaning "the host and the household," an interpretation consistent with the context.

182. Matheson, Lister M. " 'Troilus and Criseyde,' III. 2460, 'Pourynge'." *N&Q* 26(1979):203.

The line reads "Thy pourynge [*vrr*. pouryng, powringe] in wol nowher lat hem dwelle." All evidence—context, lexicographical, manuscript—indicates that it means "peering-in, gazing-in," from ME *pouren*; and not "pouring-in."

183. Shirley, Charles Garrison. "Verbal Texture and Character in Chaucer's *Troilus and Criseyde*: A Computer-Assisted Study." *DAI* 39(1979): 6118A.

Computer-generated concordances and frequency lists help in deciding which part of a character's vocabulary is especially significant. Pandarus' vocabulary emphasizes his expertise in using social and family relationships. Criseyde applies words to herself that suggest concern for her inner being, but her use of words indicates that she is more concerned with appearances than reality. Troilus' speech does not support the first impression that he is an ineffectual wailer. His use of thematically important words shows him to be a perfectly trustworthy character.

184. Sadler, Frank. "Storm Imagery in *Troilus and Criseyde*." *WGCR* 10(1978):13–18.

The storm imagery in *TC* reinforces the emotional turmoil revealed in the narrative.

185. Stevens, Martin. "The Winds of Fortune in the *Troilus*." *ChauR* 13(1979):285–307.

Chaucer uses "the winds of Fortune" as a metaphor to organize the genre and to define the characters. Troilus' perception of Fortune shifts from the divine to Criseyde, assuring his fall. The narrator opposes Pandarus' attitude in accepting the inevitability of Fortune. The traditional tragedy requires the romance to end in the hero's fall, but the Christian narrator-historian effects a divine comedy in his approach to Fortune.

186. Watanabe, Ikuo. " 'Fere' and 'Drede' in *Troilus and Criseyde.*" *Tenri Daigaku Gakuho* 121(1979):77–94. Tenri University.

The main characters in *TC* are oppressed in various senses. How to enhance and ennoble them despite their unfortunate situation is one of Chaucer's undertakings. He cannot, however, free himself from the given conditions of the Trojan cycle. Hence his own fear prevails in the whole narrative.

Book of the Duchess

187. Loschiavo, Linda Ann. "The Birth of 'Blanche the Duchesse': 1340 Versus 1347." *ChauR* 13(1978):128–32.

Argues for the later date on two counts. First, discrepancies in the records allow only the conclusion that in 1361 Blanche was at least 14 years of age. Second, the custom of early marriage makes plausible that Blanche was only 12 when married in 1359; indeed, her early marriage is highly probable given that her father was anxious to secure a male heir as soon as possible.

188. Manning, Stephen. "Rhetoric as Therapy: The Man in Black, Dorigen, and Chauntecleer." *KPAB* 5(1978):19–25.

Verbal action in Chaucer may take the form of a series of verbal encounters, as in *BD*; or a long monologue, as Dorigen's is and Chauntecleer's may as well be. Chauntecleer talks himself out of fear of dreams; Dorigen talks herself out of suicide; the Man in Black realizes what White has meant to him; and the Dreamer learns that White is dead. Rhetoric, creating shifting psychic distances, enables therapy to take effect.

189. Minnis, A. J. "A Note on Chaucer and the *Ovide moralisé*." *MÆ* 48, ii(1979):254–57.

Supports James Wimsatt's contention that the story of Seys and Alcyone in *BD* owes certain details to *Ovide moralisé* rather than to the *Metamorphoses* by offering one piece of evidence, namely, that the narrator says that, to drive away the sleepless night, he read a "romaunce," a term more likely to be used by Chaucer for a French work such as the *Ovide moralisé* than for a Latin text such as the *Metamorphoses*.

190. Robertson, D. W., Jr. "The *Book of the Duchess*." In *Companion to Chaucer Studies* [Item 3], pp. 403–13. Repr. from the first (1968) edition, with updated bibliography.

Earlier critics, led by Kittredge, read the poem as a consolation for John of Gaunt, embodied as the Black Knight; the dreamer is naive and childish. Recently, however, Robertson has denied the view of "courtly love" some see in the work. Instead, when viewed in the light of medieval literary theory, the poem is no literal reflection of John of Gaunt; rather, the knight is the "erring will" and the dreamer "reason."

191. Tripp, Raymond P., Jr. "The Dialectics of Debate and the Continuity of English Poetry." *MSE* 7(1978):41–49.

Small debates turn on method, large debates on content—goals and purposes. Chaucer's *BD* and the Old English *Solomon and Saturn* are comparable big debates. In *BD* the Dreamer is converted, not refuted, when he recognizes the "routhe" the Knight asserts. Assertion rather than logic effects Saturn's similar conversion in the OE poem.

192. Wimsatt, James I. "Chaucer, Fortune, and Machaut's 'Il m'est avis'." In *Chaucerian Problems and Perspectives: Essays Presented to Paul E. Beichner, C.S.C.* Ed. Edward Vasta and Zacharias P. Thundy. Notre Dame, Ind.: U of Notre Dame P, 1979, pp. 119–31.

From *BD* at the beginning of his career to *Sted* at the end, Chaucer made use of Machaut's ballade, 'Il m'est avis.' He drew on it for the translation of *Bo*, for

MerT, and for For. Its images appear especially in BD and in MerT, its philosophical language in Bo, and its viewpoint and social comment in Sted. All of those aspects enter into For.

See also: 37 217

Parliament of Fowls

193. Baker, Donald C. "The *Parliament of Fowls*." In *Companion to Chaucer Studies* [Item 3], pp. 428–45. Repr. from the first (1968) edition, with updated bibliography.

Substantive criticism of *PF* really begins in 1935 with Bronson, who stated that the poem is a study of contrasts between man's views of love. Later critics have elaborated this view, noting the polarities of the work: the *Somnium* and the garden, *caritas* and passion, Africanus and Cytherea.

194. Bennett, J. A. W. "Some Second Thoughts on *The Parlement of Foules*." In *Chaucerian Problems and Perspectives: Essays Presented to Paul E. Beichner, C.S.C.* Ed. Edward Vasta and Zacharias P. Thundy. Notre Dame P, Ind.: U of Notre Dame P, 1979, pp. 132–46.

Reconsideration of passages not sufficiently considered in his 1957 edition of *PF* has led Mr. Bennett to comment on Chaucer's deep and searching study of the *Somnium Scipionis*; the structure of the main part of *PF*; the central sequence of the three bird-suitors; and the roundel.

195. Cleary, Barbara A. "The Narrator and the Comic Framework in Chaucer's *Parlement of Foules*." *Delta Epsilon Sigma Bulletin* 24(1979):108–12.

There are several contrasts and incongruities in tone, style, and ideas in Chaucer's *PF*, as for example the naive narrator *vs* condescending Scipio, ideal love *vs* natural love, the love garden *vs* the discordant parliament held therein, courtly language *vs* colloquial diction of the birds. By creating a comic framework, these jarring juxtapositions help to unify the work in its mockery of all rigid views of human love.

196. Gilbert, A. J. "The Influence of Boethius on *PF*." *MÆ* 47(1978): 292–303.

The Boethian neo-platonic truth (man is immortal) gives insight into love's complexities and purpose and thematic unity to the *Somnium* precis and the love-vision. Nature's "governaunce" over the birds, like the Boethian bond of love, parallels the *Somnium's* spherical harmony. The "ryal tersel" relies on his own "trouthe"; his rivals lack a sense of higher things, a contrast like the dualities of selfishness and idealism in the *Somnium*, the entrance inscriptions, Venus's temple, and Nature's court.

197. Hiraoka, Teruaki. "Translation of *PF*." *Tezukayama Gakuin Daigaku Kenkyu Ronshu* 14 (1979):61–69. Tezukayama Gakuin University.

198. Kelley, Michael R. "Antithesis as the Principle of Design in the *Parlement of Foules*." *ChauR* 14(1979):61–73.

Antithesis is the major source of *PF*'s aesthetic unity. It arranges the poem's structural levels in a pattern of oppositions: antithetical word pairs are joined by antithetical arrangements of style, description, characterization, plot, narrative presentation, tone, and theme. *PF*'s structure is not organic but governed by a design which requires the poem's antithetical meanings and themes.

199. Mori, Hajime. "On the contrast in *The Parlement of Foules*." *Bulletin of the Department of English Literature, Teikyo University* (1979):342.

The use of contrast in *PF* is notable, as the poem begins with a suggestive contrast in 'Ars longa, vita brevis.' The main theme of the work may be considered to be a contrast of courtly love and natural love.

200. Pelen, Marc M. "Form and Meaning of the Old French Love Vision: The *Fableau dou Dieu d'Amors* and Chaucer's *Parliament of Fowls*." *JMRS* 9 ii(1979):277–305.

Structure and theme of the Vision are established not only by the *Roman de la Rose* but by Latin poems: (1) visionary setting and (2) questing love-debate for a solution to the turmoil resolved (or unresolved) at (3) a Court of Love. Chaucer's work deviates from the pattern, but it is also adumbrated by the tradition, even though there is no final resolution. Still "we can perceive all too clearly [the dreamer's] desperate need for a marriage with the cosmic love that frightens him, and that makes plain the complete irrelevance of his cunning claim to innocence of love's 'myrakles and his crewel yre.' "

See also   37   47   55   65   210

House of Fame

201. Hiraoka, Teruaki. "Translation of a part of *HF.*" *Mimesis* 2(1979):28–39. English and American Literary Society, Tezukayama Gakuin University.

202. Merlo, Carolyn. "Chaucer's Phaethon: 'the sonnes sone, the rede,' *House of Fame*, II, 941." *ELN* 17(1979):88–90.

Though "the rede" may be taken as referring to either Phaethon or his father Phoebus, Phaethon is in Ovid the red-haired boy burning in the sky, who falls to earth as a human torch; "rede Phaethon" shows fidelity to Chaucer's source and intensifies Chaucer's description of the catastrophe.

203. Shepherd, Geoffrey T. "Make Believe: Chaucer's Rationale of Storytelling in *The House of Fame.*" In *J. R. R. Tolkein: Essays in Memoriam.* Ed. Mary Salu and Robert T. Farrell. Ithaca: Cornell UP, 1979, pp. 204–20.

Chaucer questions the nature of storytelling and the possibility of writing "truth" in imaginative literature. Two words express the divergence of the problem in the Middle Ages: "sooth," which is axiomatic truth (often expressed proverbially); and "trouthe," which refers to personal worth and reliability. "The longer Chaucer went on composing, the more completely he liberated himself from the restriction of a single voice of *trouthe* imposed by oral tradition. The greater authority his *trouthe* acquired, the more voices he could speak in, so that he came to depend more and more upon his audience for the completion of the *sooth* of his stories."

204. Shook, Laurence K. "The *House of Fame.*" In *Companion to Chaucer Studies* [Item 3], pp. 414–27. Revised from the first (1968) edition, with updated bibliography.

HF is a poem about the art of poetry, for to be one of "Love's folk" was, in the medieval view, to be a poet also.

205. Vance, Eugene. "Chaucer's *House of Fame* and the Poetics of Inflation." *Boundary* 27, ii(1979):17–37.

Argues that Chaucer's concerns in *HF* are metalinguistic by drawing an analogy between verbal inflation (high style) and monetary inflation (which was rampant in Chaucer's day). Both words and coins are arbitrary signs and mediums of exchange; moreover, words, like coins, are "struck" (*aer percussus*). Chaucer shows that manipulations of language, like manipulations in the value of currency, are a form of tyranny.

See also: 37   47

Legend of Good Women

206. Fisher, John H. "The *Legend of Good Women*." In *Companion to Chaucer Studies* [Item 3], pp. 464–76. Added in the second edition, replacing Fox's "Chaucer's Influence on Fifteenth-Century Poetry."

In this century discussions of *LGW* have centered on two points: the historical occasion of the poem and its significance as a stage in Chaucer's artistic development. Not until the last decade has criticism concerned itself with the artistry of the legends themselves and not just with the Prologue.

207. Kiser, Lisa Jean. "In Service of the Flower: Chaucer and the *Legend of Good Women*." *DAI* 39(1979):4275A.

The Prologue to *LGW* reveals the God of Love's misreading of *TC* and *Rom*. The stories that follow must be read with Alceste's self-sacrifice and resurrection in mind. With Alceste's powers of *translatio*, the sinful pagan lovers rise again to live in Christian poetry.

208. Shigeo, Hisashi. "Chaucer's Idea of 'love' and 'goodness' in *The Legend of Good Women*." *The Meiji Gakuin Review* (November, 1979):19–43. Meiji Gakuin University.

Chaucer's attitude toward love should be observed in the continuity of his works. *LGW*, which comes in between *TC* and *CT*, plays an important part in this connection. Here, human love is once again taken up to be praised with some controversial criteria.

209. Sutton, Jonathan Wayne. "A Reading of Chaucer's *Legend of Good Women* Based on its Ovidian Sources." *DAI* 40(1979):2052A.

The stories in *LGW* represent a first attempt by Chaucer in a series of framed stories to deal with the relation between experience, authority, and ideal sentiment. Comparison with their Ovidian sources and close reading reveals that even though Cupid severely limits the *matere* of these stories, the variety of Chaucer's treatment is remarkable.

See also: 33   37   155

Short Poems

210. Gray, Douglas. "Chaucer and 'Pite'." In *J. R. R. Tolkien: Essays in Memoriam*. Ed. Mary Salu and Robert T. Farrell. Ithaca: Cornell UP, 1979, pp. 173–203.

"Pite" and its synonym "routhe" occur almost always in their original erotic context in Chaucer's earlier works, *Pity*, *TC*, *PF*, and *FranT*. It may be equated with "generous self-sacrifice" on the part of the lover. As Chaucer broadens the concept, there emerge comic and serious uses, as in the *MilT* and the *KnT*, but "pite" retains its connections with love, which remains fundamental to its understanding. It becomes a quality of mind desirable in the ideal knight and Christian. Chaucer the poet exhibits "pite" himself and the concept is at the core of such "pitous" tales as that of Griselda, where the conventions and assumptions associated with it are difficult for the modern reader to accept.

211. Kaske, R. E. "*Clericus Adam* and Chaucer's *Adam Scriveyn*." In *Chaucerian Problems and Perspectives: Essays Presented to Paul E. Beichner, C.S.C.* Ed. Edward Vasta and Zacharias P. Thundy. Notre Dame, Ind.: U of Notre Dame P, 1979, pp. 114–18.

Clericus Adam, a short anti-feminist poem from the twelfth century, makes one wonder whether Chaucer may not be playfully saying, "Look here, *Clericus*

Adam, you little bungler, don't you disfigure my handiwork the way your namesake disfigured that of God." The comic allusion would seem to rest ultimately on the parallel between the artist as creator and God as Creator, an idea approximated by various medieval writers.

212. Nolan, Charles J., Jr. "Structural Sophistication in 'The Complaint unto Pity'." *ChauR* 13(1979):363–72.

Pity blends the language and structure of amorous and legal complaints. Legal bills, like "The Bill of Complaint" in the second part of *Pity*, have a tripartite structure: address, statement of grievance, and prayer for remedy. Recognition of this structure shows that "The Bill of Complaint" does not extend to the end of the poem; it also shows that Pity and Cruelty are not "faint and frigid" personifications but active adversaries in legal combat.

213. Pace, George B. "The Adorned Initials of Chaucer's *ABC*." *Manuscripta* 23(1979):88–98.

A device available to Chaucer, but no longer possible in the modern printed book, the illuminated initial, emphasizes the religious nature of the poem, an alphabetical sequence of eight-line stanza prayers to the Virgin. Fourteen of the seventeen early copies of the poem make some feature of the initials, often employing "Lombardic" capitals with their religious appropriateness. The language of the letter forms was one part of the charm of Chaucer's abecedarian poem.

214. Robbins, Rossell Hope. "The Lyrics." In *Companion to Chaucer Studies* [Item 3], pp. 380–402. Repr. from the first (1968) edition, with updated bibliography.

Chaucer's lyrics, usually written in imitation of the current French forms of ballades and rondels, were, in fact, his most influential legacy to the fifteenth-century Chaucerians. Chaucer may have written his early poetry (now lost or unattributed) in French.

215. Schmidt, A. V. C. "Chaucer's Nembrot: A Note on *Form Age*." *MÆ* 47(1978):304–07.

In *Form Age* Nembrot (Nimrod), identified as King of Babylon and builder of

Babel, evokes biblical first age. This view needs modification. "ne Nembrot, desirious/To regne, had nat maad his toures hye" renders exactly a *Glossa Ordinaria* passage. Another passage is Chaucer's source for the central contrast between *nature* and *civilization*. By saying Nimrod strove to penetrate heaven "ultra naturam"—Bede says "ultra naturam suam"—Strabo makes Nimrod represent tyranny that rises with civilization.

216. Storm, Melvin. "The Mythological Tradition in Chaucer's *Complaint of Mars*." *PQ* 57(1978):323–35.

Though Chaucer obliquely refers to the positive interpretation of the Mars-Venus-Vulcan myth (in the gift by Vulcan to Harmonia of a brooch), he stresses the negative, that the martial man is best advised to avoid the temptations of love. The portrait of Mars as an inept and ultimately weakened lover is also reflected in *TC* and *FranT*.

217. Vasta, Edward. "*To Rosemounde:* Chaucer's 'Gentil' Dramatic Monologue." In *Chaucerian Problems and Perspectives: Essays Presented to Paul E. Beichner, C.S.C.* Ed. Edward Vasta and Zacharias P. Thundy. Notre Dame, Ind.: U of Notre Dame P, 1979, pp. 97–113.

The speaker of *Ros* appears to be the earliest instance of the *persona* whom Chaucer presents in full dress in *BD* and develops in all subsequent major works. This early conception is already so complex and original as to justify the scribe's admiring *très gentil*.

218. Wimsatt, James I. "Guillaume de Machaut and Chaucer's Love Lyrics." *MÆ* 47(1978):66–87.

Machaut provides the nearest precedents, the most probable chief sources, for all of Chaucer's independent love lyrics printed in Robinson except *The Complaint of Venus*, wherein Chaucer follows Graunson, and *A Balade of Complaint*, most probably not Chaucer's.

See also: 33   192

Boece

219. Fischer, Olga. "A Comparative Study of Philosophical Terms in the Alfredian and Chaucerian *Boethius*." *Neophil* 63(1979):622–39.

Comparison of the philosophical items translated by Alfred and Chaucer from the Latin *Boethius* shows that it can in no way be maintained that all the new loan words used after the Norman Conquest were needed to fill linguistic or cultural gaps in OE. After the Conquest words were borrowed which in most cases ousted already existent words; the lexical resources of OE were more than adequate to deal with the Latin philosophical terms.

220. Pace, George B., and Linda E. Voigts. "A 'Boece' Fragment." *SAC* 1(1979):143–50.

The University of Missouri-Columbia fragment (*Fragmenta Manuscripta* 150) of Chaucer's *Bo* is not in book form. This fragment is one of the few Chaucer manuscripts in North America, and the only one representing *Bo*.

See also: 192   196

Book Reviews

221. Brewer, Derek. *Chaucer and His World*. Rev. John H. Fisher, *SAC* 1(1979):170–77.

222. Burlin, Robert B. *Chaucerian Fiction*. Rev. Lee W. Patterson, *UTQ*, 48(1979):263–82.

223. Cooke, Thomas D. *The Old French and Chaucerian Fabliaux*. Rev. Glending Olson, *SAC* 1(1979):151–55.

224. David, Alfred. *The Strumpet Muse*. Rev. Lee W. Patterson, *UTQ* 48(1979):263–82; Charles Owen, Jr., *SAC* 1(1979):158–63.

225. Fisher, John H. *The Complete Prose and Poetry of Geoffrey Chaucer*. Rev. Roy Vance Ramsey, *SAC* 1(1979):163–70.

226. Gardner, John. *The Poetry of Chaucer*. Rev. Lee W. Patterson, *UTQ* 48(1979):263–82; John H. Fisher, *SAC* 1(1979):170–77.

227. ———. *The Life and Times of Chaucer*. Rev. Beryl Rowland, *Queen's Quarterly* 85(1978–79):719–20.

228. Howard, Donald R. *The Idea of the Canterbury Tales*. Rev. D. W. Robertson, Jr. *M&H* 8(1977):252–55; Lee W. Patterson, *UTQ* 48(1979):263–82; Paul G. Ruggiers, *CEA* 39(1976):38–41.

229. Miskimin, Alice S. *The Renaissance Chaucer*. Rev. John King, *MP* 76(1979):285–87.

230. Owen, Charles A., Jr. *Pilgrimage and Storytelling in the Canterbury Tales*. Rev. Robert L. Kindrick, *Rocky Mtn. Rev. of Language and Literature* 32(1978):64–66; Robert P. Miller, *ELN* 18(1979):48–51; Theodore A. Stroud, *MP* 77(1979):193–96.

231. Parkes, M. B., and Elizabeth Salter, intro. *Troilus and Criseyde: A Facsimile of Corpus Christi College, Cambridge MS. 61*. Rev. Donald C. Baker, *SAC* 1(1979):187–92.

232. Spearing, A. C. *Medieval Dream-Poetry*. Rev. Florence A. Ridley, *ELN* 18(1979):46–48.

Author Index—Bibliography

Ackerman, Robert W. 13
Adams, John F. 116
Aers, David 1, 175
Andrew, Malcolm 117
Baker, Donald C. 193, 231
Barry, Gregory L. 156
Baugh, Albert C. 14
Bazaire, Joyce 4
Bennett, J. A. W. 194
Benson, C. David 40, 157
Benson, Donald R. 118
Berggren, Ruth 104
Berry, Reginald 41, 42
Bishop, Ian 140
Blake, N. F. 73, 92, 94
Blodgett, James E. 21
Bloomfield, Morton W. 141
Boheemen, Christel van 90
Bolton, W. F. 128
Braddy, Haldeen 36
Brennan, John P. 181
Brewer, Derek S. 78, 136, 221
Brody, Saul Nathaniel 142
Brown, Emerson, Jr. 119
Burch, Beth 96
Burlin, Robert B. 222
Burrow, J. A. 23
Caluwé-Dor, Juliette de 71
Carruthers, Mary 105
Carton, Evan 176
Clasby, Eugene 97
Clayton, Margaret 158
Cleary, Barbara A. 195
Clogan, Paul M. 43, 98
Coletti, Theresa 130
Cooke, Thomas D. 223
Cosmos, Spencer 24
Crépin, André 25
Crider, Richard 143
Cullen, Dolores L. 144
Cutts, John P. 132

David, Alfred 177, 224
Davidson, Arnold B. 150
Davidson, Audrey 133
Davis, Norman 5
Dean, James 149
Donaldson, E. Talbot 159
Donovan, Mortimer J. 120
Dove, Mary 81
Ebin, Lois 79
Farrell, Robert T. 99
Ferris, Sumner 134
Fischer, Olga 219
Fisher, John H. 6, 206, 221, 225, 226
Flahiff, Frederick T. 44
Fleming, John V. 82
Frank, Hardy Long 135
Frankis, John 165
Frost, William 160
Fyler, John M. 37
Gardner, John 226, 227
Gaylord, Alan T. 137, 170
Gilbert, A. J. 196
Gilmartin, Kristine 115
Gransden, K. W. 161
Grossman, Judith 57
Gray, Douglas 5, 210
Green, Richard F. 166
Griffin, Salatha Martha 162
Hamel, Mary 106
Hatton, Thomas J. 122
Havely, N. R. 112
Heffernan, Ann Falvo 65
Hieatt, Constance B. 15
Hira, Toshinori 16
Hiraoka, Teruaki 197, 201
Hoffman, Richard L. 38
Howard, Donald R. 228
Hoy, James F. 121
Hoya, Katsuzo 26
Hunter, Michael 45
Ingham, Patricia 5

Ito, Eiko   27
Jeffery, C. D.   46
Jimura, Akiyuki   178
Jordan, Robert M.   58
Kanno, Masahiko   66
Kaske, R. E.   211
Keiser, George P.   74
Keiser, George P.   74
Kelley, Michael R.   198
Killough, George   75
Kindrick, Robert L.   230
King, John   229
Kirby, Thomas A.   7, 8, 89
Kiser, Lisa Jean   207
Kleinstück, Johannes   67
Knapp, Janet Schlauch   86
Kuhn, Sherman M.   28
Lall, Rama Rani   145
Lambert, Mark   171
Loomis, Dorothy Bethurum   100
Loschiavo, Linda Ann   187
Luecke, Janemarie   123
McCall, John P.   152
McKinnell, John   172
Manning, Stephen   101, 124, 188
Maresca, Thomas E.   153
Matheson, Lister M.   182
Mehl, Dieter   2, 17
Merlo, Carolyn   202
Miller, Robert P.   83, 230
Mills, David   4
Minnis, A. J.   59, 189
Miskimin, Alice   47, 48, 229
Miyata, Takeshi   154
Morgan, Gerald   167
Mori, Hajime   199
Mustanoja, Tauno F.   29
Nakao, Yoshiyuki   30
Newlyn, Evelyn S.   49
Nicholson, Peter   113
Nolan, Charles J., Jr.   212
Ogura, Mieko   31
Oizumi, Akio   9
Owen, Charles A., Jr.   76, 230
Pace, George B.   213, 220
Parkes, M. B.   231
Parr, Roger P.   68
Patterson, Lee W.   163, 222, 226, 228
Payne, Robert O.   32

Pearcy, Roy J.   131
Pearsall, Derek   61
Pelen, Marc M.   200
Pratt, Robert A.   114
Ramsey, Roy Vance   84, 225
Reisner, Mary Ellen   50, 125
Reisner, Thomas A.   125
Reiss, Edmund   51, 93, 151
Renoir, Alain   168
Rex, Richard   146
Rhodes, Jewell Parker   107
Richmond, Velma Bourgeois   87
Ridley, Florence   10, 232
Robbins, Rossell Hope   52, 214
Robertson, D. W., Jr.   190, 228
Roney, Lois Yvonne   91
Roth, Elizabeth   108
Rowland, Beryl   3, 60, 69, 129
Rudat, Wolfgang E. H.   85
Ruggiers, Paul G.   39, 138
Sadler, Frank   184
Sakai, Satoshi   179
Salter, Elizabeth   61, 231
Sanders, Barry   109
Sato, Tsutomu   62
Scheps, Walter   33
Schmidt, A. V. C.   215
Schöwerling, Rainer   53
Severs, J. Burke   80
Shepherd, Geoffre T.   203
Shigeo, Hisashi   173, 208
Shikii, Kumiko   11
Shimogasa, Tokuji   34
Shirley, Charles Garrison   183
Shoaf, R. A.   35
Shook, Laurence K.   204
Spearing, A. C.   95, 232
Spearing, J. E.   95
Stevens, Martin   54, 185
Stolz, Anne Crehan   63
Storm, Melvin   216
Straus, Barrie Ruth   55
Strohm, Paul   64
Stroud, Theodore A.   230
Sutton, Jonathan Wayne   209
Swart, Felix   56
Takimoto, Jiro   88
Taylor, Ann M.   180
Taylor, Paul B.   148

AUTHOR INDEX

Theiner, Paul   102
Thundy, Zacharias P.   77, 110
Tripp, Raymond P., Jr.   191
Tsuchiya, Tadayuki   12
Vance, Edward   174
Vance, Eugene   205
Vasta, Edward   217
Voigts, Linda E.   220
Wallace-Hadrill, Anne   5
Waller, Martha S.   126, 139

Watanabe, Ikuo   186
Weissman, Hope Phyllis   103
Wentersdorf, Karl P.   18
West, Philip   111
White, Robert B., Jr.   127
Wimsatt, James I.   164, 192, 218
Windeatt, Barry A.   22, 70, 155, 169
Wood, Chauncey   19
Woolf, Rosemary   20

Contributors

LARRY D. BENSON is Professor of English and Chairman of the Department of English and American Literature and Language at Harvard University. He is presently working with Robert A. Pratt and others on a revision of Robinson's *Chaucer*.

JOHN A. BURROW is Winterstoke Professor of English at the University of Bristol. He has also taught at London, Oxford, and Yale. His main publications are *A Reading of Sir Gawain and the Green Knight*, *Ricardian Poetry*, *Geoffrey Chaucer* (Penguin Critical Anthologies), *Sir Gawain and the Green Knight* (Penguin Poets), and *English Verse 1300–1500* (Longman Annotated Anthologies). He has just completed an *Introduction to Middle English Literature*, to be published by Oxford, and has been working for several years on the Ages of Man in Medieval literature.

SHEILA DELANY, Associate Professor of English at Simon Fraser University near Vancouver, Canada, teaches ancient, medieval, and renaissance literature as well as an interdisciplinary course in "Marxism and the Arts." She has published *Counter-Tradition: the Literature of Dissent and Alternatives* (1970), *Chaucer's House of Fame: the Poetics of Skeptical Fideism* (1972), and numerous articles on medieval and modern literature and culture. She is preparing a collection of essays on women in literature and a book-length socio-political reading of *The Canterbury Tales*.

EDWARD C. SCHWEITZER, Associate Professor of English at Louisiana State University, has published essays on Middle English, Old French, and Middle High German literature in such journals as *JEGP, Traditio*, and *Euphorion*. He is writing a series of essays on the poetic use of learned idea and allusion in Chaucer and Langland and preparing an edition of a Latin moralized encyclopedia, the *Liber de moralitatibus*.

Abbreviations for Chaucer's Works

ABC	An ABC
Adam	Adam Scriveyn
Anel	Anelida and Arcite
Astr	A Treatise on the Astrolabe
Bal Comp	A Balade of Complaint
BD	The Book of the Duchess
Bo	Boece
Buk	Lenvoy de Chaucer a Bukton
CkT	The Cook's Tale
ClT	The Clerk's Tale
Compl d'Am	Complaynt d'Amours
CT	The Canterbury Tales
CYT	The Canon's Yeoman's Tale
Equat	The Equatorie of the Planets
Form Age	The Former Age
For	Fortune
FranT	The Franklin's Tale
FrT	The Friar's Tale
GP	The General Prologue
Gent	Gentilesse
HF	The House of Fame
KnT	The Knight's Tale
Lady	Complaint to his Lady
LGW	The Legend of Good Women
MancT	The Manciple's Tale
Mars	The Complaint of Mars
Mel	The Tale of Melibee
MercB	Merciles Beaute
MerT	The Merchant's Tale
MilT	The Miller's Tale
MkT	The Monk's Tale
MLT	The Man of Law's Tale
NPT	The Nun's Priest's Tale

PardT	*The Pardoner's Tale*
ParsT	*The Parson's Tale*
PF	*The Parliament of Fowls*
PhyT	*The Physician's Tale*
Pity	*The Complaint unto Pity*
PrT	*The Prioress' Tale*
Prov	*Proverbs*
Purse	*The Complaint of Chaucer to his Purse*
Ret	*Chaucer's Retraction*
Rom	*The Romaunt of the Rose*
RvT	*The Reeve's Tale*
Ros	*To Rosemounde*
Scog	*Lenvoy de Chaucer a Scogan*
SNT	*The Second Nun's Tale*
ShT	*The Shipman's Tale*
SqT	*The Squire's Tale*
Sted	*Lak of Stedfastnesse*
SumT	*The Summoner's Tale*
Th	*The Tale of Sir Thopas*
TC	*Troilus and Criseyde*
Ven	*The Complaint of Venus*
WBT	*The Wife of Bath's Tale*
Wom Nob	*Womanly Noblesse*
Wom Unc	*Against Women Unconstant*

General Index

Aiken, Pauline 28, 28n
Albertus Magnus; *The Book of Secrets* 20n
Albohazen Haly; *Liber de iudiciis astrorum* 19, 19n
Albumasar; *Introductorium in astronomiam* 19n
Antal, Frederic; *Florentine Painting and Its Social Background* 50n
Aristotle; *De anima* 29n
Arnald of Villanova 21n; *De amore heroyco* 24n, 25-26, 26n, 31n; *De parte operativa* 24n, 27n
Avicenna 22n, 24n, 26, 27n, 28n, 31n
Bacon, Roger; *Opus Majus* 20n
Balzac, Honoré de; *La Comédie Humaine* 59
Bartholomeus Anglicus; *De rerum proprietatibus* 19n, 20n, 26n, 29n
Bennett, J. A. W. *The Knight's Tale* 38n
Bernard of Gordon 21n, 22n, 33; *Lilium medicinae* 26n, 27n, 28n, 30-31
Bersuire, Pierre; *De formis figurisque deorum* 24n
Best, Michael R. 20n
Blake, Kathleen 15n
Blake, N. F. 101-02, 104-06
Boccaccio, Giovanni; *Teseida* 13-43 *passim*; *De Claris Mulieribus* 50, 52; *Decameron* 77, 81
Boethius; *Consolation of Philosophy* 14-16, 20, 30-43, 45
Bokenham, Osbern; *Mappula Angliae* 65n; *Legendys of Hooly Wummen* 65n
Bradshaw, Henry 78, 111
Brae, Andrew Edmund 19n
Branca, Vittore; *Boccaccio* 50n
Brian of Lingen 66n
Bridges, John H. 20n
Brightman, Frank H. 20n
Brook, G. L. 64n
Brooks, Douglas 16, 17, 17n

Brusendorf, Aage; *The Chaucer Tradition* 99-100
Burlin, Robert; *Chaucerian Fiction* 15n
Campbell, Robert L. 82, 82n
Cavalcanti, Guido; *Donna me prega* 28, 29n
Caxton, William 77, 111
Charles d'Orléans 67n
Chaucer, Geoffrey; *CT* 77-117; *GP* 6, 8, 9; *KnT* 13-45; *MilT* 6, 8, 44-45; *RvT* 6, 9, 58, 59; *MLT* 47, 52n, 54n, 58, 59, 71; *WBT* 8, 54n, 59-60; *SumT* 54n; *ClT* 47, 52, 53, 58; *MerT* 6, 54n; *SqT* 54n; *FranT* 7; *PhyT* 47-60; *PardT* 54n; *PrT* 54n; *Th* 54n; *MkT* 44, 45, 50; *NPT* 5, 7-8, 58; *ParsT* 80-81; *Ret* 59, 80-82, 109, 113; *HF* 8-9, 59, 71, 74-75; *PF* 5, 43n, 52n; *TC* 8, 35, 42-43, 52n, 53, 54, 58, 74, 81; *LGW* 6, 8, 71-74, 75; *For* 69; *Truth* 35, 60; *Buk* 109, 110; *Scog* 69-71, 73; *Purse* 69, 81; *Astr* 8, 19
Cicero; *De Amicitia* 70
Cohen, Edward S. 78n
Cowell, F. R. *The Revolutions of Ancient Rome* 48n
Curry, Walter Clyde; *Chaucer and the Medieval Sciences* 16, 16n, 20n, 27n, 28, 28n
Cynewulf; *The Fates of the Apostles* 63; *Juliana* 63-64; *Elene* 63n, 64; *Christ* 63n
David, Alfred; *The Strumpet Muse* 15n
Delany, Sheila 58n; *Chaucer's House of Fame* 59n
Dempster, Germaine 106-08
Deschamps, Eustache 9
Dino del Garbo 28-29, 29n, 31n
Dobson, E. J. 65n; *The Origins of Ancrene Wisse* 66n
Donaldson, E. Talbot 61, 78, 78n, 99
Doyle, A. I. 102, 103-04, 112

263

Dunbar, William 66n; *To the King* 66
Eisner, Sigmund 113n
Engel, F. 60n
Esch, Arno 16n
Favati, G. 29n
Fisher, John H; *John Gower* 51
Fowler, Alastair 16, 17, 17n
Friedman, John B. 24n; *Orpheus in the Middle Ages* 34n
Frost, William 44n
Fry, Donald K. 44n
Furnivall, F. J. 66n, 78, 78n, 100n
Galeazzo de Santa Sofia; *Opus medicinae practicae saluberrimum* 28n
Gaylord, Alan T. 16n
Glosulae quator magistrorum super chirurgiam Rogerii et Rolandi 22n
Gower, John; *Confessio Amantis* 50-51, 67-69, 71, 73, 74, 77
Greenfield, Stanley B. 114n
Hammond, Eleanor P. 98n, 116
Harbert, Bruce 48n
Helterman, Jeffrey 37n
Henry IV, King of England 51, 69
Hoccleve, Thomas; *Male Regle* 66, 66n
Hopkins, David 70n
Howard, Donald R. *The Idea of the Canterbury Tales* 78n
Hume, Kathryn; *The Owl and the Nightingale: The Poem and Its Critics* 65n
Isidore of Seville; *Etymologiae* 24, 24n
James IV, King of Scotland 66
Jean de Meun; *Roman de la Rose* 33n, 47, 48-49, 52, 53
John of Tornamira 31n
Johnson, Samuel 70n
Kaiser, George R. 78n
Kane, George 67n
Kaske, R. E. 44n, 45n
Kautsky, Minna 60n
Kean, P. M. *Chaucer and the Making of English Poetry* 36n, 41n
Keep, Ann E. 109n
Kohl, Stephan; *Wissenschaft und Dichtung bei Chaucer* 21n
Laʒamon; *Brut* 64
Langer, Suzanne; *Feeling and Form* 60n
Lecoy, Félix 33n

Legge, M. D. *Anglo-Norman Letters and Petitions from All Souls MS. 182* 67n
Leslie, R. F. 64n
Limentani, Alberto; *Tutte le opere di Giovanni Boccaccio* 14n
Lindsay, W. M. 24n
Loomis, Dorothy Bethurum 16n
Lowes, John Livingston 21, 21n, 22, 22n
Lydgate, John 109-10
Macaulay, G. C. 67n
Mackenzie, W. M. 66n
Malory, Sir Thomas; *Morte Darthur* 66
Mandel, Jerome 78n
Mandeville's Travels 66n
Manly, John M. 51n; *The Text of The Canterbury Tales* 77-117
Marx, Karl 50n
McCoy, Bernadette Marie; *The Book of Theseus* 14n
Middleton, Anne 54-55
Moseley, Martha 19n
Muscatine, Charles; *Chaucer and the French Tradition* 14, 14n, 15n
Nardi, Bruno 21n
Neuse, Richard 20n
Nicholas of Guildford 64-65, 70
North, J. D. 16, 17, 17n, 18, 18n, 114n
Norton-Smith, John 109n
Ohly, F. 66n
Owen, Charles A., Jr. 45n; *Pilgrimage and Story Telling in the Canterbury Tales* 78n
Owl and the Nightingale 64-65, 72
Pais, Ettore; *Ancient Legends of Roman History* 48n
Parkes, Malcolm B. 102, 103-04, 111
Pearsall, Derek 109n
Peck, Russell; *Kingship and Common Profit in Gower's* Confessio Amantis 51n
Petrarch, Francis 50
Pintelon, P. *Chaucer's Treatise on the Astrolabe* 19n
Pratt, Robert A. 14n, 16n, 43n, 78n, 100n, 115n
Propp, Vladimir; *Morphology of the Folktale* 56-57
psuedo-Augustine; *De spiritu et anima* 27n
Richard II, King of England, 51, 70

Rickert, Edith; *The Text of The Canterbury Tales* 77-117
Robertson, D. W. *A Preface to Chaucer* 21n, 29n, 33n; *Essays in Medieval Culture* 87n
Roman de Renart 58
Rosenberg, Bruce A. 78n
Rowland, Beryl 24n
Salter, Elizabeth; *Chaucer: The Knight's and the Clerk's Tale* 15n
Schick, J. 109n
Schirmer, Walter F. 109n
Schwietering, Julius 66n
Serjeantson, M. S. 65n
Sessions, Barbara 16n
Seymour, M. C. 66n
Seznec, Jean; *The Survival of the Pagan Gods* 16n
Shakespeare, William 87n, 114-15
Shannon, Edgar 48n
Shook, Laurence 101n
Sisam, Kenneth 63
Skeat, Walter W. 17, 17n, 19n, 65n, 78, 78n, 101, 116n, 117
Smyser, Hamilton M. 16n, 20n
Stanley, Arthur P. 114
Stanley E. G. 64n, 65n
Stokoe, William C., Jr. 44n
Tatlock, J. S. P. 110n
Thorndike, Lynn; *History of Magic and Experimental Science* 26n
Titus Livius; *Ab Urbe Condita* 47-54 *passim*
Trivet, Nicholas; *Chronicle* 52n
Trotsky, Leon 60
Tupper, Frederick 100n
Usk, Thomas; *Testament of Love* 65n
Valescus of Tarenta; *Philonium* 24, 24n, 27n
Vinaver, Eugene 66n
Vincent of Beauvais; *Speculum naturale* 19n, 27n, 29n; *Speculum doctrinale* 28n
Walsh, P. G. 48n
Watson, Andrew G. 112n
Wehrli, M. 66n
Westlund, Joseph 15n
Wynkyn de Worde 77, 111